IN CLIVE'S FOOTSTEPS

Born in 1956, Peter Holt was educated at
Eton and studied journalism at Darlington
College of Technology. He trained as a
reporter on the *South London Press*, and has
worked on the *London Evening News* and
the *London Evening Standard* where he
edited the rock music column for seven
years. He has travelled extensively – from
husky sledging in Lapland to exploring the
jungles of Borneo – and was elected a Fellow
of the Royal Geographical Society in 1989.
His second travel book, *The Big Muddy*, was
published in July, 1991.

Peter Holt is unmarried, and divides his
time between London, Shropshire and Gozo.

CENTURY TRAVELLERS

IN CLIVE'S FOOTSTEPS

Peter Holt

ARROW BOOKS

Century Travellers

Published by Arrow Books Limited
20 Vauxhall Bridge Road, London SW1V 2SA

An imprint of the Random Century Group

London Melbourne Sydney Auckland Johannesburg
and agencies throughout the world

First published by Hutchinson 1990
Arrow edition 1991

© Peter Holt 1990

The right of Peter Holt to be identified as the author
of this work has been asserted by him in accordance
with the Copyright, Designs and Patents Act, 1988

Phototypeset by Intype, London
Printed and bound in Great Britain by
The Guernsey Press Co Ltd
(Guernsey CI)

ISBN 0 09 984780 9

For my Father and Mother

Contents

ACKNOWLEDGEMENTS

I could not have written this book without the co-operation of everyone mentioned in it, especially Ramesh and China, who will remain my friends until the day that Shiva says enough is enough. Heartfelt thanks also for their relentless support and encouragement to Dennison Berwick, Diane Chanteau, Catherine Harriet Cludde, Davina Howes, A. J. Quinnell and my agent Christopher Little.

Illustrations

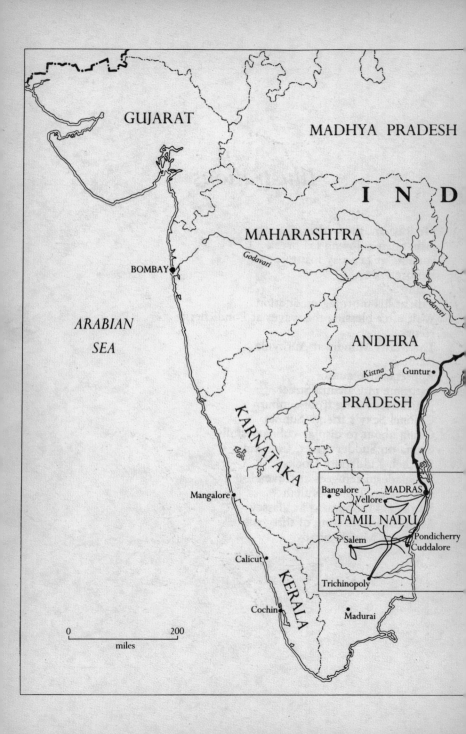

GUJARAT

MADHYA PRADESH

I N D

MAHARASHTRA

Godavari

BOMBAY

Godavari

ARABIAN

SEA

ANDHRA

Kistna Guntur

PRADESH

KARNATAKA

Bangalore MADRAS

Mangalore

Vellore

TAMIL NADU

Salem Pondicherry
Cuddalore

Calicut

Trichinopoly

KERALA

Cochin Madurai

0 200

miles

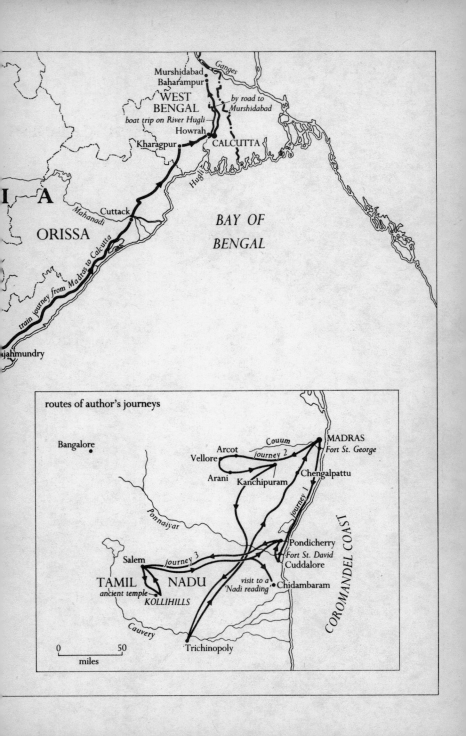

routes of author's journeys

Murshidabad
Baharampur
WEST BENGAL
by road to Murshidabad
boat trip on River Hugli
Howrah
Kharagpur
CALCUTTA
Ganges
Hugli

I A
Mahanadi
Cuttack
ORISSA
train journey from Madras to Calcutta
ajahmundry

BAY OF BENGAL

Bangalore
Arcot
Vellore
Arani
Kanchipuram
Couum
journey 2
MADRAS
Fort St. George
Chengalpattu
journey 1
Ponnaiyar
Salem
journey 3
TAMIL NADU
ancient temple
KOLLIHILLS
visit to a 'Nadi reading
Pondicherry
Fort St. David
Cuddalore
Chidambaram
Cauvery
Trichinopoly
COROMANDEL COAST

0   50
miles

Introduction

Indians called it a pilgrimage, although perhaps that is too strong a word. I called it a sentimental journey through India that progressed into a shambles.

Robert Clive, later Lord Clive, was my great, great, great, great, great-grandfather. I have always felt privileged to have had such a famous ancestor – even if he was a man whose bravery bordered on madness, who was pilloried for alleged payola on a grand scale, and whose manic-depressive tendencies led him to suicide.

When I was seven or eight years old I knew nothing of these things. As far as I was concerned, Clive was a splendid chap, who won a jolly important battle called Plassey and rode everywhere on an armour-plated elephant (the elephant bit was wrong, as I was to learn later – only the French behaved in such an ostentatious fashion). I was not interested in the politics of Pitt nor the wars of Wellington; but as soon as my teacher – Mr Morrison, I think it was – reached Clive I woke from my slumbers and reared like a cobra, devouring every morsel of information. 'Ah, Holt's ancestor has woken him up, I see,' Mr Morrison would say adding, 'Snob.'

As a schoolboy, I dreamed of seeing the places in India where Clive lived, where he fought the campaigns that were to give Britain an empire that lasted nearly two centuries.

I realised that dream in the winter of 1988–9.

> 'For a capable man, a blade of grass is a weapon.'
> 'If you see a tiger, it will die;
> if the tiger sees you, you will die.'
>
> Anon., South India.

Prelude

That was the trouble with interior designers. Dreamy pastel shades of peach and lime green might be suitable for a Chelsea pasta bar, but they were way off the mark in an eighteenth-century Mayfair mansion.

'It's too awful for words, but what can we do?' Elizabeth said. 'Of course, the walls should have been white with the cornicing picked out in gold, but these wretched interior designers always want to make old buildings look modern. I suppose they have this trendy image and they're terrified of looking fuddy-duddy.'

I was standing at the foot of the grand staircase in the entrance hall to Number 45, Berkeley Square. My guide was Elizabeth Galley, breezy personal assistant to Rafe Clutton, senior partner of London chartered surveyors Cluttons. The company had just completed an extensive programme of redecoration, having moved into the Paladian mansion eighteen months earlier.

But long before that the house had belonged to Robert Clive, the man who was to be remembered as Clive of India.

Clive lived in Number 45 from 1758 to his death sixteen years later. And he had been fussy about what it should look like. He wrote to his wife Margaret: 'I would have the Grand Flight of Rooms furnished in the richest and most elegant manner. A man of great taste and judgement should be consulted . . . I do empower you to make the House at Berkeley Square as fine and convenient as you please immediately. What can I say more?'

What more indeed, except that the hall was now furnished with Thirties-style armchairs in pale blue and baby-pink that would be more at home in a five-star hotel bedroom. 'And just

3

look at that cabinet.' Elizabeth pointed at a sort of new stripped pine, antique-style wardrobe in the corner. 'I call that distinctly MFI.'

We ascended the staircase to rooms that housed the Cluttons' employees. Smart young men in striped shirts sat behind computer terminals next to their executive trimphones. Above the modern wood and steel box-like desks were gloriously ornate ceilings bearing the original eighteenth-century plasterwork. There was an Adam fireplace, and doors made of brazil wood that Clive had had shipped specially back from India. In Clive's old dining room the girls of the typing pool pounded their word processors.

Elizabeth ushered me into the ballroom that was now the boardroom. 'At least the designers couldn't get at this,' she said. The ceiling was picked out in nine-carat gold leaf that had been put there in the eighteenth century by the architect Sir William Chambers. On the walls was the original burgundy silk covering. 'All this has listing restrictions on it like the building itself,' Elizabeth added. 'We're not allowed to touch a thing. But it's a bit of a nightmare because we're not allowed to put any plumbing in. If we need refreshments, we have to send up to the kitchen on the fourth floor.'

The tour continued up the back spiral staircase that wound its way to the top of the house. On each floor corridors led off to more rooms, once the domain of housemaids and skivvies and now a warren of offices. 'It's a bit claustrophobic, isn't it?' Elizabeth said. 'The ceilings are dreadfully low, but we can't do anything about them because of this listing business.'

On the third floor, we walked down a corridor and stopped at a door. Elizabeth straightened herself and smoothed down her flowery summer frock. She took a deep breath and adopted the manner of a castle tour guide who is about to thrill her visitors with the dungeons, complete with medieval instruments of torture.

'This,' she said, 'is the room where Clive killed himself.' And with that, she threw open the door with a flourish.

On 22 November 1774, Clive rose from his bed as usual. But he was not well. Since his twenties he had suffered from bad health, with recurring problems that were blamed on gallstones and his digestive system. Now he was plagued by acute stomach pains. That morning he took his regular, large dose of laudanum

4

– brandy laced with opium – and ordered a carriage to take him to Bath where he planned to spend a few days taking the waters. The opium seems to have temporarily cheered him up and he felt well enough to join his wife, Margaret, and two friends in the drawing room for a game of whist. At noon, the pain returned and he was forced to retire to the lavatory. On the way he is said to have passed the room of a house guest, who was attempting to write a letter. Her quill pen was blunt and she asked Clive to sharpen it for her. He took a small penknife from his pocket and, moving to the light of the window, trimmed the quill and returned it to the thankful lady. He put the knife back into his pocket before continuing on his way.

Ten minutes later, Clive had still not returned to the drawing room. Margaret was worried and made her way to the water-closet. She found her husband lying in a pool of blood having plunged the penknife into his throat. He was thought to have been struck by a particularly agonising spasm and, in a moment of sheer desperation, to have decided he could bear the pain no longer and taken his own life. He was forty-nine.

Elizabeth held the door open and I walked into the smoky fug of an office now occupied by a department responsible for managing the Crown Estates. It was a plain, insignificant, little room with a tiny cupboard-like lavatory in the corner. It was filled with clutter, old maps and cardboard boxes.

'I'm afraid it's a bit of a jumble, but we think this is where Clive committed suicide. No one can be absolutely sure about it.' I walked to the window and looked out onto the garden dotted with lily ponds. Elizabeth chattered away. 'I'm very sensitive to atmospheres, but it's funny because I've never felt anything odd about this room. The only time I've ever felt any nasty vibes was in the basement kitchen. We're certain Clive's ghost is still here. Sometimes telephones stop working for no reason and the computers suddenly go down. We blame everything on Clive.'

She showed me out and I walked across the road to sit on a bench under the trees of Berkeley Square. It was late August and there was a hint of a chill in the air. There were few people around except for suited businessmen striding across the square with their briefcases. A fat pigeon eyed me as I took notes. I could hear the clang of scaffolding being assembled on a nearby building site.

I wondered if Clive had ever sat here looking at the Portland stone facing of his splendid residence. What would he have thought about? Perhaps he sometimes wished that he was back in that strange country that brought him such great fame and riches. A country steeped in mystery; a country of many riddles.

India.

One

They were tough men of the world and they had seen it all. After a year on a supertanker, they'd signed off in Rotterdam. Now they were going home with their pockets full of cash. They were Indian merchant seamen, and by their country's standards they were rich and well-travelled.

Their leader was Albin. Life treated him well. He held a large whisky in his hand and he lounged in the seat of the Air Sabena DC10 to Bombay with a look that said he'd been around. He was surrounded in the rear of the economy class cabin by twenty-six of his men. They were drinking hard and smoking expensive Dunhill cigarettes. They kept up a relentless barrage of jokes and chatter.

Albin was seated next to me. He was a petty officer in his fifties, who was returning to his home at Cape Comorin on the southern tip of India for a month's well-earned leave. He had not seen his wife for eleven months and he was looking forward to seeing his infant son for the first time.

'She is a new wife,' he said. 'I was married before, but that did not last. It is good to have a young woman.' Albin had downed five whiskies in succession and now his eyes were tired and bloodshot. 'I like women very much,' he went on. 'I have been all over the world and I have seen many women. Best girls are in Japan – expensive, but very nice. They all have certificates once a week from the doctor. Central American girls are the best looking, but terrible diseases. Indian girls very cheap and stay in bed longer than your wife.' He cackled with laughter.

Some of Albin's boys were smuggling blue movies. They planned to sell the films in Bombay where they would be snapped up by rich businessmen wanting to impress their friends. Pornographic videos fetched a high price in India.

One of his colleagues had copies of a smut epic called *Ginger*. It had been the most popular tape in the supertanker's mess and featured three men getting to grips with a woman.

'She is called Ginger because she is hot, hot, hot. It is very dirty, very sexy.' Albin's laugh was thick with sleaze. He grinned horribly and nudged me hard in the ribs. 'Or maybe it is the hair. The hair is very good. Indians do not have ginger hair.'

The boss raised his voice so that everyone could hear. He pointed at a young Indian a few seats in front. 'My friend is keeping one of the tapes for himself. He is getting married and maybe in two years' time he will need to see a sexy movie.' This provoked much backslapping and catcalls from his men, who were now crowded in the aircraft's aisle listening to our conversation.

Albin was obviously a good bloke. He might hold petty officer's rank, but he was one of the lads at heart. He held court like a Maharajah. 'Blue movies are very good money in India,' he pronounced. 'Rich Parsis in Bombay will pay ten times what they are worth. The Parsis like dirty movies.' More raucous laughter. He gulped down more whisky and wiped his mouth with the back of his sleeve. He was enjoying the attention.

But what if the films were discovered by customs officials? 'It depends who is on the customs desk,' he said. 'Perhaps you will get a big fine and six months in jail. Or perhaps you will be lucky and the customs man will want the film himself. Then he will just take it and let you go. There are many dirty customs men in Bombay.'

Albin pointed drunkenly at me. 'Why are you going to India,' he asked. 'Holiday?'

'Well, it's a sort of holiday,' I said. 'I'm going in the footsteps of Robert Clive, going to all the places that he went to. He was the eighteenth-century Englishman who laid the foundations of the British Empire in India. He was my five-times great-grandfather. Heard of him?'

There was much chattering amongst the men. Heard of Clive? They knew him well, for goodness' sake. He was arguably the most important English name in India. Everyone in India knew about Robert Clive.

Albin and his merchant seamen had set a pattern that was to

repeat itself hundreds of times in the weeks to come. In Britain to most people the name of Clive might be a vague schooldays' memory, but in India I was to find illiterate Indian labourers who could give me a rough synopsis concerning Arcot, Plassey and Siraj-ud-daula.

'Robert Clive was a very rich man, wasn't he?' Albin said.

'Yes, he was,' I replied. 'By the time he left India, he was said to have been worth more than £600,000 – a hell of a lot in those days.'

'But he came from a good family,' Albin added. 'His father was very rich.'

'Not quite true,' I said. And I proceeded to treat my inebriated audience to a history lesson.

Robert Clive was born in Shropshire on 29 September 1725. His father, Richard, was a country squire with a respectable pedigree that could be traced back to the twelfth century. The family seat was Styche Hall, surrounded by a modest estate on the borders of the little village of Moreton Say, near Market Drayton.

But the Clives were not rich. Styche was heavily mortgaged and, although Richard practised as a part-time lawyer in London, he received few briefs on account of his fondness for the bottle. He was a disagreeable drunkard, a demanding and difficult husband who was generally unpleasant to his sensitive and slightly nervy young wife, Rebecca.

Robert – Bob – was their first child. Richard did not take to fatherhood easily. When Bob was two years old he was dispatched to live in Manchester with Rebecca's sister and brother-in-law, Bay and Daniel. Due to Richard's work the Clives spent a proportion of their time in London. Bob was a delicate child and it was thought that Manchester would be better for his health – in the 1720s Manchester was still no more than a large, busy village.

Clive was devoted to his Aunt Bay and Uncle Daniel. Being childless themselves, they worshipped him and, after he nearly died from a fever when he was aged three, devoted all their time to nursing him back to health.

Clive's biographer, Mark Bence-Jones, remarks that his early separation from his parents might have contributed to Clive's later insecurity and difficult nature. But, 'far from suffering deprivation through being parted from his parents,' Bence-Jones adds, 'it is possible that he was overspoilt by his uncle and aunt, and that this was a cause of his egoism in later life.'

All Clive's biographers agree that the young Robert grew up in Manchester as a boy who could not resist a good scrap. He was always fighting and losing his temper, and his exasperated uncle was prompted to write to Richard: 'I am satisfied that his fighting (to which he is out of measure addicted) gives his temper a fierceness and imperiousness, that he flies out upon every trifling occasion.'

Aunt Bay died, and, since Daniel was not prepared to look after the boy on his own, at the age of nine Clive was sent back to Styche. His stay in the family bosom did not last long. He distinguished himself by leading a gang that terrorised the shop-keepers of Market Drayton. Local sensitivities were further stirred by Clive's legendary adventure when he climbed to the top of the town's church tower and perched on a gargoyle. The sons of country squires simply did not do that sort of thing. Richard was furious, and shipped him off to boarding-school, first to Merchant Taylors' in London, and later to a private establishment in Hemel Hempstead, in Hertfordshire.

Albin was sleepy from the whisky. He was not listening anymore. But a few of his crewmen were still hanging around in the aisle looking quite interested. I pressed on . . .

More than a century before Clive's birth, in December 1599, a five-shilling price rise on a pound of pepper by the Dutch had led a group of twenty-four London merchants to form the East India Company so that they, too, could trade in India. By the time Clive was leaving school the Company had grown into a massive enterprise that was responsible for a fifth of all imports into Britain. Richard Clive happened to know one of the directors and seventeen-year-old Robert was sent off for an interview for the lowest possible job of 'writer', or clerk. He was accepted and assigned to the Company's settlement at Madras. He sailed in March 1743 on the Company's ship *Winchester*.

The voyage should have taken seven months, quite long enough to be cooped up in the cramped, smelly wooden world of an eighteenth-century Indiaman. But the *Winchester* ran aground off Brazil and was delayed for repairs. It was thirteen months before she eventually arrived in Madras.

I had touched a raw nerve with the merchant seamen. In their supertanker they knew all about long ocean voyages. They sympathised with Clive's plight. 'I bet Clive didn't have videos to watch,' one of them laughed. No, I agreed, eighteenth-century ships were not equipped with video players.

'Was Clive a handsome man?' the same man asked. I replied that Robert was not blessed with the looks of Adonis. A contemporary described him as being 'of the largest of the middle size; his countenance inclined to sadness, and the heaviness of his brow imparted an unpleasing expression to his features. It was a heaviness that arose . . . from a natural fullness in the flesh above the eyelid.'

I noticed that Albin also had a natural fullness in the flesh above the eyelid: he had found my little lecture so fascinating that he was now soundly asleep. The other men decided they had learned enough for one day. They drifted back to their seats to watch *A Fish Called Wanda* on the in-flight movie screen.

I changed planes at Bombay. The flight to Madras was delayed for three hours. When we eventually took off, the Indian Airlines hostesses handed out little balls of cotton wool to place in our ears. I had heard of this practice in the early days of pressurised cabins. But it seemed unnecessary to stuff your ears with cotton wool in a new Airbus 300. The quaintness that is India was just beginning.

I sat next to a young man called Emmanuel. He was in his twenties and was returning home after visiting friends in Bombay. The great wads of cotton wool with which his ears were plugged made conversation difficult: I had to shout loudly for him to hear. I explained that I planned to spend several weeks in Madras on the trail of Clive. He was not very encouraging.

'It is a very boring place,' he said. 'It is very quiet at night.' Then he thought again. 'No, quiet is not the right word. It is dead.'

My neighbour wanted to know all about Clive. 'If you are related to him,' he said, 'then you must be British. Show me your passport. I have never seen a British passport before.'

11

I handed it over. He thumbed through the pages. 'I see you are being born in Bognor Regis. What does this mean?'

It was a fair question. Why, indeed, should anyone be born in Bognor Regis? I struggled for a reply. 'It is a place on the south coast of England,' I shouted, attempting to penetrate the cotton wool. 'The name means Bognor of the King – in Latin.'

It all suddenly became clear to Emmanuel. He beamed delightedly. 'Latin! So you are Catholic then? That is good. I am Catholic also.' What more could I say? India was getting to me. This conversation was going nowhere.

Madras is the fourth largest city in India, an industrial centre and major port, with a population of around 4,000,000. It is the capital of the state of Tamil Nadu, which takes up most of the southern part of India right down to the tip at Cape Comorin.

Emmanuel wasn't joking when he said Madras was dead. Kinder locals have described Madras as a city of tradition, a place where nothing changes, where most people still dress in traditional garb of dhotis and saris. Nothing much happens either. My first impressions were of an overwhelmingly small-town atmosphere where the major entertainment was an evening stroll on the beach. During my stay, I found that by 10 pm the place was like a morgue with nothing to do except sleep. Until recently Tamil Nadu had been a dry state and it was impossible to find a drink except in bars in the large hotels, which were occupied either by tourists or by noisy, inebriated businessmen. Here was a sleepy, sprawling metropolis with only memories of a glorious past. According to Rudyard Kipling, Madras was on her uppers even a century ago. Kipling wrote in 1896:

> Clive kissed me on the mouth and eyes and brow,
> Wonderful kisses, so that I became,
> Crowned above queens;
> A withered beldame now,
> Brooding on ancient fame.

Clive may have kissed Madras, but she was courted by the British long before that.

Madras was founded in 1639 by Andrew Cogan and Francis Day, who were employed as merchants by the East India Company. Cogan and Day were looking for a place on the coast from which to trade in the cloth that was made inland. They settled on Madraspatnam, a tiny fishing village on the end of a surf-lashed sandy strip of land that was protected by the sea and rivers on two sides, making it a narrow peninsula. The company was given the site by a friendly local ruler, the Raja of Chandragiri.

The Raja must have been puzzled. What on earth did these Englishmen see in a place like Madraspatnam? There was no natural harbour and it was not a safe anchorage. During monsoon the place could be cut off for weeks. Ships stayed well away for fear of winds of cyclone force. Even in dry season vessels had to lie at anchor outside the thundering surf. Their passengers were transferred to small rowing boats to make the journey to shore.

But this wasn't going to stop Madraspatnam from turning into the seat of British power on the Coromandel Coast.

At first, Day and Cogan's base was little more than a fortified compound. They completed the main 'Fort House' on St George's Day, 23 April 1640, and gave it the name of Fort St George. Outside lay a small Indian settlement of seventy-five houses, dubbed Black Town by the British. Trade prospered, and by the time Clive arrived a century later, Black Town was a flourishing municipality of more than eight thousand houses with a population of 40,000 Indians. The British lived either in the rambling fort or in opulent 'garden houses' – small mansions surrounded by closely planted gardens – that were springing up in rapidly developing suburbs nearby. The Fort is now an army headquarters and the seat of the Tamil Nadu state government. The garden houses have long been swallowed up by the city.

The plane touched down at Madras international airport and I was plunged into chaos. The airport was awash with people arriving from all over the world for the city's annual leather fair. Indian emigrants employed in the European leather business jostled for taxis. Accommodation was going to be a problem and I wanted to avoid the touts who were quoting ludicrously high prices for rooms in what, I suspected, would turn out to be flea-pits. I took a bus into town and transferred to a cycle rickshaw in which I spent two hours looking for a place to stay. In common with most rickshaws in India, my machine was a candidate for the scrap heap. The rear wheels tended to jam solid without warning. As the driver pedalled across a busy intersection a piece of metal, that was supposed to hold up the hood, broke free and stuck in the back spokes. We slewed across the road. The traffic hooted angrily. The driver swore loudly in Tamil and removed the piece of metal. Five minutes later the same thing happened again.

I tried Triplicane, an area well-known for its bazaars and cheap hotels. Triplicane seemed a suitable place to stay. It was the first suburban village acquired by the East India Company in the mid-eighteenth century as a residential area for company servants. There is no record of Clive having ever lived there, but one can assume that he knew the place well.

There was one room left at the Broadlands Lodge, a small hotel favoured by the international backpacking brigade. The occupants were exclusively European. They spent much of their time outside under the shade of palm trees where they lolled in deckchairs and smoked joints.

The Broadlands was a rambling mansion built 100 years ago by a minor maharaja. Rickety wooden balconies looked down on a series of courtyards, which lead off to small, sparsely furnished rooms and dormitories with lumpy beds. The men on the reception desk were charming, but gloriously vague. Such was the large turnover of travellers passing through Madras that they never seemed to know if they had vacancies.

My first morning in Madras I was woken at 5 am by the call to prayer from the 200-year-old Wallajah Mosque that stood 100 yards away across an expanse of waste ground. It was a menacing building built of grey granite. 'Al . . . lah,' yelled the mullah through his microphone which led to a series of loud-speakers on the minarets. My arrival in India had coincided with the furore over Salman Rushdie's book *The Satanic Verses* and I could imagine the foul thoughts going through the mul-lah's head. 'Al . . . lah!' This time the call to the Muslim faithful was followed by a loud spitting noise and a catarrhal cough. The man was suffering from a heavy cold.

In the street outside the Broadlands, the city was waking up. Cows and goats grazed on yesterday's rubbish. Wrinkled old grandmothers hung up washing. Their daughters savagely worked the handpumps on the pavements. Naked children, their noses running, squatted in the road. A little girl of about three struggled with a bucket and poured water over her tousled head – if you are old enough to walk in India, then you are old enough to bath yourself. The women shouted. They were joined

14

by the street vendors, yelling that day's prices for melons and tomatoes. The rickshaw wallahs perched expectantly on their bicycle seats ringing their bells in the hope of attracting an early morning fare before the heat of the day. Milk salesmen, pushing churns roped to wheelbarrows, poured milk into their customers' tin cups – in India, milk does not come in bottles. Cycle repairmen sat on the pavement getting to grips with inner tubes. And outside the Broadlands, the black market money changers and dope dealers were taking up their positions in order to ensnare the first foreigners leaving the hotel.

Clive would have seen none of this activity on that first morning in India on 2 June 1744. As a trainee clerk he lived in Fort St George, a haven of calm compared to the hustle of Black Town. It is unclear exactly where in the fort Clive lived at first; he complained in a letter home, however, that he was 'wretchedly lodged'.

Life for Clive became a monotonous ritual. Each day he was woken by the bells of St Mary's Church. If he overslept, there was a loud reminder in the form of the eight o'clock canon fired from the battlements. A quick breakfast was followed by church, and at 9 am he joined his fellow clerks at the Writers' Building to begin the day's drudgery.

The work of an East India clerk was a dreary desk job that involved wading through volumes of ledgers. This was combined with visits to warehouses to check bales of cotton, a tedious task that involved interminable arguments with the Indians when figures did not tally. By the end of the day the sticky heat of Madras had drained him of all energy, and his shirt and breeches stuck to his body like damp rags. As if that wasn't bad enough, he was forced to endure another round of church.

For all this Clive was paid £5 a year, with the promise of a £10 rise if he stuck it out for five years. So it is hardly surprising that, despite occasional hand-outs from his father, he fell hopelessly into debt.

He was restless and unhappy. He had no friends and was too shy to introduce himself. In his own words, he was a 'solitary wretch'. Six months after arriving in Madras, he wrote to a cousin: 'I have not enjoyed one happy day since I left my native country.'

Clive's depression deepened. He was so miserable that he is alleged to have attempted suicide. It is a much-repeated story.

Clive locked himself in his small, whitewashed room, took a pistol to his head and pulled the trigger. The gun failed to fire. He re-cocked and tried again, still without success. At that point a colleague entered the room. Clive handed him the pistol and told him to fire it out of the window. *Bang!* The gun went off. Clive coolly remarked, 'It seems that fate must be reserving me for some purpose.' It is a good yarn but one that is doubted by contemporary historians, who say that the incident was invented later after Clive did eventually kill himself. And anyway, things like that simply don't happen in real life.

Clive needed a chap like Mr Rasnan to cheer him up. I had just returned to my room from breakfast when there was a knock on the door. I opened it to find a little man barely more than five feet tall. It was Mr Rasnan, the Broadlands' resident barber and massage wallah. Mr Rasnan walked with little steps and carried a small Gladstone bag that was packed with little bottles of cologne and hair oil. In fact, everything about Mr Rasnan was little except for his smile. It was a broad cheerful smile that left his face only at the end of his visits when he began the solemn discussions over how much I should pay him. But after I had handed over the rupees, the smile returned and Mr Rasnan showed his thanks by grasping me around the waist and giving me a huge bear-hug. I found this rather startling.

Mr Rasnan was married with a large family and had learned his barber's trade from his father. Each morning he greeted me with, 'Massage? Shave? Haircut?' And each morning I replied, 'Well, I think I'll just have the neck massage, please, Mr Rasnan.'

At which Mr Rasnan retorted, 'But you have not shaved yet and that is most untidy.' Before I could argue, he had applied soapy foam to my face and set about it with a cut-throat. He had the same tactic when it came to haircuts. I think he must have trimmed my hair every other day. But, of course, all these services represented a far greater profit to Mr Rasnan than a mere neck massage. And at the end of each session, I grudgingly paid up for shaves and haircuts I had not really wanted. Still, the smiles, if not the bear-hugs, made up for it and Mr Rasnan's morning calls became a welcome ritual.

Even if Clive did not find a friend like Mr Rasnan, at least he would have been spared the famous Madras stink.

Today Madras is blighted by the Coumm River that runs

through the city. This waterway is responsible for the overpowering smell from untreated sewage. The problem has become increasingly bad in the last twenty years thanks to the exploding migrant population, who live in slums and shanty towns along the Coumm. Thousands of people use the riverbanks as an enormous outdoor lavatory. Fish that are unfortunate enough to find their way in from the sea are said to survive for no longer than a day. The problem is worst in the hot season when the water level is low. The sand bar that separates the river from the sea prevents water flowing backwards and forwards. Thus the existing water, polluted with sewage, stagnates for weeks. The Indian Government, helped by overseas money, is planning a massive dredging and drainage project that should clean up the place for good. But in the meantime anyone with a delicate sense of smell is advised to hold their nose.

For my first steps into Clive's Madras I hired a motorised trishaw. After the rickshaw dramas the previous evening, this seemed a safer and quicker way of getting round the city. We set off from Triplicane and sped up South Beach Road and over the bridge spanning the Coumm (where Mr Rasnan's cologne helped disguise the pong) towards Fort St George.

It was Sunday and I planned to attend eight o'clock communion at St Mary's Church in the fort. Hardly had I entered the fort than I was nearly arrested for spying.

There were a few minutes to kill before the service began so I wandered into the parade ground to take photographs of the surrounding buildings. I snapped away until suddenly an Indian Army major stepped towards me. He had a huge, much-pampered moustache and was smartly dressed in spotless combat fatigues. He gestured at a row of army trucks that stood empty on the parade ground.

'You are not allowed to take photographs of the vehicles,' he said. 'Security.' And he added, 'This is very bad. You will have to be reported.'

I could not see the strategic importance of half a dozen grubby five-tonners. 'I'm awfully sorry,' I said. 'But I was only taking a few snaps of the buildings.' The major looked at me grimly. It could only be a matter of moments before he marched me off to the guardroom.

But matters of state security were not foremost in the officer's mind.

He pointed at my Nikon. 'Good camera,' he said. 'Want to sell?'

'Sell my Nikon? But I thought you were about to arrest me? No I don't want to sell.'

'You have other camera to sell?'

'No.'

The major sniffed, smoothed his moustache, did a sharp about-turn and marched away. I was rather disappointed. What might have been an exciting confrontation with the armed might of India had ended up with a brush with the black market. Even the military was on the make. Like most luxury goods imported into India, cameras carried a 300% duty. So the only way the officer would find one at a reasonable price was by tackling a tourist, who might need the cash.

The congregation of St Mary's were taking their seats for communion. After my alarming confrontation on the parade ground, the church was wonderfully calm. The trees outside in the churchyard cast their shadows through the French windows and across the pews of Burmese teak. Softly whirring ceiling fans cooled the air.

St Mary's plays an important part in the Clive story. Besides worshipping in the church as a junior clerk, Clive also married his wife, Margaret Maskelyne, there on 18 February 1753. I looked for the register that contained details of the marriage. It was no longer on display: years of exposure to the humidity of Madras had damaged the pages. It had been sent away for treatment.

St Mary's dates from 1678. It is the oldest Protestant church east of Suez and has been called the Westminster Abbey of the East due to the similar architecture, though on a much smaller scale. St Mary's was designed by a soldier, Master Gunner William Dixon, with lasting quality in mind. Gunner Dixon rated common sense higher than aesthetics. A good, solid job was needed. He constructed the church to withstand war and weather. Four-feet thick walls support a bomb proof roof.

The church quickly became the most fashionable meeting place in Madras. Services were conducted with great ceremony. The gentlemen wore full wigs and laced coats and walked into church between lines of soldiers. Here men of influence worshipped: Calcutta's founder, Job Charnock; Warren Hastings, later

the Marquis of Hastings and governor of Bengal; Arthur Welles-
ley, later the Duke of Wellington and hero of Waterloo.

The present congregation numbered about fifty. They were
smartly turned out, the women in neat, silk saris, the men in
mostly western-style shirts and trousers, although there were a
few dhotis in evidence. The choirboys and girls were gowned in
blue cassocks that matched the Wedgwood ceiling of the church.
One of the boys, a belligerent-looking urchin of about ten,
swaggered into the choir stalls wearing a pair of round, pitch
black, metal-framed sun-glasses, the type favoured by Michael
Jackson. He received a sound ticking off from Mr David, the
verger, who ordered him to remove them. Another boy appeared
to be recovering from a playground punch-up. His head was
wrapped in a large bandage.

Mr David spotted me immediately: I was a new face. Who
was I? Where was I from? I explained my relationship to Clive
and that I was on a sort of pilgrimage. Mr David was very
excited: 'So you are a sixth generation descendant of Robert
Clive. I must find the vicar immediately.'

The vicar was the Reverend Frederick Stanley. He wore thick
glasses and bright white robes that contrasted with his dark
mahogany skin. The Reverend Stanley had an unnerving habit
of encouraging newcomers to participate in his services. 'The
person who was supposed to read the second lesson has not
arrived,' he said. 'So you will read it instead.'

We sang modern hymns like *Sing Hosanna*. The Reverend
Stanley urged us on enthusiastically, bawling the words into his
microphone. The congregation responded with gusto. In the
trees outside, parakeets chattered along to the music. A pigeon
flew in through one of the open side doors. The bird studied us
through unblinking eyes as it perched on the head of a statue
erected to the memory of Adjutant-General Thomas Conway,
who died of cholera in 1837 at the age of fifty-eight. A promi-
nent Madras freemason, Conway was nicknamed the 'soldiers'
friend'. He was one of the first British Army officers to take
notice of the pitiable condition of the troops' living quarters
and to build them permanent barracks. The general's marble
head was stained with guano. He was evidently a regular stopping point for the fort's pigeons.

The Reverend Stanley prayed for Afghanistan and for an end
to the terrorism in the Punjab and Sri Lanka. He prayed for a

parishioner called Jacob, who could not find a job. He read notices for Leprosy Sunday on the following week. Posters were pinned up around the church: 'Poverty is being old at forty, dead at forty-five'; 'Poverty is having no crops to scare birds off'; 'Poverty is having no money to worry about'. The melancholy figure of Christ at the Last Supper gazed down on us from above the altar. The painting was a copy of a Raphael hanging in the Vatican, although legend had it that the chalice in the painting was executed by Raphael himself.

The vicar gave his final blessing and we adjourned for coffee and biscuits in the churchyard. The morning sun was becoming hotter and streaming through the trees. Across the road from the church I could see the large pillared building of Clive House, which stood next door to the since-demolished Writers' Building. After their marriage, Clive and Margaret rented the house from an Armenian merchant. It later became the Courts of Admiralty and it was now home to the Pay and Accounts office.

I chatted to a former vicar of St Mary's, the Reverend Ebenezer Immanuel. He was a stocky, very dark Indian, who still took lunch-time services twice a week. My ancestor held a great fascination for the Reverend Immanuel. 'Clive is a kind of hero in Tamil Nadu,' he said. 'He came here as a businessman and ended up conquering a country. Not many people in history have done that.'

Immanuel was a great Anglophile. 'What annoys me is how many people from Britain are embarrassed about what their forefathers did here. Most Indians will tell you that the British played a huge part in India's history. You gave us our law and our government.' With a glint in his eye, he added, 'Unfortunately India is now catching on to the American way of business – talking a lot and doing nothing.'

The parson introduced me to a talkative English lady called Mrs Cunningham. She was the daughter of a British Army officer and had been born and brought up in Madras. In the 1960s she left India to live in London, and now she was back for a short holiday.

Mrs Cunningham was rather tweedy and deeply nostalgic. 'Oh, you should have seen this place in the old days, you really should,' she said. 'The fort used to be so different. You should have seen it during the war. It really looked like a fort. There were soldiers everywhere and you needed a special pass to get in.

Sundays were marvellous. Wherever you looked on the parade ground there were uniforms. A brass band used to lead us all into church. Wonderful, it was. Wonderful.'

I returned to St Mary's many times during my days in Madras. The church provided a sanctuary of calm after the city and Mr David was always on hand with a cup of coffee. I could imagine Clive retreating with his thoughts to the shady courtyard whenever the rigours of clerking became too much.

I spent many hours exploring Fort St George and its maze of roads. The fort museum was a disappointment. There was a fine collection of Indian weaponry and a copy of Nathaniel Dance's famous portrait of Clive. There were also a handful of letters from Clive to his East India Company bosses mainly on the subject of the troops. Otherwise, the man was not well-represented. The people in charge of the museum obviously didn't share my view of the founder of British India.

More exciting than anything about Clive was an exhibit called the Anstruther Cage. This was a small crate that was once the prison of Captain P. Anstruther of the Madras Artillery. In 1840, Anstruther, an army surveyor, was stationed in China in the town of Tinghai when the place was overrun by Chinese soldiers. Anstruther was taken prisoner and hauled off to jail. His captors bound him hand and foot in chains and put him in a wooden cage where he stayed for a month trussed up like a chicken. 'I found my head handsomely laid open to the bone and my legs and arms covered with bruises,' he wrote later.

Anstruther was damned British about the whole affair. He was a keen amateur artist and, despite his horribly cramped position, he managed to do some sketching. The Chinese guards were so impressed by his work that they moved him to a larger cage with the generous proportions of 3ft 6in by 2ft 1in. When Anstruther was released six months later in a truce with the British, he was allowed to take his tiny prison home as a souvenir. A fierce-looking man with a shaggy beard and an abundance of red hair, he turned up later in Madras. Fellow officers could never understand why he always carried a large gold coin in his pocket. One day an ensign, just off the boat from England, arrived in the mess. Anstruther walked up to the new boy, slapped him heartily on the back and handed him the coin with the words: 'By God, sir, at last I meet someone uglier than I.'

Clive's first view of Madras would have been the battlements of Fort St George looming high above the sandy, palm-lined strip of the Coromandel Coast. I wanted to experience what Clive would have felt when he first saw his new home from the decks of the Indiaman *Winchester*. So, a few days later, I arranged a sail in one of the dinghies owned by the Royal Madras Yacht Club.

The club had seen better days. It was housed in a small wooden building on a gloomy quayside in Madras harbour, surrounded by bleak wasteland and derelict warehouses. Royal it was most certainly not, and there wasn't a yacht in sight. Instead, there was a ramshackle fleet of Wags, 13-foot clinker dinghies built fifty years ago and similar to the Waterwags still sailed in Dublin.

My host was an old sea dog called Commodore H. R. Claudius. Formerly with the Indian Navy, he was a sprightly Anglo-Indian of seventy-four, who had been the club's commodore for eleven consecutive years. Although he had never visited Britain, his voice had the trace of an English public school accent.

Commodore Claudius explained that the RMYC was going through a bad patch. It had recently been forced to move for the fourth time in its 75-year history, having become a victim of the expansion in Madras harbour. The harbour was growing every year. There were new container berths for iron ore and two new oil berths. The outer harbour had been extended to accommodate 127,000 tons of shipping.

'We're in danger of getting swamped, which is a damned shame,' the Commodore said. 'We were disgusted when the harbour was extended.' He raised a hand and pointed in the direction of the Bay of Bengal, which lay somewhere behind an ugly cluster of oil tanks. 'In the old days we could just sail round the promontory and be in open sea. Now it's a mile's trek to get out of the harbour.' He looked back at me with rheumy eyes. 'You know, there was once a time when we were untouchable, but I'm afraid that's long ago. Our old British members would have never allowed this to happen.'

Commodore Claudius was amazed that I thought I might be able to see the fort from the sea. He hurrumphed loudly. 'Ha! What you'll see is a lot of harbour and nothing else. If you sailed miles out, you wouldn't even see the roofs of the fort.'

The Commodore's sailing days were over but he arranged for

me to go out with a young female member called Roopa. Roopa was what could be described as a Madras yuppie. She was a pretty girl in her mid-twenties and married with two sons aged four and five. An engineering graduate, she was a career woman working in computers. This was unusual for an Indian mother with young children. Her husband ran his family's heavy machinery business.

We climbed into the dinghy. A pair of club boatmen had already got the Wag ready – members of the RMYC were saved the task of rigging their own craft – and they pushed us off from the jetty. A gentle breeze filled the sails and we began the trek, as Commodore Claudius put it, to the harbour mouth.

Roopa was a competent helmswoman, but quite bossy, and she put me in charge of the jib. Having had little sailing experience, I wasn't sure what to do and she kept telling me to shift this way and that and to tighten the sail. But my concentration drifted as I tried to imagine Clive's first view of Madras.

The artist-traveller William Hodges wrote in 1781 that the town presented an 'elegant prospect' from the sea. 'The approach to Madras from the sea offers to the eye an appearance similar to what we may conceive of a Grecian city in the age of Alexander,' Hodges trilled. 'The clear, blue, cloudless sky, the polished, white buildings, the bright sandy beach, and the dark green sea, present a combination totally new to the eye of an Englishman just arrived from London . . . the mind soon assumes a gay and tranquil habit, analogous to the pleasing objects with which it is surrounded.'

The January sky was clear, blue and cloudless, but that was about it. As Roopa navigated past steel gantries and derricks, dodging grubby tug-boats, it was difficult to conjure up images of a Grecian city in any age. Hodges' vision had long gone. In its place was a mess of warehouses, customs sheds and coal dumps on reclaimed land.

The wind picked up as we left the harbour. The Wag bobbed violently as we hit the strong surf. Fishermen in primitive catamarans were out after the early-evening catch of pomfret and bekti fish. The catamarans had changed little since Clive's day when similar vessels would have been used to ferry supplies to shore from the ships at anchor outside the surf.

The fishing boats had been recently banned from the harbour on the grounds that they represented a hazard to shipping. So far the fishermen were taking little notice of this tiresome rule. The catamarans crept closer and closer landward. A loud klaxon sounded whenever they strayed into the harbour mouth.

Soon we were in the middle of the little fishing fleet. The men in the catamarans had wrinkled faces, scorched from thousands of hours in the sun. They stared at us in the Wag. We were quite a novelty. Roopa explained, 'You don't see many people sailing simply for pleasure in India. Even boats like this are a great luxury and most people can't afford to sail. The only other people who do sail regularly are the fishermen and they have to do it for a living. I'm afraid that since you seafaring British left there hasn't been much demand for dinghy sailing in Madras.'

It was plain that I would not see Fort St George from the sea. Clive's view had gone for ever. Roopa gave the order to go about and we began the return tack into the harbour.

Back at the deserted club house Commodore Claudius stood us bottles of lemonade. It was like any dinghy club on the English coast. Display cabinets held an array of silver cups. Thoroughly British names like Swayne and Armstrong, the names of past cup winners, were carved on wooden boards on the walls. Claudius invited me to sign the visitors' book. It was a new book containing only a year's worth of entries. The rest of the documents dating back to the RMYC's foundation in 1911 were ruined when the RMYC moved to its present site eighteen months earlier. The records had been stored outside in a container. The container had leaked and the paper had rotted. The Commodore spread his hands in despair. 'A damned shame,' he said. 'A damned shame. Now, that sort of thing wouldn't have happened in the old days.'

The Commodore gave me a lift back into town. I thanked him for the afternoon and he dropped me on the promenade by Marina Beach. This is a strip of coastline where Clive would have been taken ashore in a massoolah boat, a flat-bottomed craft rowed by natives and made of thick coconut fibre to withstand the shock of the breaking waves. The moment the boat hit the sand, Clive would have stepped over the bows and onto a bearer, who would have carried him piggy-back the few remaining yards to dry land. English gentlemen did not get their boots wet. Then the Indians surged forward and crowded around the new arrival offering their services as interpreters. William Hodges had this to say about the Tamil welcome:

'The rustling of fine linen, and the general hum of unusual conversation, presents to his mind the idea of an assembly of females. He is struck with the long muslin dresses, and black faces adorned with very large gold earrings, and white turbans. The first salutation he receives from these strangers is by bending their bodies very low, touching . . . the forehead three times.'

Madras boasts the second longest urban beach in the world. The elegant promenade that divided the beach from the city was conceived in the 1880s by Governor Mountstuart Grant-Duff, who obviously had fond memories of bucket and spade holidays at English seaside resorts. With its trees, gardens and fairy lighting, the promenade was all rather like Worthing. Only the lines of the post-Independence statues of the likes of Gandhi reminded one that this was India.

On the sands, hundreds of families were taking their evening constitutionals. Young men in tracksuits jogged along the shore. An array of stalls offered fried fish snacks and ice cream cones. A couple of youths were running a primitive shooting gallery where customers were invited to pop balloons with rusty, antiquated air rifles.

I left the promenade and strolled across the beach. Soon I was surrounded by a group of inquisitive schoolboys. What was my name? Where was I coming from? I sat on the sand to watch the Bay of Bengal's white horses crash on the shore. The hint of the pink haze of sundown appeared on the horizon.

The boys arranged themselves in the sand next to me. One of them, aged about thirteen, was clearly the leader. He was small for his age and horribly cheeky. He was determined to show off his general knowledge learned in school. He took a deep breath and launched into a verbal assault. 'Helvetia is old name for Switzerland . . . Liechtenstein smallest country in Europe . . . Union Jack the flag of Britain.'

I interrupted him. I remarked that for some unearthly reason, known only to Whitehall bureaucrats, it was now fashionable in Britain to call the Union Jack the Union Flag.

The boy was confused. 'No, Union Jack.'

'Quite right,' I said. 'You keep calling it the Union Jack.'

He rattled through the American states: '. . . Minnesota, Missouri, Tennessee . . .'

'Very good,' I said. 'But do you know what Tennessee is famous for?'

He didn't flinch. 'Bourbon rye whisky,' he said. This kid was bright.

We reached Virginia and the boy stopped. He adopted a business-like expression. He had shown the foreigner that he was a hard worker at school; therefore I should reward him. 'Do you have any coins of your country, please, sir?'

Tourists all over India are pestered by children wanting 'coins of your country, please, sir'. Foreign coins are essential playground currency, which can be swapped for sweets and toys. There must be thousands of dollars, sterling, francs and marks circulating in schools. Perhaps even a few Polish szlotys.

I was very sorry, but I didn't have a penny on me. I resisted an urge to add that only a lunatic would lug a pocketful of British change around the sub-continent. The boy looked disappointed.

'Stamps?'

'No stamps.' Disappointment turned to disgust. The foreigner had been a waste of time. The boy got up, flicked the sand off his knees and walked away. The rest of his gang gave me a venomous look and followed after him. I sat on Clive's beach until nearly dark. I was pestered by other boys trying on the same trick. I told them to go away and leave me alone.

Clive's dull and depressing life livened up in the summer of 1746 when Madras was attacked by troops from the French colony of Pondicherry. The settlement, eighty miles down the coast, was under the command of the Governor Joseph François Dupleix, a colourful character, who has been portrayed as a scheming megalomaniac intent on winning India for France merely to boost his reputation.

Dupleix seized on the news just arrived from Europe that France was at war with Britain. In early September he dispatched a naval squadron to capture Madras. The French easily breached the defences of Fort St George and overran the garrison. Casualties numbered no more than six.

The English were rounded up and made to give their parole that they would not bear arms against the victors. Many refused, including Clive. And that night, as the fort smouldered with fires from the French bombardment, young Robert and four friends blackened their faces, put on Indian clothes, and escaped under the eyes of their French guards. They walked south, skirting around Pondicherry, to the English settlement of Fort St David.

Now that England was at war there was little clerking to do. Clive was unemployed. Rather than kick his heels, he volunteered for military service, embarking on a career that was to make him the most powerful man in India.

Clive is said to have enjoyed his time in Fort St David. The lush groves of palms, bamboo and mango provided an agreeable contrast to the sandy barrenness of Madras. Pineapples and pomegranates grew in the gardens of the East India Company's senior servants.

The settlement was established in 1690 in what can only be described as haphazard circumstances. Such was the volume of business on the Coromandel Coast that the East India Company decided they needed a second trading post after Madras. They asked the local Indian ruler if he would sell them some land to build a fort. He agreed on one condition: they could buy as many acres as would fall within random cannon shot. The English produced the largest cannon they could find and Fort St David was founded. The man put in charge of building the ramparts was Elihu Yale, and his creation was to ensure the Company's toehold in India when the French threw the British out of Madras.

Fort St David is now a suburb of the port of Cuddalore, which was originally the settlement's black town. After nine hours on a packed bus from Madras I arrived in Cuddalore to find an unattractive industrial heap suffocating under a cloud of pollution. Sensible tourists kept well away from this stained, concrete dung-hole, not least because of the limited accommodation on offer.

I checked into something called the New Arcot Woodlands hotel. I had been recommended the place by a forty-year-old Vietnam Vet called Jim, whom I had met in Madras. It was the best lodgings in town, he said. Jim was a mess, the manic-depressive victim of several Tet Offensives. Having wasted a fortune on American psychiatrists, he was attempting to get his head together in India with a life of yoga and Hindu mysticism. As I checked into the New Arcot Woodlands I reflected that he must have based his judgement of the hotel on a comparison with a fox-hole in Laos.

There were more mosquitoes in my room than in the Mekong

Delta. The air-conditioning unit clattered like a helicopter gunship. The hot water geyser in the bathroom provided an exciting element of danger as water flooded over exposed electric wiring. I took a shower wearing my trainers in the hope that the rubber soles would insulate me in the event of electric shock. The bed sheets were frayed and grey: they would have made good bandages in a field hospital. At 3 am I was forced to undertake a recce downstairs to find a mosquito coil. A man was asleep under a blanket on the floor by the reception desk. When I woke him he was very grumpy: no he did not have a mosquito coil. I returned to my room and chain-smoked cigarettes in an attempt to asphyxiate the insects. At dawn, I packed my bag and moved out.

Fort St David, on a spit partly surrounded by the sea and the River Ponnaiyar, made a welcome change after the squalor of Cuddalore. The sun was rising over a sparkling, sapphire sea. Coconut palms cast shadows over a tangle of bougainvillea.

But it no longer looked much like a fort. The outer walls were little more than heaps of rubble and it was difficult to see where the boundary had gone.

I hired a trishaw to show me round. The driver, Raja, knew all about Clive. 'Oh yes, Robert Clive. Very famous man.' I noticed that Indians never referred to my ancestor as Clive of India. That was a British affectation. Nor was it ever Lord Clive, or even just plain Clive. It was always Robert Clive. I never worked out why the use of the man's christian name seemed so important.

Raja revved the tuk-tukking engine and we motored around the fort. Pedal rickshaws and bullock carts trundled sluggishly along the streets. Children in shiny white shirts, satchels on their backs, strode on their way to school.

Raja took me to a dusty lane that bore my ancestor's name. Robert was well-remembered in Fort St David. This was where he was said to have lived when he first arrived.

Clive Street was a picture of typical rural South Indian life. Paan salesmen sat cross-legged on the pavement making up their little parcels of spices wrapped in betel leaf. There was an abundance of hardware merchants and coffee stalls. Cows ambled up the street leaving piles of dung behind them. Goats scuffled for scraps in the gutter. Limping dogs sought refuge from the sun in shady doorways. A gentle sea breeze kicked up piles of dust.

The houses had changed little since Clive's time. They were small terraced bungalows, fronted with pillared verandahs and rusty iron railings. Once they would have been smartly white-washed. Now the walls were smeared with grime, the shuttered windows bleached with sunlight.

Perhaps this was where Clive's famous duel had happened. Like his suicide attempt, the duel was another of those dubious stories. Clive had been playing cards when he accused another man of cheating. The man challenged him to a duel. They stood back to back and walked twelve paces. Clive turned and fired. He missed. His opponent walked up and placed the gun against Clive's head demanding that he withdraw the accusation. Otherwise he would fire. Clive refused. There was a nasty moment while the man's finger tightened on the trigger. Then he lowered his weapon and walked away, muttering that Clive was mad.

I told Raja this story. Raja thought for a moment. Then he said, 'That sounded like a very foolish thing for Robert Clive to do.' I agreed with him that it was stupid to argue with a loaded pistol at your head.

Raja left Clive Street and we headed for the Garden House, the mansion where Clive later lived as the fort's Deputy-Governor in 1756. It was a splendid building with a grand, colonnaded loggia, and was set in a peaceful garden. Clive's occupancy was remembered by a stone commemorative plaque in the entrance hall. The property was now used as offices by the Cuddalore local authority. It was in surprisingly good order although none of the upstairs rooms were in use.

Raja motored on to the mouth of the river. Fishermen were lazily mending nets. Their wives, bent double, worked hard on the sand dunes sorting through a carpet of fish that had been laid out to dry in the sun. Their daughters, some as young as six, helped them in this unenviable task. As the day hotted up, the smell of stinking fish drifted across the beach. It was an unrewarding job. The 2,000-plus fishing families were the poorest people in the fort with each man earning barely ten rupees a day.

Raja stopped the trishaw at a large, decaying bungalow over-looking the river. Here was more proof of Clive's occupation. Clive built the house as his headquarters when he was appointed

Deputy-Governor. According to legend, a tunnel underneath the building once went as far as Pondicherry eight miles away. This seemed like fanciful nonsense. Some British soldiers, victims of an epidemic, had been buried in a mass grave in the garden. There was nothing to mark the spot, but gardeners had unearthed skulls and bones.

Danish missionaries occupied the bungalow until the 1960s when it was taken over by the Lutheran church, who used it occasionally as an educational retreat. The building was depressingly dilapidated. On one side, the massively buttressed walls were in danger of collapse and threatened to sink into the river. I met a carpenter doing some rudimentary repairs on the broken shutters. He did not know much about the place. I should speak to Bishop M. Samuel of the Arcot Lutheran Church; he could tell me more.

I found Bishop Samuel at his office in a quiet tree-lined road not far from Clive Street. Purple ecumenical robes enwrapped his portly body. A huge wooden cross dangled from a chain around his neck. He was in charge of thirty pastors, who ministered to a total congregation of 30,000. The church had more than 100 schools, three hospitals and three orphanages.

Bishop Samuel sat me down next to him on the verandah while one of his flock made coffee. The Bishop was recovering from a circulatory illness and found it difficult to stand for any length of time. He had a disconcerting manner of not looking one in the eye when he spoke. I told him what I was doing in Fort St David. He looked over the top of my head and promptly stuck out his metaphorical begging bowl.

'It is very good you have come at this time,' he said. 'I was only just saying that it would be good if some descendants of Robert Clive came up with some money to save the house.'

Good grief! The man wanted me to write out a large cheque!

Bishop Samuel gazed into the distance behind me. He pressed on. 'I have even thought of asking my congregation to buy me a ticket to England so I can find some relatives of Robert Clive to help pay for it. If we had the money we would use the building as a permanent religious centre for teachers. It badly needs money spending on it to make it decent. We love that building very much and we do not want it to fall down. It would cost maybe 300,000 rupees to repair.'

This was about £12,000, an optimistic estimate in my view.

I shifted awkwardly in my chair and wondered how I was going to get out of this one. I told the Bishop that I couldn't think of anyone prepared to come up with that sort of money. But I would ask around the family. He seemed satisfied by my reply. 'That would be very kind of you,' he said. 'But please urge upon them about the importance of this task.'

The fund-raising speech was over. The conversation turned to British history. The Bishop explained that he remembered Clive well from his schooldays.

'We were taught one very good story,' he said. 'Clive was having difficulty teaching his Indian sepoys their left and right. So he tied pieces of cloth to their left legs and palm leaves to their right legs. The Tamil for cloth is seelay and palm leaf is wallay. Leg in Tamil is kal. Then Clive marched his soldiers up and down and they all shouted 'Seelaykal, wallaykal, seelaykal, wallaykal.'

For the first time in our conversation, the Bishop made eye contact. He said, 'That is a good story, is it not?' I agreed. It was an excellent story.

I returned to Cuddalore with the sepoys' chant of 'seelaykal, wallaykal' ringing in my ears. After Fort St David, the town looked more miserable than ever and I did not fancy another night in the New Arcot Woodlands. I was temporarily leaving Clive for the trail of Dupleix and I boarded the bus to Pondicherry.

Two

If Paris is for lovers, then Pondicherry is for seekers after truth. The former French colony has a long metaphysical tradition and the earth beneath it is supposed to hum with spiritual vibrations.

Pondicherry's ancient name was Veda Puri, the City of Learning. The area is home to the graves of more than thirty Indian spiritual gurus, who are said to have reached Nirvana. Many more have visited the place over the centuries. Even today there are three schools of yoga in the town with a legion of gurus leading wealthy Indians and Europeans along the path towards enlightenment.

Before I reached Pondi, as locals call it, I had not considered for one moment that there might be a spiritual angle to Clive. But that all changed. Here Clive's achievements took on a whole new meaning. For it was in Pondi that I descended into the mysteries of India.

And it was all Walt's fault.

Walt was a faith healer and Methodist pastor from Cleveland, Ohio. He had been told by half a dozen Indian holy men that he was the New Messiah. There was no doubt about it, said the mystics. Walt was a spiritual time bomb about to explode. 'According to all these mystics and astrologer guys I've met,' he explained, 'I will be world famous by the mid-1990s with a universal religion that will unite the world.'

I met Walt at Madras bus station where we were both catching the coach to Pondicherry. Madras bus station was not where one expected to meet the New Messiah. And would the world's saviour come in the form of a man approaching sixty with grey beard, glasses and an Ohio accent? Could an American who chain-smoked fifty cigarettes a day lead us towards a new revelation? But at least Walt showed no signs of Bible-bashing. He was a straight-speaking, modest man with none of the makings of a raving telly evangelist.

Walt had just spent a weekend in Hyderabad with a holy man, who came up with the theory that Walt was the reincarnation of the North Indian sage, Agasthyar. Agasthyar lived several thousand years ago and was one of the most famous Indian spiritual gurus, who came south to establish a centre of learning in Pondicherry.

Walt didn't know what to think. He had been in India for less than three weeks and this messiah business was baffling him. 'I am a totally unlikely candidate for the New Messiah in that I have no ambitions of power,' he said. 'I am just a Methodist pastor, nothing more.

'I'm writing a book about faith healing, so I suppose that might make me a little famous. Anything bigger – no way! I certainly can't see myself as the new Moses starting a new church.

'But I've been told I'll be able to speak many languages and I might even be able to levitate. And I'll spend the next twenty years travelling the world spreading the word.' Walt drew hard on a cigarette and laughed loudly. 'My immediate response was bullshit with a capital B – before I came to India I'd never even travelled outside the States.'

How would his congregation back home in Ohio react if they knew they had a new prophet in the pulpit? 'I guess they'd be pretty dubious,' he said. 'It was bad enough when I started faith healing five years ago. They were pretty shocked.'

We boarded the bus and began the four-hour journey down the coast to Pondicherry. I told Walt about my project. In common with other Americans I had met, he had never heard of Clive. 'You say this guy came to India as a clerk and ended up as the most powerful man in the country? That sounds to me like a case of Indian destiny. I wonder if any holy men told him that he was a sort of prophet.'

Walt was carrying a video camera. 'It belongs to Henry,' he explained.

'Who's Henry?' I asked.

'Henry's the guy I'm travelling with. I guess you could call him a millionaire playboy. We're both staying with a guy in Pondicherry called Ramesh.

Walt lit another cigarette. 'Ramesh is a doctor, who's experimenting into human energy fields. He's come up with this way of detecting cancer by studying the human aura.' Walt thought for a moment then added, 'Hey, why don't you come and stay as well? Ramesh won't mind and you can sleep on the floor.'

I had a feeling that if I spent much longer with this American I was going to be hopelessly sidetracked from my Clive quest. But I was intrigued by the idea that Clive's life could be connected with Indian mysticism and destiny. I accepted Walt's invitation. The prospect of spending a few days with the New Messiah and his intriguing friends was too good to turn down.

We arrived at Pondicherry bus station and took a trishaw to Ramesh's home in a suburb outside the town. The doctor welcomed me as if it was perfectly normal for one of his guests to invite a strange Englishman to stay. 'I am getting good vibes off you,' he said, adding with a wave of his hand, 'stay as long as you like.' Ramesh was twenty-nine. He was descended from a family of Rajputs, the caste of gallant Indian princes that once ruled Rajasthan and the Hindu equivalent to the knights of Arthurian legend. Most of his face was covered in a heavy, black beard that gave him the look of a warrior. He was obviously very bright. When he discussed subjects about which he cared deeply, his voice became progressively louder, ending in a Churchillian roar as he slapped his hands together to make a point.

Ramesh lived in a simple first-floor apartment with virtually no possessions except for some much-loved potted plants. There were cushions and fold-up garden chairs to sit on. The only decorations were a carved wooden Hindu lintel above a door and posters depicting the various guises of Krishna. In one corner of the living room was a small statue of the Hindu god Shiva. It was Ramesh's shrine and he prayed to it each morning.

It was quite crowded in that small flat. As well as Walt and me, there was Ramesh's wife Malla and their two-year-old daughter Sunaina. Ramesh always spoke to Sunaina in English. 'If she can speak English as well as Hindi, it will make her life easier later on,' he said. Malla was slim, serene and immensely beautiful. She dressed in silk saris and moved with the grace of the catwalk. She was obviously devoted to Ramesh, who had given her the name Malla on their wedding day. It meant flower garland in Hindi.

In keeping with the Hindu tradition of married women, Malla wore a red spot on her hairline, bangles on her wrists and rings on her toes. The Hindu system of spots, bangles and toe rings dates back hundreds of years when it had a practical purpose. A pubescent girl always wore bangles and a red spot on her forehead. As she walked along the noise of the bangles told any man she approached that she was a virgin. Thus the man knew he could view her as a prospective wife when she passed. When the girl married she moved the red spot to her hairline and added rings to her toes. The noise of the rings clinking on the road now warned any man that she was unavailable and therefore he must lower his eyes. The Hindu male of earlier times must have had a keen sense of hearing.

Of Henry, the mysterious millionaire playboy, there was no sign. He was still asleep in the spare room, having flown in from Malaysia the night before. Apparently India had been getting him down and he had taken a few days off to sample the entertainment in cosmopolitan Kuala Lumpur.

I was keen to continue my Clive journey. That afternoon I went into town to look at Dupleix's former power base in old Pondicherry. I was joined by Walt, who wanted to stretch his legs after the bus journey from Madras.

The French arrived at Pondicherry in 1673. They were led by a man called Martin, who was in search of a place to trade on the Coromandel Coast. Like Madras, Pondi began life as a small fishing village around which Martin built a fort. The town prospered and by the end of the seventeenth century, the 'Pride of France' was the most important French possession in India. After Martin's death in 1706, the place deteriorated until the 1720s when commerce began to flourish again under the governors Lenoir and Dumas. It was Dumas who began to build the army that would eventually challenge the position of the English in India.

And then, in 1742, Joseph François Dupleix arrived as the new Governor-General of the French Indian possessions.

In French Dupleix is pronounced with a hard 'x' – as in complex. And that is a fair assessment of the man's character. By the time he arrived in Pondicherry, Dupleix was fifty. He had entered the French East India Company thirty years earlier with the aim of making his fortune. 'One can see him,' says Mark Bence-Jones, 'as an intensely patriotic Frenchman who loved *la gloire* and regarded himself as the instrument of Providence in establishing French power in India. His cold, taciturn aloofness, the rather worried look in his portraits . . . stemmed from a pathological need to believe that success was near at hand, although every indication may have been to the contrary.'

In India Dupleix had married Jeanne Vincens, a lady who had Indian blood via her Portuguese mother. Madame Dupleix – a 'remarkable woman, a beauty with the eyes of a lemur and the head of a politician', according to Bence-Jones – was even more ambitious and avaricious than her husband. She showed him that the way to Empire lay in playing off local nawab against nawab in a game the pair called *Le Grand Jeu*. Dupleix saw that if he played the game right he could be a very rich man and the most powerful person in India. The Mogul Empire was at an end and the empire in the south was a loose federation of hereditary local chiefs squabbling amongst each other. India was up for grabs and the only stumbling block was the English, who also fostered imperial ambitions. But, in the eyes of Dupleix, the English were an undisciplined rabble and no contest when faced with the military might of France.

Of course, Dupleix lost in the end. He spent the last years of his life a broken man, discredited and ignored. He died in Paris in 1763 almost penniless. While approaching the end, he remarked, 'I gave my youth, my fortune, my life to enrich my country in Asia.' But in defeat he found his 'services treated as fables, and I as the vilest of mankind'.

Following the war with Clive, France lost Pondicherry to the English. The town was restored to the French as part of the Treaty of Paris 1763 – but not before the English razed the place and Dupleix's grand palace to the ground.

Today's Pondi dates mostly from the end of the Napoleonic Wars when the French created a coastal colonial town from which to trade quietly without threat to the British. It was built in the sleepy French provincial style with rows of white houses, all shutters and porticoes, on a grid system of wide boulevards.

The French finally quit India in 1954, but the Gallic influence continues to live on in old Pondi. The local authority have strived hard to preserve the sleepiness. Strict laws have kept out the shops and bazaars that litter Pondicherry's black town across the canal to the west. You will still see old street names like Rue St Louis on the signposts, although the Tamil translation now lies underneath the French. When I asked for directions, I was often answered in French (although it was heartening to discover that the Indians' knowledge of the language was as poor as mine). Similarly, French is still spoken in shops and cafés. And in the sandy churchyard outside Our Lady of the Angels, you will find groups of Indian men playing boules.

Walt and I strolled along the promenade past the French consulate, above which flew a huge Tricolour. The Bay of Bengal's surf thundered onto the shore. Walt removed his shoes and walked into the sea. He raised his arms above his head and muttered a prayer.

'What are you doing?' I called down from the promenade.

'I am healing the waves, calming them.' Several minutes passed. The ocean appeared to take little notice.

'King Canute tried that,' I said. 'He didn't have much luck either.'

Walt looked up and smiled. 'Well, it was worth a try. It can do no harm for man to attempt to come together with nature.'

We were joined by an ice cream salesman, who sold his wares from a wooden box attached to the front of his tricycle. Walt offered to treat me to an ice. I refused and pointed out that eating ice cream bought from an Indian street vendor was a surefire way to get poisoned. Walt looked at me as if to say, 'What can possibly be wrong with an ice cream?' It wasn't going to stop him from having one. He bought a two rupee vanilla tub.

We sat on a bench while Walt dug into his tub with a wooden spatula. The waves pounded on monotonously. There were few people around except for the occasional rickshaw wallah tinkling his bell. A large cat came and sat next to us on the bench. Pondicherry seemed to be home to a lot of well-fed cats, an unusual sight in India. There also appeared to be more domestic dogs here than anywhere else. Perhaps this was something to do with the spiritual nature of the place. One of the best sights I'd seen was that of a rotund, bearded yoga swami taking his afternoon constitutional along the promenade with his immaculately-groomed Yorkshire terrier. The guru cut a camp figure in his saffron robes while the Yorkie, its hair tied in a pink bow, scampered at his heels.

I asked Walt about faith healing. He explained that, in common with other healers, he radiated God's 'love energy' at

37

an 8.00 hertz electromagnetic frequency. He was matter-of-fact about this, as if talking about God's love energy while eating an ice cream was the most natural thing in the world. There was not a trace of Billy Graham hallelujah in his voice.

Walt went on. 'Faith healing is known in every community on earth, from South America to Africa to India . . . Scientific instruments show that we all give out energy when we pray. Healing is a process that acts like an antibiotic. God's love energy begins the healing process. It then accelerates healing by eight times normal, taking eleven hours to reach full strength. The healing diminishes over the next thirty-six hours and needs to be replenished by more prayer.'

Walt swallowed the last scoop of ice cream. 'You seldom get instant healing, maybe one time in 1,400. God certainly doesn't zap people with a bolt of lightning. But you don't need to be very holy to offer or receive healing. You just need to deeply love the other person and pray hard.'

Did he have a satisfactory success rate? Walt shrugged. 'I can heal most illnesses, but healing is a process that often requires daily doses of prayer until a person is well. About thirty per cent of those I pray with are healed within forty-eight hours. The rest need further prayers and are healed over a period of time. Thankfully, God's healing can be imparted into clothing or jewellery. I hold things in my hands and then the sick can place them next to their bodies. The healing flow can last for months.

'People often report that they can feel heat flowing from my fingers. Or the sick say they can feel heat in the ill areas of their bodies. Most people experience a sense of well-being and peace that lasts up to two days. Sometimes they even report a white light in the mind. There's no great mystery about healing. You can do it yourself. You just need a deep compassion for the person who is hurt and a oneness with prayer and God. I am just lucky that I was born with a genetic potential to offer a more powerful flow of energy to others.'

I looked sceptical. Walt offered me another of his boyish smiles. 'I may be completely wrong about all this,' he said. 'But I reckon I am ninety-six per cent right.'

We left the promenade and took a trishaw back to Ramesh's apartment. It was time to meet the famous Henry.

Henry was the last person you expected to see travelling in India. The son of a tycoon who owned a billion-dollar chain of department stores along America's east coast, Henry was, in his own words, 'sort of like retired'. He was thirty-five. He came from the clinical suburban comforts of Charlotte, North Carolina, and, as far as I could make out, he couldn't wait to get back there. Booze and birds, he happily admitted, were the most important things in his life. And it must be said that it is not India you go to if you want booze and birds.

'Shee-it,' Henry said as we introduced ourselves. 'I keep asking myself what I'm doing in this goddam country. First thing I do when I get back home to Charlotte is catch me a blonde.'

Malla made tea and we sat on cushions in the living room. Sunaina hovered in the doorway to the kitchen, eyeing these white-faced intruders with curiosity through deep brown eyes.

Henry had a crooked nose and a blasé drawl that you expected of an American playboy. When he laughed he sounded like Dudley Moore in the film *Arthur*.

He had travelled to India to keep Walt company, but he did not feel at home. 'It's not that it's so goddamed backward,' he said. 'It's just that there are so many people out on those streets giving one so much shee-it, always hassling you. But I can't find an earlier plane home, so I guess I'm just gonna have to carry on.'

The video camera Walt was carrying belonged to Henry's father, an old friend of Walt's. Henry had brought it from America to film Ramesh's aura experiments.

'Shee-it. I don't know why I'm here. My father wanted me to come and film all this stuff that Ramesh is doing. I did it for my dad. I guess he thought that three weeks with Walt in India would reform me.'

I asked, 'Has it changed you?'

Walt interrupted. 'No, it hasn't,' he said bluntly.

But didn't Henry enjoy travelling? 'Hell, who needs to travel when you've got Charlotte? All those bars, man! They're sure going to be losing money while I'm away.'

Malla cleared away the tea cups and prepared dinner. We settled down to a relaxed evening. I wrote up my notes. Walt practised the mantra he had been given to recite by the Hyderabad holy man. Sunaina sat on Ramesh's lap while he studied a thick folder of medical research material.

39

Henry went about the important task of his personal grooming. He took a shower and smoothed aerosol styling mousse into his hair – 'it makes the hair fuller, the girls like it that way' – before slotting Wham!'s Greatest Hits into his Walkman. The tones of George Michael failed to hold him for long. Wham! gave way to the Rolling Stones. 'Come alive, Mick,' he yelled. The Walkman's headphones chattered with the opening bars of *Brown Sugar*.

Walt and I went on to the balcony to smoke – Ramesh had banned smoking inside the apartment. Across the street a woman was emptying a pail full of rubbish onto the waste ground. This was garbage disposal, Indian-style. By next morning the rubbish would have gone: cows, pigs and dogs would have devoured everything.

Walt talked about his career in the Methodist Church. He had been a pastor since the age of twenty-five. 'I don't regret it,' he said. 'But it would have been nice to have had a higher level of income. Even the lowest paid teacher in America earns fifty per cent more than I do. Methodist pastors are at the bottom of the heap.' This was said without bitterness.

I joked that when he was the New Messiah the money would roll in. Ramesh heard this remark. 'Don't even think of it, Walt,' he called from the sitting room. 'If you bitch with spiritual forces they will desert you.' Henry joined in: 'Go for the money, Walt. Hey, when you're the Messiah it will do wonders for your sex life.' The New Messiah smiled tolerantly. This is what was expected of Henry.

Walt did not look well. He had been uncharacteristically quiet ever since we returned from our stroll on the promenade. He screwed up his face in pain. I asked him what the matter was. 'It's my stomach,' he said.

'You can blame it on the ice cream,' I replied rather unkindly.

'Nah. You don't get a stomach ache from ice cream.'

'Well, American ice cream is probably all right. But I wouldn't touch the stuff here. I remember an aunt of mine once saying that ice cream could be very dodgy. You never know what sort of bugs can lurk there.'

Walt grimaced again. I wasn't being very helpful. 'In that case I will have to heal myself,' he said. He clasped his hands together so that they were about six inches from his stomach. He closed his eyes and went deep into thought. A smile swept across his face. 'Ah, that's better,' he said. 'I can just feel the energy flowing out of my fingers. God's love energy. Ah. I can feel it going into my stomach.'

'Has it worked?' I asked.

'I feel much better. My stomach is beginning to heal itself.'

We stood in silence on the balcony for a couple of minutes while Walt held his hands in front of him. Then he opened his eyes. 'Not all healers can heal themselves, you know,' he said. 'But I find it works well. I seem to have the knack for it.'

Walt had spoken too soon. At the time we never realised the significance of that innocent-looking vanilla tub, but it was to have a devastating effect on Walt's psyche. A few scoops of Pondicherry ice cream were to almost destroy Walt's faith, and his powers of healing along with it.

I spent the next day with Ramesh at his laboratory in Pondicherry's Jipmer Hospital. A large complex set in pretty landscaped grounds with splashes of purple bougainvillea, it was regarded as one of the best hospitals in India.

Hundreds of people were milling around outside the building. Mothers cradled newborn babies, children limped on heavy plaster casts, barefoot old men, bent double, shuffled into the Outpatients Department. Ramesh shouted good morning to his colleagues as he led me down a long corridor to his lab. On the door was a sign scrawled in felt pen: 'Derision will never help in the development of true knowledge'. And it was here that Pondicherry's long tradition as a place of spiritual advancement was being kept alive.

Ramesh was conducting his human energy experiments in spartan conditions. There was no hi-tech furniture here. His lab was a boffin's lair, a shabby room with piles of paper stacked on broken chairs with sagging seats. A mess of wires led to contraptions that looked like they had been built by a schoolboy Meccano fan. On the walls were more slogans: 'Don't go where the path leads. Rather go where there is no path and leave a trail'; 'There are no incurable diseases, only incurable people'. Ramesh said the words gave him inspiration.

Ramesh specialised in what he described as bio-electrography. It was about as far removed from conventional medicine as you could get and he had developed the idea after studying ancient Indian scriptures. He had built a machine that used high-voltage, high-frequency electrical currents to photograph the aura – or energy field – surrounding the fingertips. It was possible to see from a photograph if a patient had cancer. The advantage of this technique over conventional methods of diagnosis such as smear tests was that cancer could be discovered much earlier.

Ramesh sat me down on one of his rickety chairs and, as he explained how it all worked, his eyes burned brightly. I had a feeling that his brain worked twice as fast as anyone else's.

Thousands of years ago the Indian sages believed that the physical body was surrounded by four energy bodies: the aura, the astral body, the mental body, and the body of cosmic consciousness. They concluded that anything happening to the physical body was first reflected in the energy bodies.

'It's a very ancient concept,' Ramesh said. 'Look at pictures of your Christian saints and you will see a ring – or halo – around the head. In almost all cultures, particularly Hinduism, the holy men and women had halos. The halo was the energy field that the old philosophers were talking about. But when the halo changed shape it meant something was going wrong in the physical body.

'I thought that maybe the halo could have a medical use,' Ramesh said. 'If we had some insight into what was happening to the physical body, we would not have to employ expensive medical techniques. My researchers and I started observing these energy fields through various filters. We had some very interesting correlations. In children, for example, there is very little difference between the sexes when you look at the aura. But in adults you find a definite female and definite male pattern. The man has a cigar, or phallus-shaped, energy field; an oval pattern surrounds the woman.'

Ramesh paused. Was I keeping up with him? He put his hands together as if in prayer and stormed on.

'I was looking for ways to fight cancer when I was struck with an idea. We have excellent methods of surgery and radiation or chemotherapy but the trouble is we are still unable to diagnose cancer early enough. By the time the patient comes to the doctor the cancer is already well advanced and you can't give a curative treatment. You can only keep the person up and alive for a little while.

'There is no method that can tell us about a cancerous process going on in the body before the symptoms appear. It suddenly became obvious that we should get this information from the energy body before there was a change in the physical body. Inside the body is a micro-electrical circuit with a large number of electrical changes taking place. These are probably responsible for the formation of the cancer. That is the basis of the whole thing. Stress, for example, can trigger off the process.

'We started by doing experiments using hypnosis to change the speeds of neuro-muscular conduction, or nerve transmission. We put people into trances and waited to see what happened. In several of the sessions the subjects went to such deep levels of trance that they became spontaneously clairvoyant and they started describing all kinds of colours coming out of the body. I had read about the aura and here were subjects – all medical students, perfectly sane people – suddenly describing colours no one else could see.

'One day a strange incident took place. A medical student, whom we had put into a trance, began to describe something very funny about one of my technicians. The student was burbling away and said he could see strange colours coming from the technician's body. I didn't take much notice. But the next day the technician didn't turn up for work. I eventually went round to his house. The man had gone down with a fever and was quite ill. He said that after he'd got home the previous evening he had developed a mild headache, which had turned into a full-blown fever.

'He came back to work a week later and I put the original hypnotised student into another deep trance. This time the student didn't find anything odd about the technician. This gave me a big clue. The student had reported something odd about the technician's aural emissions and in a way we had actually known what was going to happen to the person in the next few hours. It was fascinating, and that is when I started looking into the ancient Indian scriptures to find out more about what they had to say about energy fields.'

Hypnotising a person into a clairvoyant trance is a slow, tedious process. So Ramesh looked for other ways to see the aura. He came across the works of an English doctor called Walter John Kilner, who died in 1941. Kilner was the King's physician and worked at St Thomas's Hospital in London. All of a sudden Kilner abandoned conventional medicine and plunged into the field of aura research – much to the disgust of his colleagues, who refused to believe in such hocus-pocus.

Ramesh went on, 'Most of what I had recorded through clairvoyants matched what John Kilner had described in his books. This man had discovered a particular dye that could be used as a filter and through which one could see the aura.'

Ramesh tried out the same process, but now another problem faced him. He could not record the data. And that was when he stumbled across the works of the famous Russian engineer, Simon Kirlian. In 1934, Kirlian discovered that it was possible to take photographs of the human aura using high-voltage, high-frequency electrical currents.

'I thought it would be fantastic if I could build such an instrument. I'm not an engineer and if you're a medical man in India you're not even expected to understand your own household's electricity. I got a few ideas off some people who understood these things and I built a machine similar to Kirlian's.' Ramesh pointed at his Meccano kit. 'I started taking pictures of people's fingertips. I discovered there was a great difference between the photograph of the aura of a normal person and a cancer sufferer.

'In a healthy person the aura shoots out in fountains of light in an organised way. In cancer, the fountains are completely disorganised. That is not enough proof of cancer, so you have to feed the pictures into a densometer, which converts them into digital information.'

Ramesh discovered that cancer victims all displayed the same changes in the aura around their fingertips – irrespective of the type, size or location of the cancer.

'They had one particular pattern that was different from healthy people. We compared healthy individuals with people who had other kinds of illnesses. Cancer always came out differently. It was uncanny.

'The point is that once you know a person is developing cancer, it is easy to use other kinds of tests to pin-point it. You are no longer groping in the dark. It gives doctors much more time to treat people rather than screen dozens of people just to find out if they have cancer in the first place. Also you can use an aura test as many times as you want without the dangers of chemicals or radiation.

Ramesh's machine was also cheap. 'You can build one for about £6000 and each test would cost no more than fifty pence in the West. I come from a poor country where eighty per cent of the people cannot afford even the nominal costs of visiting a doctor. Many families have to go without food for a day if one of them wants to visit a doctor. We have lots of Government hospitals in India, but the treatment is generally bad. So even poor people go to private doctors even if they can't afford it. I believe that everybody should have a right to health. There should be no distinction between the rich and the poor.

'Medical investigative procedures in India are very expensive. Hi-tech techniques like magnetic resonance imaging cost several thousand pounds. There you can pick up a tumour of two centimetres in diameter. My method costs a fraction of that, it is much more efficient and it can pick up much smaller tumours.'

The lecture was over. Ramesh started plugging various wires into his machine. It featured a small perspex screen with a multitude of smaller wires running through it.

'Now I am going to test you, Peter,' he said. I looked horrified. 'Do not worry, you will not feel much.' He turned off the lights in the room so that we were in pitch darkness. I could feel him placing my index finger on a small perspex screen. Under my finger he slipped a piece of film. The screen was attached to what looked like a transformer for an electric train set.

'How many volts do you put through this thing?' I asked.

'Oh, about six thousand.' Ramesh flicked a switch. I felt a strong tingling sensation. I prayed that the instrument was earthed properly. Sparks flew out from around my finger. They formed a sort of multi-coloured circle. 'That is your aura,' Ramesh said. 'Bet you didn't even know you had it.' He flicked the switch again and the sparks died. We waited in darkness while he developed the film.

Ramesh switched the light on. He studied the negative. There was a perfect, unbroken circle around the area where my finger had been. 'This is a healthy reading,' he said. 'There is no sign of cancer.' I fumbled in my pocket for a packet of cigarettes. It was a reflex reaction, and anyway it wouldn't hurt to smoke one more.

I felt that we would be hearing a lot more of the name of Dr Ramesh Singh Chouhan. He was no crackpot scientist indulging in his whims. The Indian government was taking his experiments seriously and was pouring money into aura research. Statisticians at America's Princeton University had tested his data. They judged it ninety-eight per cent correct.

He was in regular contact with American and Russian doctors. Ramesh showed me a letter from Professor Victor Adamenko, head of the Soviet Academy of Physics. The professor had written that Dr Singh Chouhan was further ahead than anyone else in the world in the field of human energy research.

So this was the Pondicherry of the weird and the wonderful; a place where the spiritual reverberations rumbled with the force of a Californian earthquake. But where did Clive fit in? I was to find out the next weekend.

Ramesh had a dream.

Two months earlier the doctor was treating a woman for terminal cancer. He was approached by an uncle of a patient who was desperate to find a final, last-hope cure. The uncle told Ramesh that he had heard of an old sadhu – a man who had given up all material possessions for a life of spiritual search – who lived as a hermit in Kollihills, part of the Eastern Ghats, the range of mountains in inland Tamil Nadu. This sadhu was also an alchemist with supernatural powers. And he could cure cancer.

The uncle asked Ramesh if he would join him on an expedition to find the sadhu. Ramesh agreed. 'All that mattered to me was the welfare of my patient,' Ramesh said. 'Obviously I was sceptical, but the woman was about to die and if anything could be done to save her, that was fine by me.'

The uncle arranged to meet Ramesh at his home at 4 am one morning. Then they would drive together to Kollihills. Ramesh set his alarm and went to sleep. At about 3am. he had a dream in which the god Shiva came to him. Shiva is one of the three incarnations of Krishna, the omnipresent Hindu god: Brahma is the creator, Vishnu is the preserver, Shiva is the destroyer and reproducer.

'Lord Shiva stood in front of me and told me to come with him,' Ramesh went on. 'I was to accompany him to a temple in Kollihills. It was more of a vision than a dream. I could see Shiva clearly standing by my bed – and I can promise you I am not the sort of person who looks for visions.'

The uncle arrived and they drove six hours to Kollihills. They inquired about the mysterious sadhu, but no one knew where he was. Kollihills was famous for the medicinal herbs that grew on the hillsides and the holy man was believed to be far away searching for new potions.

'We were told we might find out more at an old temple that stood deep in the hills in a valley by a river. The temple was supposed to be four thousand years old, one of the oldest in South India. When we got there I discovered it was dedicated to Shiva. This hit me like a sledgehammer.

'We arrived at the temple at about 3 pm. I met a group of people coming from the temple and they said there was no point trying to get in as the doors were locked. I decided to try anyhow. I walked up to the doors to find that they were unlocked. This was the first surprise. I walked into the outer temple and tried the gate to the holy of holies in the centre.

'You must remember that, if the priest is not in, the holy of holies in any Indian temple is always firmly locked. But this gate was also open. I sat in the temple and got the most extraordinary feeling that I had been there before.'

Ramesh and his friend returned to Pondicherry having still not found the sadhu. And tragically, the woman died a few days later. Ramesh thought no more about the experience.

Until Bala arrived.

Bala was a sixty-six-year-old student of yoga, and a retired construction engineer from Sri Lanka. He had recently emigrated to Australia to join his grown-up sons. Bala returned annually to India to study yoga and meditation at one of the Pondicherry ashrams. This is where he had met Ramesh.

'The moment we met I felt that I had known Bala for years,' Ramesh said. 'We hit it off immediately.

'Bala asked me if I could introduce him to an astrologer friend of mine in Madras. This astrologer specialised in telling people about their past lives. We both went to see the man. We sat around a table and the astrologer began to talk.

'He told Bala that in one of his previous lives he had been a yoga student in a temple. The temple was in a place called Kollihills. The astrologer added that he'd never heard of Kollihills, the name had just come to him that moment. I was aghast. I'd never even heard of the place until a month before and now everyone was talking about it. This had to be more than mere coincidence. The astrologer told Bala he must go to the temple immediately. There he would have a revelation that would change his life. I told Bala that I could show him where the temple was because I too had been there in strange circumstances.'

And so we set out on the journey towards Bala's revelation; a jolly charabanc ride was to lead me deep into the heart of Indian mysticism. And a little closer to Clive himself.

We took the bus from Pondicherry to the town of Salem in the foothills of the Eastern Ghats. From here we would eventually make our way to the Kollihills. We were a bizarre tour group: Walt, Henry, Ramesh and me. And, of course, Bala.

Bala's name meant small in Singhalese. He was indeed small, a few inches over five feet, and one of the most delightful characters I had ever met. He was kind and gentle with a funny little face, a sort of male version of Mrs Tiggy-winkle. He spoke in a high, musical voice. When talking about someone he liked, he would say: 'He seems a decent sort of fellow. Oh yes, very decent.' Asked in the morning whether he had slept well, he would put on a slightly puzzled look and reply, 'I believe I did,' as if to say that you can never be sure of anything when you are asleep.

His inner peace left him only once when we talked about arranged marriages. I remarked that the arranged marriage was old-fashioned nonsense and unacceptable in the 1980s. Bala strongly disagreed. He was angry. 'You are quite wrong,' he said. 'I went against my parents' wishes and married for love. My mother was very against my marriage, but my father was quite open-minded and accepted my decision. My marriage ended sixteen years later. I wish I had taken my mother's advice and gone for an arranged marriage. It is a question of obligation, you see. Your family finds someone from the same background with the same outlook and ideals as you. Therefore the marriage has the greatest chance of surviving. There is no question about it.' I never broached the subject again. This was not a matter for argument.

The bus set off on the five-hour journey to Salem. We settled down in our seats as we rolled out of Pondicherry. I sat next to Bala. Walt had forsaken his mantras for a good book. He spent the trip with his nose stuck into *Battlefield Earth*, the sci-fi blockbuster by L. Ron Hubbard, late leader of the dubious Church of Scientology. He was still complaining of stomach pains and had undergone several more self-healing sessions.

Henry wasn't feeling very mystical. He sat across the aisle

from me, his Walkman headphones clamped to his ears. Someone in Pondi had given him a tape of traditional Indian music, but he was not enjoying it. He tore the headphones from his head. 'Shee-it,' he said, 'can't stand it. Sounds like the tape's gone speed crazy.' He changed the cassette. The Rolling Stones resumed service.

Henry was totally out of place in an Indian bus. Earlier he had told me about his most prized possession, a Chevrolet Speedbird sports car. Henry liked cars. He also owned a Porsche, but the Chevvy was his favourite. 'Hey, you should see it when I hit 100 mph with the roof down. I take an open can of beer in one hand and the slipstream just sucks it out and turns it into a vapour trail. Man, that Chevvy is *sleak*.' The bus backfired noisily, the springs groaned as we trundled over a pothole. Henry looked uncomfortable. He was accustomed to better transport.

I chatted to Bala, who was perched cross-legged on his seat. He had been studying yoga for six years. Meditation had changed his life. 'When I lived in Sri Lanka I was not good to myself,' he said in his soft sing-song voice. 'I used to smoke a tin of cigarettes a day, drink whisky and chase women. My life was not good. But through yoga I have found peace. I have learned that human beings are no more than a microcosm in the great macrocosm, we are part and parcel of nature. Yoga is a way of life, a method of teaching people to lead a sane life in an insane world.'

The bus driver kept his hand hard on his horn as we headed into the Tamil Nadu countryside. The noise was deafening. The conductor came down the bus to check our tickets. He shouted at a woman carrying a small child. She had the wrong ticket. She would have to get off at the next stop. Was this the insane world Bala talked about?

We waited for the disturbance to quieten down. Bala went on intensely. He was a leading light in yoga in Pondicherry. At the World Yoga Conference, held in the town the previous year, he had proposed a motion to take yoga to the next Olympic Games. He maintained that yoga had performance-enhancing qualities that could replace drugs like anabolic steroids.

'India does not have much to offer the world, but she does have yoga. And with it she will last until doomsday. Some spiritual gurus have predicted that India will conquer the world in the next century. It won't be a conquering in the normal sense of the word, with weapons. It will be a conquering through cosmic consciousness and the science of yoga. There was once a time when yoga was practised all over the world. There is proof, for example, that a few thousand years ago, it was common all over South America. But with the start of organised religion it declined.' Bala paused and smiled happily. 'Now yoga is coming back, and that is good. When we learn that we are all part of nature, things will be better.'

It was nearly midnight when we arrived at Salem. We were hot, sticky and tired. Even at that late hour the coach station was madness and we were pushed and jostled as we left the bus. As far as I could see there was little to recommend Salem, a modern town with a large amount of concrete buildings. It was one of the biggest centres for the country's jewellery industry. More than 50,000 people were employed making silver ankle chains that were sold all over the subcontinent.

We spent the night in a concrete lodging house that pompously called itself the Hotel Hema International. Or rather what was left of the night – we had an early start the next morning to catch the bus to Kollihills. I woke at 4 am and peered out of my room to see Henry sitting on the floor of the corridor.

Our millionaire playboy had been unable to sleep. Because of a shortage of accommodation, Henry had been forced to share a double bed with Bala. And Bala was not an easy person to share with.

'That guy chants mantras in his sleep,' Henry said. 'What the hell's going on? These Indians are crazy.'

I pointed out that Bala was Sri Lankan. It didn't make any difference to Henry. 'Sri Lankan, Indian, Hottentot . . . shee-it, they're all the same to me, man.' I looked into the room. Bala was already awake. He was sitting bolt upright on his bed doing his yoga breathing exercises – short puffs of air accompanied by little grunts.

It was time to catch the bus. Ramesh woke up Walt. The New Messiah was not a happy man. His stomach problems had reached epic proportions. He thought that perhaps an old stomach ulcer had flared up again. Either that, or it was the dinner of curried chicken the night before. Oh no, it's not, I thought, it's the Pondicherry ice cream.

Walt was very depressed and looked miserable. He had not

slept well and was wearing ear-plugs to keep out the noise of the traffic. He had been trying to heal himself with no luck.

'I don't know what is going on,' he moaned. 'I seem to be losing my power. This food is causing havoc to my stomach. I guess the Indians don't know what a bland diet is.' Ramesh tactfully suggested that, rather than faith healing, Walt should try some good old-fashioned antacid tablets.

'Yes, Walt,' Bala said. 'I think tablets are what you need. And you should really try to do some yoga, you know.'

Henry disagreed. 'Hell,' he said, 'what you need, Walt, is a good, long, slow massage with a Californian blonde.'

'Well, you won't find one of them in Salem,' Ramesh said. 'In fact, you won't find any blondes here.'

'In that case he can kill the pain with a bottle of whisky,' Henry said.

Walt lay on the bed moaning. Blondes, whisky, antacid tablets – he wanted none of them. He had another try at directing the love energy to his stomach. He shook his head sadly. He could feel no heat in his fingers. By God, I thought, this Pondicherry ice cream is vicious stuff.

Walt was not well enough to accompany us to the Kollihills. Henry said he would stay behind and keep Walt company. I suspected that Henry couldn't face another long bus journey. 'Don't worry about me,' he said. 'I'll just hang loose and have a few iced teas.' This was Henry's euphemism for beer.

Ramesh, Bala and I walked to the bus station. This was going to be a day to remember. Bala was dressed specially for his revelation. He wore a white shirt and traditional dhoti, a long piece of material tied around his waist. I felt that I was letting the side down in my empire-building, knee-length shorts and a T-shirt promoting Nutbourne Manor, a vineyard in the south of England.

It was still dark as the bus left Salem and began the twisting climb 4,000 feet up into the Eastern Ghats. As the light came up, a blue mist appeared over the mountains. The first rays of the sun appeared. It cast long shadows across the palm trees at the side of the road. The purple light turned to orange and then quickly into daylight.

I did not have much faith in the bus. It was a battered heap, about twenty years old. The route to a remote hamlet like

Kollihills was evidently not important enough to warrant a decent vehicle.

We had hardly gone ten miles when the bus filled with thick, oily smoke. Bala coughed violently and Ramesh held a handkerchief over his nose. The driver stopped and got out to inspect the damage. It transpired that no one had remembered to grease the back axle. The rear wheels were about to seize up.

Some of the passengers joined the driver at the rear of the bus. They stood around talking and prodding the wheels. I stayed in my seat and lit a cigarette. The conductor glared at me. 'Smoking is prohibited,' he growled.

'But the whole bus is full of smoke,' I said. 'One cigarette's not going to make much difference.'

'That is not the point. No smoking.'

The driver returned to his seat and drove to a garage where a posse of mechanics swarmed under the bus. We set off again two hours later. The road became steeper and the scenery took on an Alpine look as we wound through valleys of lush vegetation. Either side of the road were fields of rice, tapioca, sugar cane and pineapples. Cows with bells around their necks grazed under the shade of massive jackfruit and banyan trees.

The Eastern Ghats are home to one of the most productive agricultural areas of South India. Here, above the parched plains of Tamil Nadu, the air is cooler. Crops like rice and tapioca flourish in these mild conditions. Rivers run down the steep hillsides and in the early hours each morning a heavy dew adds more moisture to the ground. The farmers are less lethargic than their counterparts down in the steamy, dusty heat at sea level. The fields are tidier, the cultivation more efficient.

The road left the valleys. The gradient increased as we twisted around the mountainside past rocky outcrops and eucalyptus plantations. The bus swerved dangerously at the tight corners. Signs warned drivers to 'Leave early, get there slow'. Two thousand feet below, a heat haze shimmered over the brown, sunburnt plains.

It was a magnificent view . . . marred only by the presence of the man in the seat in front of me. He was determined to have a conversation with the only white man on the bus and he kept turning round to talk. He explained he was headmaster of a school near Kollihills.

I was holding my camera, attempting to take pictures of the

view, but the movement of the bus made photography impossible.

'Take photo!' the man urged as we trundled over the craters
in the road. 'Take photo – now!'

I pointed out that the bumpy bus would mean blurred pictures. 'No good for photos,' I said.

This had no effect. 'Take photo,' he insisted. He was becoming quite agitated. 'I give you my address and then you send
photo to me.'

The man changed tack. 'Drink!' he said. 'You give me drink.
Brandy!' I could see Ramesh smirking in his seat. Trust my luck
to be button-holed by the most boring man in South India. The
man then grabbed a novel I was reading. 'You give me,' he
raved. 'Present!'

I snatched the book back. 'No it's not a bloody present. It's
my book and I'd appreciate it if you left me alone.' The headmaster turned round and shut up. I felt deeply sorry for his
pupils.

The rocking motion of the bus lulled me into sleep. I awoke
an hour later as we reached the sprawling hamlet of Kollihills.
It was little more than a cluster of mud and thatch huts, vegetable stalls and a couple of lean-to shacks that functioned as
cafés. I looked out across the valleys to a glorious panorama of
rolling hills.

Bala could not wait to get off the bus. He was shivering with
anticipation and could hardly contain his excitement. Was this
where he had spent one of his past lives?

He turned his face towards the sky and sniffed the mountain
air. He was like an angel returning to heaven. This was his
firmament. 'Ah,' he said, 'ah, Peter, I feel that I have come
home. Oh, this is beautiful, very beautiful.' I felt a lump in my
throat. At that moment Bala was the happiest man in the world.

The temple lay near a giant banyan tree at the end of the
village. As we approached the temple walls, Bala softly repeated
a mantra. We stopped by a small stall. Ramesh and Bala each
bought coconuts, lemons, bananas and incense sticks. These
were for their puja, the offering to God that they would make
inside the temple. But before puja, Hindus must cleanse themselves. A river ran through a gorge below the temple. We
climbed down over the rocks. Ramesh and Bala stripped off
their clothes and bathed in the cool water.

The ancient Hindus chose their temple sites with great care and they sometimes spent years looking for a place with the right power and energy. They would search for an area where cattle liked to graze. In a big pasture the cows always had a favourite place. Likewise, dogs were considered to be a good sign. If dogs were found wandering among the cattle, then the site was perfect. But any sign of a cat in the field, and the site was abandoned. According to the ancients, dogs and cows attracted positive energies, whereas cats were definitely negative. The priests tethered the cows and left them there for forty-one days. Then they slaughtered the cows and checked their internal organs. If any of the beasts showed signs of disease then the priests looked for another place. If the cattle were all healthy, the construction of the temple went ahead.

I joined Bala and Ramesh in the river where I washed off the dust of the journey. A barefoot sadhu in orange robes was sitting on the rocks by the water's edge. He was a tall, thin man, and he suffered from a skin disease. His gaunt face was partially white and covered with moles. He smiled broadly and beckoned us over. He asked us what we were doing in Kollihills?

Ramesh told him our story. He explained how Shiva had come to him in a dream and how Bala was searching for clues to his past life. But where did the Englishman fit in? Ramesh told him about my relationship to Clive. The sadhu listened intently. He stood up and began to talk.

Kollihills was one of the oldest temple sites in South India. The sadhu added that it was well-known as a place of intense spiritual vibrations. And we had come here on one of the most auspicious days in the Hindu calendar. That night there would be a full moon, an event that traditionally marked Shiva's birthday. We would all have great luck in the future because we had travelled so far on such a special day.

'This is no coincidence,' the sadhu said. 'Everything has clicked. Everything has coincided to your advantage.' He pointed at Ramesh. 'Shiva himself has brought you here.' He turned to Bala: 'You are searching for your past life.'

Finally, the sadhu looked at me. 'Your ancestor was Robert Clive, a man who had a great effect on the destiny of India and you are searching for his past. I believe that Robert Clive has brought you to this special place. Such a powerful man with such a great mission in India can never go away. His vibrations will be felt until the end of time.'

I remained silent. What could I say? Was the sadhu talking superstitious nonsense? But who was I to argue with the mysteries of a civilisation thousands of years old?

Ramesh was convinced the sadhu was right. 'This can only be some kind of divine game, a message, a play of destiny. There are too many coincidences. You are tracing the footsteps of your forefather, a truly great man in India, and suddenly you turn up out of the blue on my doorstep. You meet Walt, who is supposed to be the reincarnation of Agasthayar and who lived his past life as a great rishi in India. Then Bala turns up looking for his past and Shiva tells me in a dream to come here. For such things to happen to four people travelling together is no coincidence.'

Ramesh stared hard at me. 'Why did we all meet like this? Can you explain it?' I could not.

The sadhu took Bala's arm and led him up the riverbank. It was moving to see these two peaceful, elderly men, walking arm in arm and linked by the common bond of devout Hinduism.

Ramesh and I followed them into the temple. Ramesh repeated our story to one of the brahmin priests. The priest said nothing, but merely nodded and prepared for the puja. I stayed at the back of the temple while Ramesh and Bala stood by the entrance to the holy of holies. They presented their offerings. The priest chanted mantras and placed the coconuts and lemons before the statue of the temple god. Then he placed a garland of lilies around the deity's neck.

The ceremony lasted for ten minutes. At the end, the priest invited Bala into the holy of holies. Bala sat on the floor cross-legged and began to meditate. He descended into a trance. Ramesh rejoined me and we left Bala alone in the temple. The sadhu brought us tea and we drank it under the shade of the banyan tree.

Bala returned an hour later. He was a man at peace, his mission was complete. 'I can honestly say I had a feeling of *déjà vu* in the temple,' he said. I have a wonderful sense of well-being and I look forward to the future. I could never understand why I became so interested in meditation. But now I understand that it is my mission in life to go deeply into yoga.'

The bus to Salem turned up and it was time to go. We said

goodbye to the sadhu. He clasped our hands and gave us his blessing. We boarded the bus. Workers from the fields were loading bananas and pineapples onto the roof. The hills were turning honey-coloured in the late afternoon sun. The sadhu waved. 'Perhaps one day we will meet again and you will tell me about the luck you found in Kollihills,' he shouted as we began our descent back down into the valley.

Back in Salem, Walt and Henry were showing signs of recovery. Henry's iced tea had put him into an excellent mood! 'Shee-it, some of these Injun girls are pretty.'

Walt had taken Ramesh's advice and had resorted to antacid tablets. His healing powers were still temporarily out of action and the tablets were having a slightly soothing effect on his stomach.

After the journey from the Kollihills the thought of another five-hour bus ride was too much. But Ramesh needed to get back home for work the next day and we all left the hotel and boarded yet another coach back to the coast.

I spent a week in Pondicherry relaxing by the sea and avoiding the ice cream salesman. Walt and Henry flew back to the States (would we ever hear of the New Messiah again?) and I was left with the company of Bala and Ramesh. Old Pondi was a soothing place where you could sit in cafés and watch the world go by. The streets were immaculately clean by Indian standards and the crowds stayed away in the heaving bazaars across the canal in black town.

But beneath the surface of this sedate old *grande dame* lurked a cesspool of back-biting and bitchiness.

The biggest landlord in Pondicherry was the Sri Aurobindo ashram, which owned many of the buildings in the old quarter. This centre of yoga and modern science was founded in 1926 by a Bengali called Aurobindo Ghosh. Aurobindo was born in Calcutta in 1872 and in his teens came to England where he studied at Cambridge University. On his return to India he became a writer and revolutionary in the extremist wing of the Indian Independence Movement. In 1908 he was jailed by the British for his part in a bomb plot. While in prison he discovered yoga and meditation. When he was released two years later, he fled south and took up residence in Pondicherry where he began teaching the Hindu scriptures to local people.

Aurobindo had the gift of the gab. Word spread quickly that here was a guru who could lead his pupils on the road to enlightenment. Other Bengalis began to trickle into Pondi and an ashram was built around Aurobindo's teachings. By the 1950s he was a cult figure and the ashram was on its way to becoming one of the most affluent in India. Now Aurobindo's Indian followers were joined by Westerners, who were only too happy to hand over their money in return for spiritual advancement.

After Aurobindo's death in 1950, his divine power passed to one of his devotees, a French woman known as 'The Mother'. Mira Alfassa, born in Paris to wealthy part-Egyptian parents, who themselves were deeply spiritual and religious, first came to India in 1914 with her husband, a French diplomat. She was granted an audience with Aurobindo and that meeting was to change her life. The outbreak of the First World War forced her to return to France, but by 1920 she was back, minus her husband, in Pondicherry. And when Aurobindo went into seclusion in 1926, The Mother, as she was now called, took charge of the ashram.

The Mother had a vision. She dreamed of a utopian city, an 'experiment in international living where men and women could live in peace and progressive harmony with each other above all creeds, politics and nationalities'. It would be shaped like a lotus flower, the sacred bloom in the ancient Hindu scriptures. It would be the City of Dawn.

And so the town of Auroville was born. The Mother and her ashramites bought a 12,000-acre site to the south of Pondicherry. At the height of flower power in 1968 a vast building project was launched. The Mother stood up and announced that Auroville was the way to world peace. In a ceremony brimming with sincerity and good vibes, the representatives of 121 nations came to pour soil from their countries into a symbolic urn. Money poured in from overseas, including contributions from international agencies like UNESCO.

But in 1973 The Mother died. And with her went the love and peace of the old days. A bitter struggle broke out over the ownership of Auroville. The Sri Aurobindo Society said it was theirs. The people living in Auroville said they owned it.

The two sides sniped at each other. The Aurovillians claimed that the Society had misused funds meant for building. The

Society fired back. They refused to pay the bills for the project, accusing the Aurovillians of corrupting The Mother's teachings and indulging in free sex and drugs.

The squabble drifted on for more than a decade until the Indian Government stepped in. Ownership passed to the Government with the Auroville Foundation Bill of 1988.

These days the Pondicherry locals have little time for either the ashram or Auroville. Both are populated by foreigners and rich Indians from outside the town. Local people, who cannot afford the large donations required to join, are ignored.

'You need lots of money to be an ashramite,' one Pondicherry shopkeeper told me. 'Give them a big donation and you are treated well. But if a common man turns up at the ashram without money . . . well, dogs are treated better.

'Aurobindo himself was a good man. But the horrendous thing about these people who claim to represent him is that foreigners think they are an example of how human beings should behave. Actually, they are evil money-grabbers with octopus tentacles. They've managed to buy half the property in the town by conning rich Europeans and Americans into believing their so-called divine messages. Actually, the ashram is about as alien to regular Indian culture as you can get.

'You only have to go into one of the ashram shops to see what's going on. Everything costs twice as much as it would elsewhere because it's supposed to have been blessed by Aurobindo and The Mother. No one can understand how these supposedly intelligent foreigners can fall for it.'

Auroville, meanwhile, continues to exist as if the hippy dream of the 1960s never went away. Outsiders say that drug-taking is as rife as ever and the township suffers from a serious heroin problem. The shopkeeper in Pondicherry alleged that Auroville was no more than one big red-light area where European girls plied their trade to fund their drug habits. But the most outrageous claim I heard was that Westerners visiting Auroville were responsible for the first cases of AIDS in India.

I spent a day there with Bala, who was still in a state of spiritual euphoria after his pilgrimage to Kollihills. But even the tolerant Bala couldn't work out what was going on.

'What are these people trying to do?' he asked. 'With yoga I can live within myself and take outside influences in my stride. Why do people need to shut themselves up in Auroville?'

Auroville was like an exclusive club. The blurb proclaimed it was for 'those who thirst for progress and aspire to a higher and truer life'. There wasn't much progress here. And nearly two decades after its foundation, the place looked like a building site.

We started at the visitors' centre where I found a copy of the charter: 'Auroville belongs to humanity as a whole. But to live in Auroville one must be a willing servitor of the Divine consciousness . . . Auroville is for those who want to do the Yoga of work. To live in Auroville means to do the Yoga of work. So all Aurovillians must take up work and do it as a Yoga.'

This was hippy gobbledygook at its most inspired. But the names of the surrounding townships were even better: New Creation, Gratitude, Hope, Sincerity, Quiet, Existence, Fertile Forest.

I chatted to Eleanor, an Aurovillian in charge of the information office. She was a former journalist, a no-nonsense lady in her fifties, who left her native Canada ten years ago to pursue The Mother's dream. Eleanor had been an active Christian all her life. 'But I found that a bit narrow,' she said. 'I had read about The Mother and I thought that this was exactly where I was on my spiritual journey.'

Eleanor explained how Auroville worked. Newcomers were expected to put £1,000 into the kitty. This entitled them to live in Auroville for three months. After that, they had to find a job in anything from electronics and accountancy to teaching and farming (macrobiotic only, pesticides most definitely not allowed). When you found work, you were entitled to free food and pocket money.

'We provide maintenance for everybody depending on how much they can earn from their work,' Eleanor said. 'If, for example, you can make clothes, you'll make a bit of money selling things in our visitors' shop. But if you work in our health centre you're not going to make anything and will have to rely totally on our maintenance fund.'

Eleanor conceded that no one was going to make a fortune in Auroville. 'I suppose that half of us have private money. If you don't and you have a family to support, you might have to work abroad for a few months once a year. In the Gulf, for example.' Aurovillians were encouraged to build their own houses. 'Once you've built it, it is yours,' she added. 'But the moment you leave for good, it belongs to Auroville. No, we do not encourage holiday homes!'

So was Auroville just one big, permanent hippy commune where everyone could do as they pleased? Was there free love under the palm trees? Could you smoke marijuana until it came out of your ears?

Eleanor said: 'There are no rules, except one – no drugs. We're getting tough these days. I've heard the rumours about a heroin problem, but they're completely untrue. We've thrown out two or three people and if people don't behave we don't let them come back. The same thing happens if you don't work. There was one man who had a large private income. He thought he could sit back in the sun and do nothing. He didn't last long.'

'What about the local Indians?' I asked. 'There can't be many of them who can afford £1,000? What happens if they want to live here?'

'There are many Indians living in their villages on the site,' Eleanor said. 'They earn money like we do and are mostly employed as labourers.'

Great stuff! The Westerners ran the place while the Indians worked as labourers. Imperialism was not dead! Dupleix would have loved it!

Eleanor showed us the main auditorium and conference hall. It was a remarkably hideous piece of 1960s concrete architecture designed in the 1970s by an Indian Government architect. I remarked that this grey blockhouse with its ski-jump roof made London's National Theatre on the South Bank look quite beautiful. 'Yes,' said Eleanor. 'We think it's dreadful too. But the Indian Government very kindly built it for us so what can we do?'

But the most outrageous construction was the enormous meditation hall known as the Matri Mandir that was designed to be Auroville's spiritual centre.

We walked across an acre of parkland. Bala and I stared up in a mixture of awe and horror. 'What are these people doing?' Bala asked for the second time that day.

The Matri Mandir was a 100-foot high concrete golf ball. It was vast and bulbous and it dominated the countryside. Beside it a towering crane swung about with more chunks of concrete. Indian workmen swarmed over the sphere. It was a revolting display of expensive nonsense in a country where most people were on the breadline. But even worse was the Aurovillians' plan to install in the centre of this thing a crystal ball. Not just any old crystal ball, but the world's biggest crystal ball, that was being made by a German glass manufacturer for £50,000.

Despite its claims of oneness and collectivity, Auroville seemed to be trying to be a little piece of Western civilisation in India. Far from being 'utopian', the place had a depressing atmosphere. The Aurovillians wore intense looks and I wondered whether many of them had simply escaped the stressful West to recover from nervous breakdowns. It was certainly a place for the rich. Most of the young people looked rather yuppy-ish in tidy, designer clothes. Button-down shirts and Italian loafers outnumbered T-shirts and sandals. Frankly, after the hocus-pocus of the 1960s, I was surprised that Auroville had any relevance today.

What was the future of Auroville? The inhabitants were optimistic. They cheerfully talked about a final population of 50,000. But they were unworried by the fact that well under 1,000 seekers of truth and all things macrobiotic had decided to settle here.

Bala and I left in disgust. On the way out we stopped at the souvenir shop. Here you could buy the products of Auroville: fancy little children's romper suits, arty-crafty wooden toys, hand-painted greetings cards and scented candles. The prices were three times as much as you'd find anywhere else in India. It was like walking into a National Trust gift shop.

I had one final mission before I returned to Madras. Ramesh suggested that if I wanted to discover more of the secrets of India – and, indeed, myself – I should go to a Nadi reading.

The Nadi is the world's most mysterious system of astrological prediction. Here you find Indian mysticism at its deepest.

The Nadi dates from around two thousand years ago when a rishi called Brighu produced a vast series of personal horoscopes on palm leaves called saraswathi, after the goddess of knowledge. He dictated his predictions to a team of scribes, who wrote them down in Mundu Tamil, the ancient form of Tamil.

Rishi Brighu is said to have had the power of divine insight and he was able to write down the past, present and future lives of individuals, who would make their stay on this planet in years to come.

It seems difficult to believe, but the Nadi readers claim there is a palm leaf for nearly everyone in the world. It seems mathematically impossible that Brighu would have had the time to write down the past, present and future of billions of people. But the Nadi readers counter this argument by saying that many people share the same palm leaves. Therefore, on that basis there are perhaps thousands of people out there with the same past, present and future as yourself. Likewise, Brighu based his philosophy on the fact that when a person died his or her spirit would pass to another person.

The Nadi differs from other horoscopes in that it uses no intuitive, instinctive skills of clairvoyancy. First you provide your date of birth and an impression of your thumbprint – the right thumb for males, the left for females. Then you are asked a few questions as a sort of index: Are your parents still alive? Do you have brothers and sisters? Then the reader looks for the palm leaf corresponding to you. All the Nadi reader does is relate exactly what is written on the palm leaf. Nothing else. Ramesh was able to read the ancient Mundu Tamil script. When his Nadi was read a few years ago, he asked to look at the palm leaf afterwards. 'What the man had just told me was exactly the same as what was written down,' he said. 'Just from my thumb print, the palm leaf got my whole family history absolutely accurate as well as my life to that point. As to whether the future was accurate, I have yet to find out.'

If you don't believe in horoscopes, then all this will sound like nonsense. But it must be said that the Nadi is one of the great mysteries of India. And Indians take their readings very seriously indeed.

The Brighu Samhita, or collection, was duplicated 150 years ago. And one of the sets of inscriptions had ended up in the little town of Vaitishwaran Koil, thirty miles south of Pondi. The palm leaves were kept in a small terraced house in the centre of town.

When I turned up, a minibus load of rich Indians from Madras were crowded on the verandah waiting to have their leaves read. A man in the office seemed amazed that an Englishman had heard about the place. He arranged for me to see a reader immediately. The problem was that no one spoke much English.

Help appeared in the form of a well-to-do-tea-planter and his wife from Ootacamund, the hill station on the western boundary of Tamil Nadu. They had travelled 250 miles specially to have their fortunes read. They spoke good English and they agreed to sit in on my reading and translate what the reader told me.

We sat down on the floor in a large room with shuttered windows. It was dark and gloomy and lit by a single candle. The Nadi reader was called Mr Chellian. He sat on a cushion behind a low lectern. He took my thumbprint and asked a few questions about my family. Then he disappeared into a backroom and returned with a set of palm leaves. They were long strips, measuring about one inch by a foot, and tied together with leather thongs. They were covered in the neat, tiny script of Mundu Tamil.

Mr Chellian flicked through the leaves and came to the one that corresponded to me. He began reading it. I have to admit that although he was not entirely accurate about my childhood and immediate past, he got most of it right. It galled me to be reminded, for example, of my lack of academic study at school. He also correctly identified my father's occupation – farmer – and informed me, correctly again, that my sister was an actress.

Mr Chellian moved to my future . . . and then to the end of my future. And this was the bit I had not wanted to hear.

He lowered his voice. My interpreter, the tea-planter, did the same. Suddenly everything had become very solemn. I had a nasty feeling about what was going to happen next. The Nadi reader continued. The tea-planter translated: 'At the age of . . . you will leave this life. It will be in a hospital on the . . . of . . . and you will go peacefully.' That was enough for me. I stood up, thanked everyone for their time and handed Mr Chellian his fee. He looked puzzled. Why was I in such a rush to go? I muttered something about needing a breath of fresh air. Not for a moment had he thought there was anything wrong in telling a person when and where he was going to die.

And that put an end to my metaphysical meanderings. It was time to return to Madras and get stuck back into Clive's trail. Bala was preparing to leave his yoga studies to fly back to Australia and I promised Ramesh that I would look him up again before I left India.

I was sad to leave Pondicherry. The place had given me an insight into what India could offer the world. That nothing should be clear-cut; that we should take nothing for granted; that it is too easy to explain events as mere coincidence; that the forces of destiny are guiding us all.

Three

It was a great idea at the time. Find a bullock cart and travel in it to Arcot. What better way to get the feel of India? What better way to capture the atmosphere of Clive's march to the town that was to make him a hero?

The siege of Arcot was the turning point in Clive's military career and the first positive step towards the foundation of the British Empire in India.

By 1751 Clive had risen to the rank of captain. He had received his baptism of fire three years earlier when the French attempted to capture Fort St David. Clive was still an East India Company servant and only a part-time soldier, but he distinguished himself in further actions against the French and was quickly gaining the attention of his superiors. Here was a formidable commander.

The politics of the time are complicated. Briefly, France and England were each trying to promote their own puppet ruler in order to secure a lasting foothold in India and all the treasures that went with her. The prize was the throne of the Nawab of the Carnatic, a kingdom that encompassed a large expanse of South India. The support of the Nawab was vital for a foreign power wanting to trade unhindered. The English candidate was a prince named Mohammed Ali. Down in Pondicherry, Governor Dupleix was backing a pretender called Chanda Sahib.

By the summer of 1749, the French were winning the political game. Chanda Sahib was confirmed as Nawab and Mohammed Ali's forces were under siege in the town of Trichinopoly. It could not be long before Mohammed Ali surrendered. And where would the British be then? They would have no Nawab to support and the control of South India would fall into the hands of the French.

Swift action was called for. And it was Clive who came up with the plan. It was bold and dangerous, a desperate, final gamble.

Clive suggested that, to relieve the pressure on Trichinopoly, the English should attack and occupy Arcot, capital of the Carnatic. This would force Arcot's new ruler, Chanda Sahib, to turn his attention elsewhere. After all, the Nawab could hardly stand by and see his capital lost. 'It was a suggestion,' says the historian Philip Mason, 'of which the direct results lasted two hundred years and the indirect may last as long again.'

On 26 August 1751, Captain Clive set out from Madras across the Choultry Plain, the boundless sweep of arid scrub and desert that lay inland. His army consisted of no more than 200 Europeans and 300 sepoys. They were backed up with three field pieces for their artillery.

It was the height of the monsoon, the worst time to travel in India. But despite the intense heat and sudden downpours of torrential rain, the army covered the sixty miles to Arcot in barely six days. They arrived to find the town undefended. The garrison had fled. The enemy had no intention of tangling with a superhuman army who had marched on regardlessly, paying not the slightest attention to the appalling weather.

Clive took the town. His plan had the desired effect and the infuriated Chanda Sahib began to move troops up from Trichinopoly to lay siege to Arcot. The odds began at 2–1 and soon rose to 40–1. The English held out for more than two months. At dawn on the seventy-fifth day, the enemy made their final assault only to be repelled by musket fire. The fighting went on until the early hours of the following morning. Then, frustrated by their efforts and hearing that English reinforcements were on their way from Madras, Chanda Sahib's hordes lost faith and fled. News of Clive's success spread fast, not least because of his age. This was the sort of achievement expected of grizzled veterans with years of battle experience. Captain Robert was a mere twenty-six.

The bullock cart wheeze started over a few beers with a chap called Christopher whom I met in Madras. Christopher was overseas sales manager for a London publisher. He was on business in India persuading bookshops to stock his paperbacks.

Christopher understood the sort of things that sold travel books. 'You've got to have an original angle,' he said. 'Walking to Arcot is no good because everyone's written about walking in India. Bicycles are old hat too.'

We were sitting in the bar at the Connemara, an ex-maharaja's mansion, now the smartest hotel in Madras. After his fourth bottle of Kingfisher lager, Christopher suddenly found inspiration.

'What about a bullock cart? No travel writer has ever made a journey in India with a bullock cart. Clive's army would have used bullocks to pull the artillery and carry supplies. A bullock would be quite in keeping.'

'Great idea,' I said. 'First thing tomorrow I'll find a chap with a bullock cart and get him to take me to Arcot.'

'Yeah, great idea,' Christopher said. And that is what it was: a great idea.

Next morning I was nursing a hangover in a café next to the Broadlands. A bald man with dark shiny skin sat down at the table opposite me.

'Where you from?' he demanded.

I did not feel like company. 'England,' I replied tersely.

'You want to sell anything?'

'No.'

'Good price for cameras.'

'No'

The man squinted at me through opaque, watery eyes. His teeth were stained red from chewing betel nut. I did not like the look of him. He shifted in his seat.

'Grass? You want grass? Best stuff from Kerala. Kashmir black hash?'

'No.'

'Opium?'

'N-O spells no.' I decided to play the dealer at his own game. 'You can keep your drugs. But here's a thought. Any idea where I can find a bullock.'

'A bullet?' The dealer looked dumbfounded. Was this tourist a travelling hit-man?

'A bullock – with a cart. I want someone with a bullock cart who can take me to Arcot. If you can find someone, I'll give you an introduction fee. Now, that can't be bad, can it?'

The man cocked his head to one side. He was confused. I was

not getting through to him. 'You want to change money? Good black market rate.'

'The only thing that I want is a cart with a bullock. You know, a sort of cow. You see them all over India.'

'Bullock cart? I have no bullock cart.' The dealer spat the words. He was completely flummoxed and quite cross. He got up and left the restaurant in disgust, convinced that the foreigner was not firing on all cylinders.

I returned to my room at the Broadlands. Mr Rasnan arrived clutching his Gladstone bag. He smelled faintly of eucalyptus oil. Did he know where I could find a bullock cart? Mr Rasnan took the question in his stride. There was nothing odd about wanting to take a bullock cart to Arcot. But no, he did not know of one. None of his friends owned a bullock. Perhaps I should ask a farmer.

I tackled dozens of people on the street and in shops and restaurants. The answer was always no. In the end I took Mr Rasnan's advice. I took a bus to the outskirts of Madras and found a farmer who could speak a little English. He owned a bullock cart in which he brought vegetables into the city.

The farmer soon put an end to my ridiculous idea.

'No one will take you with their bullock cart to Arcot,' he said. 'Arcot is sixty miles away and that is too far for the bullock. Perhaps the bullock will die and that is bad because bullocks are very costly animals.'

I explained that I did not want to cause unnecessary suffering to an innocent bullock. I merely wanted to use the same transport as Clive's army.

'Pa! In those days it would have not mattered if the bullock died,' the farmer said. 'The army would have eaten it. But I am vegetarian and I would not wish to eat my bullock.'

It was cheering that the welfare of the farmer's animal was more important to him than my offer of a fistful of rupees. The idea that had been dreamed up over a few beers was simply not feasible – unless I planned to eat steak for a month. In the end I swallowed my pride and took the bus to Arcot.

These days Arcot could not withstand a 75-day siege without the occupying force dying from water poisoning.

The largest industry in Tamil Nadu is the production of leather, with tanneries centred around Arcot and the neighbouring town of Vellore. Tamil Nadu's treated hides end up on the West's fashion market where they are turned into clothing, handbags and shoes. Such is the demand for leather that factories have sharply increased their output in the last five years. This has led to the inevitable problem of pollution. There are more than seventy chemicals and salts in tannery effluents, which are harmful when mixed with water or soil.

Pollution control does not rest high in the consciences of the Indian leather barons. Thousands of gallons of untreated chemical-ridden effluent have ended up in the Palar River which runs through Arcot and Vellore. When I arrived in Arcot the level of bacteria in the water had reached such a point that local people were demanding that tanneries be shut down unless effective treatment plants were installed. Brain and liver diseases were rife. Cattle were dying after drinking contaminated water. I heard one story about a man who turned on his tap only to be rewarded by a flow of green slime.

The state government was taking little action save for agreeing that there was a problem. Licences were still being granted to new tanneries. After all, who wanted to rock the boat when such a profitable industry was at stake? But one thing was clear: if conditions had been as bad 250 years ago, Clive's small army would have been poisoned.

The bus left Madras on the main Arcot highway, a limitless ribbon of tarmac stretching across the Choultry Plain. Madrassers warned me that it was one of the most dangerous roads in Tamil Nadu.

As early as 6 am it was crowded with lorries thundering to and from the tanneries inland. The ancient vehicles were overloaded with stinking animal hides, great masses of dripping, gelatinous skin. On the back of one of the trucks someone had stuck a sign – 'Do not follow me, I am lost'. Judging by the erratic way they swerved and jostled for position on the road, the drivers looked as if they were losing themselves to sleep. They were over-tired and under pressure. The tanneries paid on piece work. The more trips made the more money the drivers earned, until exhaustion forced them to stop.

The Choultry Plain was flat, hot and dull with rice paddies stretching into the distance. Two and a half centuries ago, cactus would have covered the landscape. Now it was dotted with ugly billboards. A poster advertising a make of motorbike advised us to 'Go for a pick up not a pack up'. Another promoted the merits of 'Bisleri Club – the quiet soda water that bubbles gently'. I wondered what advantages there were in having a silent soda with your whisky. The Church of South India had erected a hoarding made to look like an endorsement for Coca Cola. Written in the famous Coke script, it proclaimed, 'Things go better with Jesus'.

We passed soft drinks factories and a ceramics works. Six miles out of the city the Madras Sports Trust was building a new motor racing track conforming to international standards. The Trust claimed it would rival Brands Hatch and Monaco. What would the locals make of Formula One machines in a country where the speed on the roads was seldom more than 40 mph?

In Clive's day, the Choultry Plain would have been sparsely populated with a few villages of thatched huts. But deep wells and twentieth-century irrigation had made it home to thousands. There were people and animals everywhere. Families clustered around roadside shrines and small boys splashed in water butts. Peasants carried calves around their necks. They barely glanced at the broken trucks and coaches that littered the ditches under the avenues of tamarind trees. In the fields, men trained oxen on leading reins and ducks feasted on green stalks of rice. The bus stopped at a village to make way for a marriage procession. A ten-piece brass band in multi-coloured home-made uniforms marched like toy soldiers in front of an elderly Morris Minor convertible containing the bridal couple.

Three hours after leaving Madras, the bus rumbled across the long bridge spanning the Palar River and entered Arcot, a third-grade municipality with a population of about 100,000. It was congested with traffic and typical of a Tamil Nadu rural town. Around the bus station was the inevitable collection of soft drinks stands, banana barrows and stalls selling flimsy sandals. Arcot featured a type of cycle rickshaw I had not seen before. They were little covered wagons with canvas awnings and used for carrying light loads like bundles of sugar cane.

I had heard there was a museum in Arcot. I hung around at the bus stand asking people for directions. A museum? Never heard of one. Try asking someone else. What d'you say? Museum? Sorry. Might be up that street over there.

I walked and walked until I met an old man with silver-grey hair. He seemed to understand what I was talking about and agreed to show me the way. The museum turned out to be in a small house tucked away down a back street.

The curator, Mr Thulariram, was making tea when I arrived. I introduced myself and explained my reasons for visiting Arcot. Mr Thulariram listened patiently and then exploded with enthusiasm. He shook my hand until it threatened to fall off. Here, at last, was someone who had travelled miles specially to see what was becoming his life's work. For he was taking his role as Arcot's chief archivist very seriously indeed.

Mr T. was an anxious man with great plans and practically no resources. His museum was a dusty, ill-lit chamber of about twenty five feet square. The exhibits consisted of fragments of pottery, rusty swords and daggers, a few Hindu sculptures and some faded black and white photographs of nineteenth-century Arcot. The chipped, plywood display cabinets were an example of DIY gone horribly wrong. It was not an impressive collection. But the museum was less than two years old and Mr T. hoped that in time he could move to larger premises.

Mr T. pointed at his hoard of treasures. 'I am collecting all these things with heavy pain,' he sighed. 'I have collected everything myself. Everyday I am out begging, borrowing or stealing things of interest from local people. If persuasion does not work, then I pay a few rupees out of my own pocket. Sometimes I take my lunch to Arcot fort and look for old cannon balls.'

Mr T. showed me his collection of coins. Many dated from the eighteenth and nineteenth centuries when the Nawabs issued currency in collaboration with the East India Company.

Clive was noticeable by his absence. He did not feature any-where in the museum. Mr T. apologised for this. 'I would like to have a special corner for Clive since he is very important to Arcot. But everything to do with him is in the museum in Madras and they will not let me have anything. When you return to England, please send me a picture of Clive. And maybe even some good books. I am very desperate for new artifacts.'

Mr T. was not overburdened with work and agreed to take the afternoon off to show me around the old fort. Arcot, sur-rounded by two miles of walls, was one of the biggest forts in Carnatica. And it is only when I saw the place that I realised what an enormous task Clive had to defend it with so few men. The defences consisted of an outer 'city' fort, which in the eighteenth century would have been home to most of the inhabitants. Further in there was a moat, which surrounded the Nawab's 'palace' fort.

Mr T. found a taxi and we set off to the south of town. Here, on the outskirts, was the Delhi Gate, the only section of original fort wall still in one piece. Clive is said to have made his siege headquarters in the room above the arch. It was a moment of irony that Clive gave it the name Delhi Gate. The city of Delhi, powerbase of India's Moghul rulers, was more than 1,000 miles to the north. But Clive believed – rightly, as it turned out – that the capture of Arcot would eventually lead to a British victory over the Moghuls. From Arcot, the road led to Delhi and final conquest.

We walked half a mile to the site of the Nawab's palace. The entrance was marked with a large black cannon, but the ramparts had gone. They were no more than lines of stone poking up through tufts of grass. After serving its purpose, Arcot had been left to fall down. There was no sign of the palace except for a huge empty 'tank', or pond. 'This is where the royal ladies took their baths,' Mr T. explained. I looked at the layer of green sludge in the bottom. No self-respecting water buffalo would bathe there now. Next to the tank was a small structure. 'Maybe it was the ladies' changing room,' Mr T. added.

The only other building of significance was the Nawab's mosque. It was unused and decaying fast. It would not be long before the mosque joined the rest of the ruins.

Clive's bravery at Arcot wrote him into South Indian folklore. He lived on the battlements in the stinking heat, seldom leaving the sides of his men. He went the rounds with a sergeant. Three times enemy muskets were aimed at him. Three times it was the sergeants who took the fatal bullets. As Clive was said to have remarked after his failed suicide attempt in Madras, the fates seemed to have greater things planned for him. At least, that's what the superstition-hungry Indians thought. By the end of the siege, Clive's name was legend. A grateful Mohammed Ali presented the young man with the robes of a Moslem warrior and called him Sabit Jang – 'steady in war'. The Tamil scribes wrote down tales of his bravery so that they could be told to future generations. Two and a half centuries later the name of Clive lived on in the fort of Arcot.

I ended my tour at the tiny village in the centre of the fortifications where women were filling gleaming copper water carriers from a handpump. The village was still known as Clive Bazaar. But had you listened carefully to the locals, you would have heard them talk about Kalava Bazaar. Kalava was a corruption of Clive. But the word also meant town chief in Tamil.

Was this more than just a remarkable coincidence? Were the forces of Indian mysticism playing their little games again? Was this part of Clive's destiny? Whatever the answer, there can be no doubt that the extraordinary mystique surrounding Clive was strengthened by the fact that his name was so similar to the Tamil word for 'leader'.

After Arcot my journey took me twenty miles south to Arani. Here Clive began the mopping up campaign that followed the siege. Arani was Clive's first victory in the field. The English met Raza Sahib's forces across a huge paddy swamp outside the town. Clive wisely placed his artillery and troops on high ground so that, when the enemy charged, the English were able to shoot them down easily. Two hundred of Raza Sahib's troops, including a detachment of French infantry, were killed or wounded. Losses to Clive's army amounted to only eight sepoys. But more significant was the fact that the French panicked during the action, suddenly retreating under the fusillades of musket fire. The enemy troops were so disgusted by this display of cowardice that next morning many offered their services to Clive. The tide had turned against the French; far better for the Indians to be on the winning side.

During my travels I had been told by several people, including a yoga guru in Pondicherry, that Clive had presented a temple in Arani with two valuable rubies to be used as the eyes of the resident god.

Clive would have had no problem paying for a pair of rubies. The grateful Nawab Mohammed Ali was said to have given him a present of 40,000 rupees, and the Captain was also making a small fortune in his role as commissary. As well as leading the troops, Clive was also responsible for feeding them. His bosses in Madras had given him an allowance of half a rupee a day for every European soldier under his command. With a certain amount of haggling, Clive was able to procure supplies for much less than his allowance, allowing him to slip the difference into his own pocket. This was a recognised perk – and a substantial one: and a year later Clive was able to return to England with a fortune of £40,000.

Like so many things in India, the rubies story was rather muddled. No one knew exactly which temple the stones were presented to. Nor could anyone tell me why Clive suddenly had this fit of generosity. Perhaps the gift was a way of saying thank you for his victory. The yoga guru in Pondi swore that the rubies existed, so I decided to make my way to Arani to find out for myself. This turned out to be a big mistake.

On the basis that Clive was doing rather nicely after Arcot, I splashed out on a taxi to take me to Arani. Lolling in the roomy back seat of a cab made a refreshing change from standing up in a crowded country bus. My driver was a man of twenty-one called Ravi. He had a shaved head, possessed a smattering of English, and was convinced that Singapore was a suburb of London. He had stuck a plastic statue of Krishna on the cab's dashboard and a garland of flowers hung from the rearview mirror. One of the rear doors had a tendency to fly open without warning.

As I climbed into the vehicle, Ravi demonstrated his knowledge of my language. 'Four wheels,' he said proudly, pointing at the car. I was glad to hear it.

Ravi spent five minutes revving the engine until it was firing on all four cylinders. We headed out of town. As we drove through the streets he leaned out of the window, waving wildly at friends on the pavement.

'English boss,' he yelled. 'Good money.' Ravi looked back at me, laughing through yellow teeth. He found this hugely amusing. I cringed in embarrassment as people stared at me through the car windows. We stopped by a house and Ravi hooted on the horn. We were joined by a friend of his called Gopal. Ravi moved over to let Gopal take charge of the driving. Gopal crashed the taxi into gear and we were off again. It turned out that Gopal was a seventeen-year-old schoolboy, and Ravi was teaching him to drive. This was unnerving.

Ravi went to sleep, which was not what one expected of a driving instructor. Gopal was left in charge to negotiate around the scores of water buffalo on the road.

Our route took us via the tannery town of Vellore. It was in the huge fortress of Vellore that Raza Sahib rallied his troops after his defeat at Arcot. One of my guidebooks gushed that

Vellore was a picture book rural Tamil Nadu town with endless subjects for photography. My attitude was that if you were after pictures of stray cows and plastic flip-flop salesmen, why leave Madras?

But it has to be said that the fort, dating from the sixteenth century, was highly impressive. It was a sinister looking place, grey and forbidding, and straight out of Hollywood. I could imagine Raza Sahib pacing the dungeons and dreaming up the most terrible tortures for his English enemies.

The fort had ceased long ago to be a means of defence and the moat now provided coarse fishing courtesy of the Tamil Nadu Fisheries Department. Inside the walls was a collection of run-down army barracks and a police training college.

Gopal stopped the car and I explored the fort temple. It was an unhurried, peaceful place. A cat sat on a wall languidly cleaning its face. Outside the holy of holies a man was playing an elongated, clarinet-type instrument. It was a slow, soulful melody that conjured up images of a smoky jazz club. And I could swear that the tune – presumably an ancient Hindu melody – contained snatches of Acker Bilk's *Stranger on the Shore*.

During Clive's campaign against the French, the temple enjoyed a brief moment of notoriety. In the weeks after Arcot, the English employed a prostitute to spy in the fort. The girl was discovered and murdered in the temple, which was immediately closed. The British later used the building as an arsenal and it was only reopened for worship in 1982.

From Vellore, I continued to Arani. Ravi surfaced from his slumbers and began to chat. He told me that he earned the equivalent of £50 a week with his taxi – good money by Indian standards. The snag was that he was the only breadwinner in a household that included his parents and seven brothers and sisters. He was spending more than half his wage feeding them all.

Ravi asked for my life history. After I had told him, he announced, 'You are thirty-three and not married. You need to enjoy ladies.'

It turned out that taxi-driving was not Ravi's only occupation. He was a part-time pimp in Kanchipuram, the next town after Arani on my itinerary. I was quite taken aback by this news since he looked so innocent.

Ravi was determined to clinch a deal. His favourite 'girlfriend' was a sixteen-year-old called Misty. She would cost me thirty-five rupees, but the cost of the room, tiffin and tips would bring the total to three hundred. I explained that because we could sleep with our girlfriends in England without breaking social taboos I had no need for a Kanchipuram hooker. Ravi looked sad. What a waste of a potential customer.

We reached Arani after a dusty, two-hour drive past sugar cane and banana plantations. Arani seemed to be big in brick-works. Little kilns dotted the red, sandy soil on the outskirts. A small electronics factory was the only sign that the twentieth century had reached here. The town was a flea-bitten dump, another of those so-called photographer's dreams, but hell for anyone living there permanently.

Now to find the temple with Clive's rubies!

The taxi crawled along streets crowded with the usual cows and pigs. Gopal had a near miss with a bullock cart. We tried two small temples. No one spoke a word of English and they certainly didn't know about any rubies. And no, they had no idea there'd ever been a battle at Arani. Maybe I should try one of the temples on the south side of the town.

We tried three more, all reached by narrow dirt tracks. No luck. At the third temple, we found a man who spoke reasonable English. He said we should go back into town and try the temple by the bus stand. By this time, it was midday, hot and dusty and we were all fed up. Ravi turned the car round and we headed back to the town centre. We passed a large, former British Army Parade ground. In the middle was a massive stone obelisk. I hoped vainly that this was a monument to Clive's battle, but it turned out to have been erected more than 100 years later to the memory of a soldier called Kelly, who had died of cholera. The monument had been paid for by Kelly's fellow officers. Judging by its size, he must have been a popular chap.

We arrived at the temple by the bus stand. A pretty girl in a pink sari sat behind a typewriter in the temple office. I churned out my story for the umpteenth time.

The girl looked blank. She fetched one of the priests. The priest said something to Ravi, who muttered something that I took to be the Tamil equivalent of 'sod this for a game of soldiers', and we all got back in the car.

We tried the last temple in town. I was shown to the temple office where I met a Mr Bose, who was president of his devotees' association. I felt that at last here was someone who could help me. Mr Bose spoke good English. He looked businesslike and he sat behind a tidy desk. I had great confidence in Mr Bose.

I launched into my story again '. . . in India following the footsteps of my ancestor Robert Clive.' Mr Bose looked serious and nodded wisely. 'Have you heard of Clive?' Another nod. 'I believe that Clive presented one of the temples at Arani with a gift.' Mr Bose was nodding again. 'I understand that they were rubies.' Another nod. 'Deity's eyes . . .'

I sat back. 'So Mr Bose, I wonder if you know which temple has these rubies.'

Mr Bose studied me for a moment. Then a horribly blank expression clouded his face. 'I do not understand,' he said. 'What do you mean?' At that point I gave up. I was not going to waste any more time. Arani had turned into a nightmare.

I mumbled a 'Thanks very much, Mr Bose,' and turned to go.

Mr Bose suddenly said, 'Stop. Do not hurry. You must go to Kanchipuram.'

'Kanchipuram?' What was the man talking about?

'I do not know anything about rubies at Arani, but I do know that Clive presented a temple at Kanchipuram with a valuable necklace. Go there and you will find it.'

I felt a fool. I turned to Ravi. 'Okay, now we will go to Kanchipuram. There is no time to waste.' Ravi raised his eyes to heaven. The Englishman was mad.

It was late afternoon when we finally arrived in Kanchipuram. Kanchi is one of the seven sacred cities of India with a vast complex of temples, whose towers, or gopurams, can be seen from miles away. When I arrived, the place was teeming with pilgrims and tourists.

I paid off Ravi and checked into an hotel. I intended to sleep off the memories of Arani before looking for Mr Bose's necklace. One wild goose chase in a day was quite enough.

The next morning I tried the Devarazeperumal temple on the outskirts of Kanchi at Little Kanchipuram. It was in this temple, a 22-acre complex surrounded by high walls, that a detachment of French troops sought refuge after the Battle of Arani. The

French were making a nuisance of themselves to the English, attempting to disrupt communications between Madras and Arcot. Clive brought up his cannons and, after two days of bombardment they fled.

I walked into the temple past rows of souvenir salesmen and a succession of interminably boring people offering to act as my guide. I brushed them all aside and went in search of the Executive Officer.

The Executive Officer – or E.O. for short – is the man you need to speak to if you want to find out anything about a temple in India. The E.O. is all powerful, almost one step down from the deity itself.

I tried the E.O.'s office. A clerk listened to my story. He confirmed that Clive had indeed presented a necklace to the temple. It was about ten inches long and made of gold inset with rubies, diamonds, sapphires and emeralds. And it was displayed in all its glory on special feast days when it was brought out and hung around the neck of the temple deity.

Fantastic, I said. Will the E.O. give me permission to see it?

Ah, problem, said the clerk. The E.O. was on business in Madras. But if I cared to wait for half an hour I would meet the treasurer, Mr T. Ramaswami. He also had the authority to let me see the necklace.

Wonderful, I said. I will wait for Mr Ramaswami. The clerk gave me a little bow and left me alone in the temple office.

The room was a Dickensian Mess. A fan squeaked overhead. On one wall was an ancient pendulum clock that had long ceased to function. Piles of old papers and ledgers were stacked around the edge of the floor. I doubted whether they had been touched for thirty years. Like everywhere else in India the Hindu temples suffered from a surfeit of bureaucracy. A collection of old milk powder and Horlicks boxes contained even more ledgers, all thickly coated with dust. Through the door into the next office I could see the clerk clattering away on a pre-war typewriter.

Mr Ramaswami turned up an hour later. He had overslept and his eyes were still bleary. He was wearing a grubby vest and white dhoti. He told me to sit down and I explained my mission. The treasurer knew all about the necklace. It was known as the Gemset Makarakanti and he showed me a black and white photograph of it.

He did not know of the circumstances in which Clive presented the necklace. It would have been unusual for a European to present a valuable piece of jewellery to a temple and a great honour for the temple elders. Certainly it was a brilliant PR move by Clive, who was trying to attract more Indians on to his side. The Indians saw him as an awesome warrior with a charmed life and this gift would have done no harm to his image. Perhaps it was his way of saying sorry for knocking the walls down with his cannons.

Or did Clive believe in the Hindu attitude to destiny? I thought of the sadhu in Kollihills. Did Clive see himself on some sort of spiritual mission? Did he think that by presenting these jewels he would come a little closer to the mysteries of India? Certainly it gives an insight into his religious tolerance. Most Europeans in eighteenth century India regarded the Hindus as heathens, who should be converted to Christianity at the earliest opportunity. They would have most definitely not wasted their money on presents for Hindu temples.

'We don't know anything about the history of the necklace or why Clive presented it,' Mr Ramaswami said. 'But he's the only European ever to have presented anything to this temple.'

'So can I see the necklace?' I asked.

'Of course.'

I couldn't believe it. Everything was going too smoothly. Mr Ramaswami added, 'Mr Clive's ornament is locked up in a box in the temple. But I will get it out for you. You wait here and I will send word to you to come and see it.'

I waited in the office for another hour. Various temple employees came and went. Mr Ramaswami returned. He sat down at his desk and looked official. So where was the necklace?

'There is a problem. The E.O. is not here.'

'Yes, Mr Ramaswami, I know that. When I first arrived your clerk told me the E.O. was in Madras. But you've just said yourself that you can show me the necklace.'

'The E.O. is not in Madras. He is in Lucknow for two weeks.'

'I couldn't care less where the E.O. is. You're the treasurer of this temple and you said you could show me the necklace.'

'It is locked up.'

'Yes, you told me that only an hour ago.'

'And the E.O. has the only key.'

I gritted my teeth. My voice rose to a frustrated whine. 'But,

Mr Ramaswami, you are the treasurer of this temple. I thought treasurers were in charge of things like keys.'

Mr Ramaswami looked rather pathetic. I felt sorry for him.

'I know, I know. But look at this place.' He gestured at the junk littering the office. 'How am I expected to find anything here? There is a key somewhere, but I am afraid I will never find it.'

So I never saw the necklace. I was disappointed, but at least I knew the thing existed. At least it wasn't a figment of the imagination of a half-baked guru in Pondicherry. I said farewell to Ravi, turned down another offer of a Kanchipuram tart, and caught a bus south for the town of Trichinopoly.

Dupleix's dream of a French India was shattered once and for all at the temple of Sri Ranganathaswami at Srirangam outside Trichinopoly.

In March, 1752, Clive set out to relieve the Nawab Mohammed Ali, whose troops were still bottled up in Trichinopoly by Chanda Sahib and the French. Clive's force was now under the command of Major Stringer Lawrence, the man who has been described as the father of the Indian Army. Back in the early days at Fort St David Lawrence had been Clive's military Svengali and had recognised the lad's potential. Now the Major had returned unexpectedly from England as Commander-in-Chief of the English forces in India.

Clive's demotion to second-in-command must have been a disappointment to the young man. Certainly, some of his jealous fellow officers were delighted to see control of the army taken out of his hands. But Lawrence was a friendly sort of chap and he gave Clive a free hand to do whatever he thought fit.

The French were under the command of one of Dupleix's young officers called Jacques Law. When Law heard that the English were marching on Trichinopoly he retreated into the vast temple complex of Srirangam.

Srirangam is one of the largest temples in India and its twenty-five foot-high walls provided a good defensive position for the French. But Law had made a disastrous move. Srirangam was almost surrounded by water in the form of the Cauvery River to the south and the Coleroon to the north. Lawrence agreed to Clive's proposal that they should split the army and cut off Law's supply line to Pondicherry. The French were trapped. By the beginning of June their position was hopeless and Law was forced to surrender. Chanda Sahib's troops had been deserting in their droves and the old warlord was a broken man. He was caught and beheaded by one of Mohammed Ali's Indian allies while trying to escape.

Dupleix's days of pomp and power were over. When the news of the débâcle at Trichinopoly eventually reached France seven months later, he was stripped of his governorship and ordered to return home in disgrace.

These days Trichinopoly is known by its post-independence name of Tiruchirappali – a mouthful, so it's not surprising that locals call it Trichy. The town is home to a thriving boiler industry and is dominated by the famous Rock Fort Temple, which rises from a huge outcrop of rock in the centre of the old city.

It was late when I arrived in Trichy. In an attempt to find something from the old days of the British raj, I checked into the Ashby, a faded heap of a hotel that might have been quite modern at the turn of the century. Like Jacques Law, I had made a big mistake. The place looked as though it hadn't been dusted since the 1930s and there was the unmistakable smell of marijuana around the reception desk.

The staff smiled a lot, but that was about it. A boy with a sleepy grin found me a room. It was furnished in chipped, Edwardian bric-à-brac and memorable only for the quaintness of the plumbing. The lavatory was operated by standing on a chair and reaching into the cistern high on the wall. The shower had given up years ago, but someone had thoughtfully provided a plastic bucket with which to sluice oneself down. Still, these shortcomings were made up for by the cavernous entrance hall, which featured stuffed animal heads and heavy, leather club armchairs from which the springs had exploded long ago.

The bar was quite lively. It was packed with inebriated Trichy businessmen. I was cornered by a television repairman called Danny, who insisted on buying me a beer. Danny's party trick was the system of Indian fortune telling called numerology. By adding and subtracting the numbers of a person's birthdate, you could work out their horoscope. Danny tried it on me and got everything hopelessly wrong. Then I gave him Clive's birthdate.

'Oh, dear,' Danny said. 'This person was ruled by Saturn. He had the potential for being a great man, but he would have been prone to suicide.' So numerology did have something going for it, after all.

Danny was downing large brandies. He was keen to talk about England. In the early 1980s he had spent three years in London working in a Kilburn off licence. He was fascinated by the intricacies of the London underground system.

'Dollis Hill,' he said. 'Now that is on the Bakerloo line.'

'No,' I said. 'Dollis Hill is on the Jubilee.'

'Then Willesden Junction must be on the Metropolitan?'

'No, Bakerloo.'

'And you change onto the Circle line at Paddington for Edgware Road.'

'Right in one,' I said.

We discussed the noisy traffic in India. Danny had the theory why Indian motorists used their horns so much. 'It is because the pedestrians always walk in the middle of the road,' he said. His voice began to slur from the alcohol. 'The bullockshh also walk in the road and the drivers must avoid them if they do not want a bad accident. The pedestrians see the drivers avoiding the bullockshh and think that if the bullockshh can do it so can we. Indian people are stupid. They think they are like bullockshh and that they can walk in the road without coming to harm. Therefore the drivers must hoot a lot.'

Danny was verging on incoherence and I found it difficult to follow his conversation. I turned down his offer of another beer. It was time for bed. Two Australian Hare Krishna devotees, a man and a woman, were haranguing the man on the reception desk. They looked under-nourished and pasty-faced. They wore saffron robes and the remaining hair on their shaved heads was tied in pigtails. They were very cross.

Apparently they had gone to bed only to be woken an hour later by the 'bug man'. This was the hotel employee whose job it was to go round the rooms spraying them with insect repellant from a Flit spray. These Hare Krishnas might have travelled to India to worship an Indian god, but they understood little about Indian ways. Anyone who stays in cheap Indian lodgings should know that the bug man is an unpredictable character. He enters your room without knocking and he doesn't think twice about turning up at midnight. It is also the custom in Indian hotels, both grand and modest, for servants to enter your room at all hours with offers to turn down your bed, refill the water flask or, most annoying, ask what you want from room service when you never even rang. In five-star establishments you are likely to be pestered by the house astrologer asking if you want the day's predictions. Westerners accustomed to staff blending into the woodwork are often irritated beyond all belief.

The Hare Krishna couple were failing to make their point to the man on reception. They shouted and raved, but he just grinned and waited for them to go away.

Next morning I took a rickshaw to the temple of Srirangam. More like a town than a temple, it was a vast complex covering 650 acres. Seven massive concentric walls surrounded the holy of holies that was dedicated to Vishnu, the creator in the Hindu trinity. The roof above the inner sanctum was crowned with a golden dome.

The complex dated from the fourteenth century and was built of granite. The site was declared a municipality in 1871 and was now home to nearly 100,000.

The streets between the outer four walls were packed with bazaars. I paid off the rickshawman and walked towards the main temple entrance up a street lined with coffee stalls and buildings that once housed temple servants. They were now occupied by tradesmen and souvenir vendors selling garish pictures of Vishnu. I was plagued by small boys peddling everything from cheap plastic hairslides to moth balls. For fifty yards I was pursued by an urchin selling elastic bands. I could stand his persistent chatter no more. I surrendered, and bought a packet.

Near the entrance to the temple I stopped by a roadside cobbler to have my sandals mended. He hand-stitched a piece of rubber that looked like part of a lorry's mudflap onto the soles. As he was getting started on the second shoe, a mother and son came up to him. She said something to the cobbler in Tamil. He stopped stitching and stood up. It transpired that the boy was sick with a fever and that the cobbler was well-known as a freelance faith healer. The cobbler took a bunch of leaves and started waving them in front of the boy's face. He muttered a prayer. This went on for about five minutes. Then the cobbler tightly closed his eyes, screwed up his face, spoke a few final words of mumbo-jumbo and hit the boy hard over the face with the leaves. The blow must have stung like hell. The boy flinched, rubbed his cheeks and, for no apparent reason, began doing kung fu drop kicks in the middle of the road. He was healed.

The woman gave the cobbler a couple of coins and the pair went on their way.

A gaggle of guides surrounded me, all offering their services to escort me around the temple. From my experience, guides in Indian temples knew about as much as the tourists they were supposed to be guiding. I brushed them aside and went in search of the temple office.

The E.O. was not in. I was not surprised. I had learned at Kanchipuram that E.O.s were never in when you wanted them. A bored clerk sat behind a desk piled with paper. I told him about my quest. Did he know anything about Law's last stand at Srirangam? He did not. In fact, he swore categorically that the temple had never even been used as a defensive stronghold. The only British connection with the place, he said, was a gold drinking vessel in the holy of holies that had been presented in 1875 by the Prince of Wales, the future King Edward VII. The clerk was a clot. I gave up and set off to wander around by myself.

Srirangam still functioned according to ancient tradition. And, as in all Hindu temples, there was a strict daily ritual. The priests begin work at 6.45 am. First, a cow and one of the temple elephants are made to stand next to each other looking towards the holy of holies. The sanctuary is unlocked, the premises cleaned and the lamps refilled. It is time to wake the god. A man responsible for music plays the zither while two priests pour sacred water into the five ritual vessels kept in the sanctuary. Then the curtain hiding the sanctuary is drawn so that the god can see the elephant and the cow. The temple astronomer reads aloud the astronomical signs for the day. The curtain is closed again while various ceremonies take place.

Caring for the daily needs of a Hindu god is similar to coping with a bed-ridden invalid. At midday the god is given a hot bath and annointed with saffron powder. Sandal paste is applied to the statue's breast and feet. It is clothed in clean garments and decked with jewels and garlands of flowers. When the god is ready, the curtain is reopened so that the god can be seen by the devotees. Next comes lunch, specially prepared by Brahmin cooks in the temple kitchens. Baskets of food are placed before the god. Finally the statue is offered quids of betel nut and its mouth is washed with water.

Srirangam was a perfect example of temple administration in

ancient times. The temple had a huge staff consisting of ten categories of officials ranging from sacred water bearers to weavers responsible for making fly-whisks. Most of these posts were hereditary but holders needed to be highly qualified. Some employees were voluntary and others were paid for with donations from rich devotees and revenues from the temple farms.

At the top were the Brahman priests. Below them came accountants and treasurers. Then there were potters who made the god's food bowls and coppersmiths who were responsible for the drinking vessels; tailors sewed the god's clothes and goldsmiths designed the jewellery. A regiment of barbers shaved the priests and visitors. There was a complete health service with a doctor, surgeon and nurses and a fifteen-bed hospital with a large pharmacy. The god was entertained by actors, singers and dancers. Until the end of the nineteenth century, the dancers performed another function – as prostitutes for the male staff.

I strolled around the temple. Near the holy of holies was a party of young Frenchmen dressed in saffron robes. They were sitting crosslegged on the ground with that 'aren't I being spiritual' look on their faces.

I remembered a conversation with Ramesh back in Pondicherry. Westerners in saffron robes irritated Ramesh beyond belief.

'Those people are fakes. I have seen people like them all over India,' Ramesh had sneered. 'How dare they wear those holy clothes?'

We talked about Westerners who handed over large sums of money to fashionable Indian gurus like the Bagwan Raneesh.

'Perhaps I should become a guru,' Ramesh said. 'Look at me, I'm perfect. I've got the beard and it won't take long to grow it a bit longer. With a bit of talk I reckon I could have people following me in a couple of years.'

'I'll be your manager,' I said. 'We'll hire one of the top London public relations people and I'll go twenty per cent on the loot.'

Ramesh laughed. This was a great idea. He went on, 'I'll tell my followers that there's not just one god, but that they can all be gods. Everyone would fall for that. Think of it. You could just pray to yourself wherever you were.'

Ramesh stroked his beard. 'I'd have to bring in some sex.

Rather than encouraging my followers to have sex with lots of people, I'd show them hundreds of ways to have sex with the same person. It wouldn't take much to get a good slide show together. No one's tried that one before and it would overcome the AIDS problem.'

A cinch. The fleet of Rolls Royces was looking good. 'And when I get denounced as a fraud, who cares?' Ramesh spread his arms wide. 'The money's in Switzerland, home is an island in the Bahamas and there will still be some followers stupid enough to keep believing in you. Most important is not to get greedy so that the tax authorities get onto you. That's where the Bagwan went wrong.'

I looked at the Frenchmen. They looked pretty guillible to me – putty in Ramesh's hands.

Later that day I put myself again at the mercy of the Indian bus system and headed for Chingleput, an old fortified town between Pondicherry and Madras.

Chingleput played a minor part in the Clive story. The fort was occupied by the French and even after Jacques Law's surrender at Trichinopoly the bastion continued to hold out. Because of Chingleput's proximity to Madras, the Council of Fort St George decided they could stand this annoyance no longer. Clive was ordered to send the enemy packing. The French commander, who was keener on his food than matters military, had heard of Clive's reputation and decided it was not worth tangling with him. He surrendered on condition that he was allowed to keep his stock of turkeys and snuff. By Clive's standards, it was not a glorious victory.

But if Chingleput was insignificant to Clive, it is now home to one of the most important medical establishments in India.

A mile from the ruins of the fort lies the large hospital complex of the Central Leprosy Research and Training Institute. In India there are an estimated four million sufferers of leprosy with the majority in the south.

The Institute's director, Dr P. K. Neelan ('but everyone calls me Neelan'), was casual and relaxed for a man who had spent nearly thirty years working with lepers. 'It is a very fascinating disease,' he said. 'I think you can call it one of the world's great mysteries. We simply don't know why some people get it and others don't. Did you realise that the only animal that can get a disease similar to leprosy is the armadillo? Why should God have wanted to discriminate against the armadillo? It is such an obscure creature.'

Leprosy is a disease of many myths. Contrary to popular belief, patients' limbs do not simply drop off. Nor will you catch leprosy by contact – shaking hands, for example – with a sufferer. Leprosy is listed in the *Guinness Book of Records* as the world's least infectious disease; it is also one hundred per cent curable. Despite that, it continues to bear an unbelievable stigma. The sight of a man or woman swathed in bandages, minus their fingers and toes and their face horribly disfigured is enough to send most people running for cover. But it is the legal position of the leprosy sufferer in India that makes everything much worse. He is rejected as an outcast. There are seventeen laws in India discriminating against lepers, the most iniquitous being that a married person can be automatically granted a divorce if their partner develops the disease. Even the so-called caring Christian Church accepts this legislation without question.

The Chingleput Institute was founded by the British in 1926 as a leprosy sanitorium. The Indian Government took the hospital over after independence and it is now the main leprosy research and training facility in India attracting patients from all over the subcontinent. The annual £6,000,000 running costs are split between the Government, the World Health Organisation and UNICEF.

I talked with Neelan in his office that looked out onto the eighty-acre hospital site, a tranquil garden setting of bougainvillea and palm trees. He was a charming man with a good sense of humour and a look of Peter Sellers about him. He sat in his shirtsleeves and an orderly brought us coffee while we talked about the disease that, after AIDS, is the world's most anti-social affliction.

After qualifying as a doctor, Neelan joined the Institute in 1960. 'My family were fairly horrified when I told them I was going to work in leprosy,' he said with the hint of a smile. 'I think my parents were slightly embarrassed. Let us call it a peculiar reaction.'

Neelan described himself as part-surgeon, part-social scientist. 'The best way to educate people about leprosy is for me and my staff to demonstrate that there is nothing wrong with it, that we can handle patients without catching it. It's the same as with AIDS. We can now cure leprosy in the early stages, but for older patients with disabilities the stigma will be with them until they are dead. I would like to think that things are changing for the better and it is becoming less of a stigma. I don't want charity for my patients – that leads to pampering and is too patronising – but I want understanding.'

Leprosy attacks the victim's periphery nerves – not the skin as is generally believed – and is caused by micro-bacteria that are transmitted in the same way as tuberculosis – by mucus and closeness. The incubation period from infection to disease can be anything from two months to five years.

First the patient loses feeling in his nerves, usually at the extremities like fingers and toes. Lesions appear on the arms, legs and face. The loss of sensation leads to injury. For example, the sufferer may break a finger, but he will feel nothing. His finger will become infected and may, in serious cases, lead to gangrene. In the worst stages of the disease the limbs at the extremities fall off.

'But the bacillus does not effect the bones directly,' Neelan went on. 'There are some special bones in the nose that will collapse, but if a hand appears to have dropped off, there will still be a stump and you will always see the fingernails. In the feet it will be a combination of nerve damage and motor paralysis.

'The central nervous system is not affected. The reaction can destroy vital organs like the kidney and liver and that can kill, but this is very rare indeed. Only twenty per cent of leprosy cases are in the serious form – lepromitis – with the potential to infect others. Most cases show only minimal lesions and can be cured in six months.'

Neelan paused to sip his coffee. He stood up and paced the room. He was getting into his stride.

'Leprosy has a lot in common with tuberculosis. The living condition, for example. For me to transmit the infection to you, you will have to be very close. I will have to cough, sneeze over you, share a bed. You will be very poor, undernourished and live with me in the same crowded mud hut for several years before you catch it. But many people in India live in crowded mud huts and eat badly and that makes for favourable conditions for leprosy. Five hundred years ago you had similar conditions in Europe – and you also had leprosy.

'Patients used to be kept in leper colonies until they died. I wonder if the people who put them there realised how stupid they were. If you put a large number of people together in one place, the disease just spreads even more.'

I asked where leprosy originated. 'Ha!' Neelan said. 'Where did any disease start? There is no record of the disease in India before two thousand years ago. The earliest cases recorded were in central Asia in 600 BC. Before that, there is no history of leprosy.' He laughed. 'When you can't trace something you put the blame on an innocent group of people. Civilisation, or organised living, started where Europe and Asia meet, so we say that leprosy also started there and was taken around the world by travellers.'

The disease is treated by using multi-drug therapy with serious cases taking up to five years to cure. Since the introduction of new drugs in the early 1980s there has been a dramatic reduction in the number of sufferers. But as yet, treatment is the only weapon for control. There have been experiments with vaccines – but the results will not be known for ten years. The leprosy bacillus was one of the world's first organisms to be identified – but to this day scientists cannot find a way to grow it in a laboratory.

'As I pointed out at the beginning,' Neelan said with a gleam in his eye, 'it is a very fascinating disease.'

He was confident that leprosy was on the decline. 'To reduce the spread, we must reduce the number of active cases, but I believe we will be down to 500,000 sufferers in fifteen years' time, which is a big drop from 4,000,000. I believe that leprosy will be eradicated in India in fifty years.'

But social conditions apart, no one really understands why there is virtually no leprosy in the West. There *are* a few thousand lepers in Europe and America, but they are mainly confined to ethnic groups like Africans and Puerto Ricans.

'Do not worry, Mr Holt.' Neelan chuckled. 'You will not catch it by being in this hospital. Even Europeans who work for years with leprosy sufferers never, and I repeat never, get the disease. There are studies being carried out in genetics and molecular biology. But until we learn more, we simply don't know why.'

What would Neelan do if he caught leprosy from his patients? Had he ever caught leprosy? He leaned back in his chair. 'This is a delicate subject. It is a difficult question to answer.' He thought for a moment before speaking slowly and deliberately. 'If I got any evidence that I had leprosy, if I found a lesion on my body, I would start taking the drugs and cure myself. I am lucky in that I could identify the disease. No, I would not tell anyone. There is no need. Why worry people? Why cause anxiety?

'It would be the same with my staff. For all I know, some of the doctors working here may have developed the disease at some time or another. I do not know and I do not care. They can take the drugs and cure themselves. End of story.'

Before I left, Neelan remarked that he hoped I was now better informed, that I would not go away thinking I was about to catch the disease myself. He returned to his work and left me in the hands of Mr Morthi, the Institute's secretary, who took me on a tour of the hospital.

There was a peaceful and unhurried atmosphere. Much love and dedication had gone into tackling one of the most undignified diseases known to man. The grounds were well-kept with paths leading to a series of bungalows that housed the wards. There was a recreation centre and a coffee shop run by the patients themselves and an open-air stage where patients put on shows during Hindu festivals.

'Just because these people suffer from leprosy, it doesn't mean they can't enjoy themselves,' Mr Morthi said. He was a bright little man, who walked rather quickly. Like Neelan he held a deep concern for the hospital inmates. 'We try to treat them as much like ordinary human beings as possible.'

He showed me the outpatients department. Posters on the wall warned sufferers about the dangers they faced in everyday life: take extra care – wear gloves even – when picking up hot cups of tea or coffee. The loss of feeling in the patient's fingers meant that he could burn himself without even knowing it. Likewise, when smoking a cigarette be careful that it does not burn right down to your hand. 'Healthy people like us take these things for granted,' Mr Morthi said. 'But they could lead to infections, maybe gangrene.'

I was introduced to a woman of twenty-two, who had just been admitted with the first signs of lepromitis, the more serious form of leprosy. For a fortnight she had been suffering from painful nodules on her body. Now the first signs of lesions were appearing on her ears and thighs. She was in great pain, and very distressed having only just learned that she had the disease. At least this woman understood that there were genuine medical reasons for her plight. 'Indian people can be very superstitious,' Mr Morthi explained. 'They often think that leprosy is a curse from God or that they caught it after eating fish.'

We moved to the clinical laboratory where half a dozen technicians were examining skin scrapings in microscopes in order to find leprosy bacilli. Then on to the physiotherapy department where splints and plaster casts were being used to straighten disfigured limbs. More than seventy-five per cent of deformities caused by leprosy can be cured by physiotherapy at a fraction of the cost and far less pain than surgery.

A boy of thirteen was receiving treatment for his crippled left hand, which resembled a claw. He had suffered from leprosy for five years. He was now rid of the disease, but it would take nearly a year before his fingers were back to normal. Each day he was coming to the hospital for physiotherapy and to have a new plaster cast applied to his hand. The boy was very patient. He said he was happy with his treatment at the institute. One day he would like to be a doctor himself and help other sufferers.

The institute was a model of self-sufficiency. It even boasted its own micro-cellular rubber factory, which produced ultra-soft shoe rubber that caused as little friction as possible to the feet thereby preventing ulcers. A leprosy sufferer may have no feeling in his foot.

'This might be a little upsetting for you,' Mr Morthi said as we entered a long bungalow. It was the amputees ward where about thirty men were about to undergo or had undergone, removal of limbs. One man was having a bad reaction after losing his right leg. He was in terrible pain and groaning. He was being given tablets and the pain would eventually go.

Mr Morthi took me to the bus stop and we said goodbye. All too quickly the kind little world in the hospital would be replaced by the cruel reality of India.

The bus arrived and I got on with several outpatients, some with bandaged feet and hands. The bus was already full and the lepers and I were forced to stand in the aisle. It was a pitiful sight to see an old man, his hand horribly crippled, attempting to hang on to the overhead rail with a fingerless, bandaged stump.

A young man – presumably because I was the only foreigner on the bus and a guest of his country – offered me his seat. I declined and suggested that perhaps one of the legless lepers would appreciate the seat more than I. The young man shrugged. If I did not want his seat, it certainly did not mean that he would give it to anyone else. Least of all one of *them*.

His reaction spoke for itself: in India, lepers are dirt.

Four

The hero of Arcot returned to Madras in triumph . . . and fell in love.

Clive is said to have lost his heart to Margaret Maskelyne when he saw her miniature on the desk of her brother Edmund, a fellow East India Company clerk.

Edmund was a keen match-maker and Clive's closest friend. So when Margaret arrived in Madras in June 1752, he wasted no time in introducing her to the man they were all talking about. It is unclear how the battle-weary Clive took to this petite seventeen-year-old with huge, grey eyes. But Margaret was well-educated with lively, intelligent conversation, and Robert quickly realised that she was a cut above the giggling teenagers who arrived off the ships from England in search of a husband with good prospects.

Yet Clive dithered over what to do about Margaret. His biographer Mark Bence-Jones says that by 15 February the following year the hero had booked a single passage home to England. Some time in the next three days he must have changed his mind and proposed. For on 18 February they were married in St Mary's. The ceremony was performed by John Fabricius, the jovial Danish missionary responsible for the first Tamil-English dictionary. Margaret joined her new husband on the voyage home. The seven months at sea cannot have been a pleasant honeymoon.

Bence-Jones adds that the indecision was Clive's rather than hers. 'We know from her letters that the marriage was a love match as far as Margaret was concerned, and that she worshipped Clive for the rest of his life . . . For his part, the fact that he married her after deciding to go home would indicate that he loved her.'

Perhaps Clive courted Margaret at one of the many balls held in Madras in 1752. There was an exhausting round of parties to celebrate the French defeat and the walls of Fort St George echoed to the sound of minuets, jigs and gavottes.

These days, balls are thin on the ground in Madras. But a lack of formal gatherings is made up for by the annual Guild of Service Evening of International Song and Dance. Indeed, the spirit of the raj lives on at this sparkling affair that marks the height of the Madras social calendar and raises thousands of rupees for charity. Here you will get the closest in India to the traditional English summer fête.

The evening is run by the Guild of Service, a sort of cross between the Rotary Club and the Women's Institute. The organising committee is made up of the city's grandest ladies and representatives from the foreign consulates.

I became involved in this gala after meeting the committee chairman Mrs Indira Kothari and her husband D. C. Kothari. The Kotharis were my only contact in Madras, old friends of my brother-in-law's parents. They were great Anglophiles and on their bookshelves was a copy of just about every book published on British India. They agreed that Clive's name was remembered with greater affection than any other British Indian leader. D.C. was one of the most successful businessmen in India on the scale of a Rowland or Goldsmith. He was very rich and came from an old monied family – the first Kotharis had arrived in Madras in 1815 and they had been a driving force in the city ever since. Indira was a leading light on the local charity scene. She stood for no nonsense and she ruled her committee meetings with a rod of Thatcherite iron.

When I returned from Trichy I gave Mrs Kothari a telephone call. She said she did not have time to meet me socially, but, if I cared to, I could come along to one of the Guild's committee meetings. They were busy sorting out the finishing touches before the big night.

The meeting was in progress when I arrived at the Guild's headquarters. Mrs Kothari, large spectacles balanced on the end of her nose, was seated on a stage surrounded by her henchwomen. Beneath the stage were the helpers: wealthy

94

Indian ladies smartly dressed in saris and a smattering of Europeans.

I sat at the back of the hall. The main topic of discussion was how much milk would be needed for two thousand cups of coffee – the huge population of India means that even a relatively minor charity event will attract thousands of people. More than five thousand people were expected to turn up at the sports stadium where the evening was to take place. And considering that the party was in less than a week's time, it seemed ridiculously late notice to be working out how much milk would be needed. The committee appeared to be tackling the thing as if it were a village jumble sale.

'I am very worried about the ice cream,' said a young, pretty woman in a bright orange sari.

Mrs Kothari stared down from her throne. 'And what is the matter with the ice cream?' she asked.

The younger woman swept a strand of black hair back from her forehead. The bangles on her wrists jangled loudly. 'An ice cream company has donated a lot of ice cream free. I think we should sell it for a high price so we can make more money for charity. But I am worried that we are going to get unofficial ice cream sellers inside the stadium. They will try to undercut us.'

Pirate ice cream salesmen were the scourge of Indian charity events. Mrs Kothari took charge. 'Then we will make sure the security guards keep them out,' she said.

The younger woman was not convinced. 'But they will take no notice. They are very determined people and they will get in over the railings.'

'No they will not.' Mrs Kothari was firm about this. She made a note to the effect that all unofficial ice cream men were to be slung out on their ears.

The meeting over, I introduced myself to the powerful Indira and offered my services.

'Excellent,' she said. 'I am sure they will need help on the British stall.'

The British stall was being run by Agni Morey, wife of the consulate's Deputy High Commissioner. I got the impression from Mrs Kothari that a shortage of volunteers meant that the British always needed help on their stall.

A cloud passed over Mrs Kothari's face. She made me promise one thing: 'On no account must you handle money. There will

95

be a lot of people pushing and shoving and I would not like to think of you, a visitor to Madras, being robbed. You have to keep an eye on these people all the time or you will find money going astray. Much better that it is handled by people with experience of this sort of evening.'

The following Saturday I arrived at the sports stadium a few hours before the gates opened. The dusty arena buzzed with activity as charity ladies hurried to set up their stalls.

The Madras Round Table had a hoopla stall and biryani stand: the Rotarians were running something called a Coin Game. Large, chunky ladies from the Russian Consulate fussed around in tight bulging skirts and crimplene tops. They were preparing gallons of kvass, a soft drink made from black bread. It had an evil taste and left a cotton wool coating on one's tongue. The Germans were determined no one would go hungry. They had produced 120 kilograms of potato salad and 1,000 sausages.

At the Sri Lankan tent a group of women were noisily putting up flimsy tinfoil Christmas decorations of the kind found in Woolworth's. They chattered wildly as they laid out brightly-coloured souvenir wooden elephants, packets of tea, pastries, and string hoppers, the Ceylonese equivalent to the crumpet. The American Consulate had demanded no less than three tents from which to sell their hot dogs, pizzas and chocolate brownies. They planned to lure even more punters with a raffle with prizes of hampers of tinned food flown in specially from the States.

And the British? Well, the British were British. In the great tradition of the garden fête, our contribution to the evening was a cake stall. Having conquered India with glorious campaigns like Arcot, we were now trying to win her people back with flapjacks and Victoria sponge.

'Home-made English cakes are very popular with the Indians,' insisted Sheelagh Humphreys, one of Agni Morey's happy band of helpers. 'We tried selling teddy bears a few years back, but they didn't go nearly as well.'

Agni was delighted that I had turned up. The British cake stall needed all the help it could get. Agni was an attractive woman, dark and part Greek with a deep Oxbridge voice. She wore a flowery Laura Ashley frock. She was obviously highly intelligent and I gathered that cake stalls were not quite her thing. The Moreys had been in Madras only three months, having come from the British Embassy in Moscow. Agni hadn't yet got the hang of Indian shindigs like Guild of Service evenings.

She nominated me head cashier. 'But Mrs Kothari said I mustn't handle money,' I said. 'She said I'll be robbed.'

'Nonsense,' Agni said. 'Sheelagh and I will hand over the cakes and you can take the cash.'

Sheelagh was an old cake stall hand. Daughter of an Indian Army Officer, she had lived all her life in Madras. She and her husband George ran a flower arranging business aimed at the Indian wedding market.

She gave Agni and me a little pep talk. There were strict rules about which cakes were to be sold whole and which could be cut into slices. A Victoria sponge, for example, could go in slices, whereas a coffee gâteau commanded a higher price in one piece. 'You'll get people insisting that you sell them a slice from a cake that is supposed to be sold whole,' Sheelagh warned. 'You have to be very firm and say no. Loudly.'

British Airways had donated thirteen Fortnum and Mason fruit cakes – a strange number, but thirteen it was. We debated how much to sell them for. They still had English price labels on – £6.95, the equivalent of 150 rupees. This was too expensive, said Sheelagh. You could buy similar cakes for a third of the price at a shop in Madras called Bake-A-Cake.

Agni overruled her. 'I think we should have a bash at 150 rupees,' she said. 'There'll be a few people from the other consulates and maybe they'll be prepared to spend that much for a cake from Fortnum's. It's quite a good name, after all.'

Sheelagh wasn't happy. 'Fortnum and Mason won't mean much to the Indians,' she pointed out.

We removed a vast assortment of cakes from their tins and arranged them on the trestle tables. Unfortunately, Sheelagh had been unable to lay her hands on any doilies on which to place the cakes so as to make them look more interesting. Not one doily was to be found in Madras. 'Never mind,' she said. 'I have cut some butter paper into circles and that will have to do.' Agni was unimpressed by the Government issue table cloths provided by the High Commission. They were dotted with moth holes. 'Dreadful,' she sighed. 'I should have brought some of my own.'

We decorated the tent with paper Union Jacks, the type sold in English seaside resorts to stick in sandcastles. Someone from the British Library in Madras had donated a wad of English Tourist Board posters. I pinned up pictures of Buckingham Palace and Windsor Castle. It was an exceptionally humid evening and the exertion of pushing in drawing pins brought droplets of sweat to our brows. Sheelagh had dug out some tinsel to give the stall a 'jubilee feel'. We wrapped it around the tent poles. Finally, we crowned the stall with a large sign saying 'British Cake Stall'. It hung at a slight angle.

Agni surveyed our handiwork. 'I'm afraid,' she said, 'that it all looks rather English and home-made.' Sheelagh thought the effect was marvellous. 'Very cottagey,' she added.

Next door, the Americans were unloading a small Chevrolet truck piled high with fridges and cooking equipment. A young man with a G I Joe haircut was assembling a portable generator. Agni looked at the US tent with disdain. 'The Americans make 50,000 rupees each year whereas we're lucky to manage a grand,' she sniffed. 'I'm convinced they cheat. We think they make up their figure by putting in a large donation at the end.' The Soviets were also taking the American threat seriously. They had reduced the price of their kvass so that it appeared better value than the hot dogs.

The gates opened at 7 pm. People flooded in. The crowd was predominately middle-class and well-off enough to pay the fifteen rupees entrance fee. The teenagers wore jeans and there was a profusion of Michael Jackson T-shirts.

A brass band with an unnecessarily loud bass drum struck up with *Colonel Bogey*. The smell of hot dogs wafted across the dusty arena. The Sri Lankans chattered louder than ever. I took up my position by the cash box. Several of the Union Jacks had fallen down.

Agni and Sheelagh prepared to do battle. Suddenly the British stall was swarming with Indians. Agni launched into a hard sell on the Fortnum and Mason Dundees.

'Special fruit cake from London,' she yelled. 'Only 150 rupees each. A bargain!' The Indians didn't seem to think so. They were after the flapjacks at three rupees each. Agni persisted. She adopted the manner of a circus ringleader. 'Roll up! Roll up! Special English cake,' she shouted.

Hurrah! a buyer came forward. He was a Japanese business-man. Outside London, Fortnum's only other branch is in Tokyo, and this gentleman knew his brand names. He bought two

Dundees and I slipped 300 rupees into the cash box. I soon discovered that the job of cashier presented the usual problem you find all over India – an absence of change. I never seemed to have enough of the right notes and coins to hand back to customers.

After their earlier exertions with *Colonel Bogey* the brass band had succumbed to lethargy. They stumbled over the theme to *Chitty-Chitty-Bang-Bang* and rambled into what sounded like the RAF fly past. Up on the main stage, the evening's entertainment was underway with a series of Tamil comedy sketches.

Tony Morey popped by to give us moral support. He played the part of the keen, young Deputy High Commissioner with gusto. He patted children on the head and chatted to a trio of English back-packers. He blew up balloons to give to the children. Indian balloons can be rather naughty. They were black and phallic with red blobs at the end.

There were all manner of cakes on our stall: fairy cakes, gooey gâteaux, Victoria sponges and chocolate Swiss rolls (although I noted an absence of Battenburg). There was much deliberation by large ladies over whether to buy cakes filled with butter or honey. And while they poked and prodded and poked, their children munched on macaroons.

William Hodges described the eighteenth century Tamils as 'delicately framed'. 'Their hands,' he wrote, 'are more like those of tender females, and do not appear to be what is considered a proper proportion to the rest of the person . . . their manners are mild, tranquil, and sedulously attentive: in this last respect they are indeed remarkable, as they never interrupt any person who is speaking, but wait patiently till he has concluded, and then answer with the greatest respect and composure.'

The Tamils around the cake stall were not acting with the 'greatest respect and composure'. They clamoured and jostled. Grabbing, less than feminine hands swooped on the flapjacks.

The British Consulate's commercial attaché, a bon viveur named Brian, kept us supplied with cans of diplomatic issue Heineken. 'I get it shipped in specially,' he said. 'Can't stand this pissy Indian muck.' Due to Tamil Nadu's strict alcohol laws, there was no beer tent in the arena, although I spotted several men with pocket-sized bottles of brandy. A gang of youths hung around the stall looking longingly at our beer. I suggested that next year the consulate should run a tombola with bottles of alcohol for prizes. Tony was not keen. 'The Tamil Nadu government wouldn't like it,' he said stiffly. Agni thought it was a brilliant idea. 'That would give the Americans something to think about,' she said.

There was great excitement when the Governor of Madras, Dr P. C. Alexander paid our stall a visit. Agni tried to tempt 'P.C.' with a slice of walnut gâteau. 'No, thank you,' he said rather priggishly, 'if I eat something here, I will have to accept something from every stall. Then I will not have room for dinner.' A banquet was being thrown in the Governor's honour later that evening.

Dr Alexander had a mixed reputation in Madras. He was famous for never being able to sit still for longer than an hour. He was known to suddenly get up and leave official dinners before the pudding.

After what seemed like an eternity, the last slice of walnut gâteau disappeared. Agni and I totted up the takings: 3,400 rupees. It had been the most successful year in the history of the British Cake Stall. The Fortnum and Mason fruitcakes had done the trick.

Towards the end of my stay in Madras, I met up with friends from England, Maurice and Jean Bourcier. Maurice was an old India hand, who had spent much of his early life in Madras working for a British company. They were on a holiday of nostalgia in India, staying at the Madras Club, and asked me to join them one day for lunch.

The Madras Club was one of the last vestiges of Clive's legacy. It was a long, white building with a magnificent eighteenth century cupola and one of the few remaining 'garden houses' in Madras. The mansion was built in 1780 by a man called Moubray, who arrived nine years earlier as Government Accountant and acquired 105 acres on the banks of the Adayer River.

The club had long been a revered Madras institution. And this was where mulligatawny, the British colonial answer to Tamil pepper soup, was said to have been created. Despite post-Independence financial blues the establishment had managed to struggle on and now boasted an almost exclusively Indian membership.

But the spirit of the raj was being sorely tested. There was still a full-sized table in the billiards room and a barber's chair

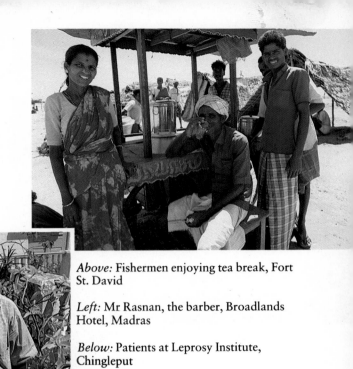

Above: Fishermen enjoying tea break, Fort St. David

Left: Mr Rasnan, the barber, Broadlands Hotel, Madras

Below: Patients at Leprosy Institute, Chingleput

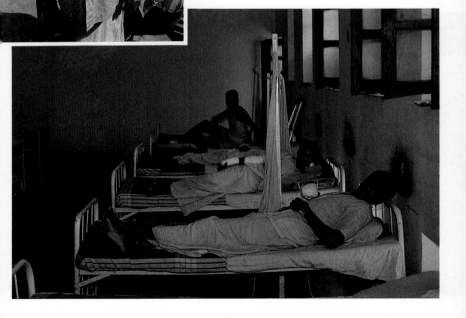

Vellore Fort

Right: "Clive's vibrations will be felt until the end of time." – Sadhu I met in Kollihills

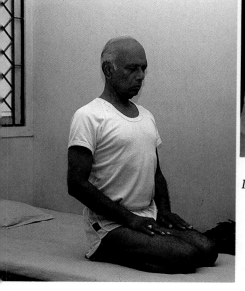

Left: Bala at his morning meditation

Henry

Above: The Matri Mandir at Auroville, home to the world's biggest crystal ball

Left: Walt after blessing the waves at Pondicherry

Ramesh *(Above left)* and an apprehensive author, *(Above right)* whose aura is about to be tested in Ramesh's lab

Bathtime in Calcutta street

Above: Janice recovering from sunburn in evening cool on Hughli

Below: Colonel Sexy's friend, Sumita, Kiddapore

Above: China about to display culinary skills on boat trip up Hughli

Right: "Don't worry, baba." – China, Sudder Street, Calcutta

Below: Brothel, Kiddapore Docks

Bangladeshi refugees at Clive House, Dum Dum

Shantys on Tolly's Nullah, Calcutta

Battlefield monument at Plassey

Momentous meeting of the clans: author, five-times great grandson of Clive, and Syed Mol Iman, eight-times great grandson of Mir Jafar. Murshidibad

Sunset at Murshidibad

in the gents, but the magnificent dining room had last been decorated in the early 1970s. The wallpaper bore hideously complicated patterns with that Berni Inn look.

Much worse, the club was recovering from an eighteen month strike. The staff had been called out by their union after the management demanded that blood tests must be conducted on everyone who worked in the kitchens. With the onset of HIV and Hepatitis B, the management thought it prudent that all those people handling food must be submitted to thorough medical tests. The union objected on the grounds that their members were poor, often undernourished men, who could not spare a drop of their precious blood. The club was plunged into a strike.

Everyone walked out, including the gardeners. The club's grounds leading down to the Adayer River were overgrown with coarse grasses. The herbaceous borders, once a sea of colour, looked sadly threadbare. Paint was peeling off the building's grand pillars and the window frames were rotting. The place was miserably neglected.

Hardly had I entered these hallowed portals and shaken hands with Maurice and Jean than I committed a huge social blunder. The steward in the bar scowled at me. He looked down at my feet. I was not wearing socks.

'It is a rule of the Madras Club,' he sniffed, 'that everyone must wear socks.'

'Good God,' said Maurice, 'I've never heard of that one before.'

'Socks compulsory!' The steward was not prepared to argue. Maurice grumbled and disappeared upstairs to fetch me a pair of his socks. 'I've never heard of anything so ridiculous in my life,' Jean remarked. 'I doubt that five per cent of this country wears socks.'

We downed a couple of gins and moved into the dining room for a lunch of curried fish followed by fruit salad. We were served by white-suited servants, who, I noted with surprise, all wore socks. They bowed and scraped as the other diners, all Indians, bellowed orders.

Lunch over, we returned to the bar for coffee. Maurice talked about the strike. The members had kept their chins up and things were getting back to normal. The chief complaint was that they had been able to get nothing to drink but beer.

'People were crosser about that than anything else,' Maurice said. 'Trouble was there was no one to do proper stock-keeping so the committee thought it best to dispense with the gin and tonics. It's much easier to keep track of a few crates of beer.' No G and T? Times had been hard indeed.

Archetypal British institutions like the Madras Club would have never existed in the first place had it not been for the British resolve to gain absolute power over India. But for men like Clive, the Indian people might have been brought up on French patisserie rather than Victoria sponge.

After their wedding, Clive and Margaret returned to England. News of Clive's success at Arcot had preceded him and his reputation as a swashbuckling adventurer was born. The couple stayed in England for nearly three years while Clive spent much of his small fortune earned after Arcot on courting politicians like the Earl of Sandwich and standing unsuccessfully for Parliament. In the end, he decided politics was not for him. He was promoted to Lieutenant-Colonel and agreed to return to India as Deputy-Governor of Fort St David. In March 1754, Margaret gave birth to their first child, a son called Edward, and a month later the couple sailed.

Clive's deputy-governorship was short-lived. In August 1756 the English received appalling news from their East India Company fellows in Calcutta. A month earlier the city had been attacked by the French-backed Nawab of Bengal, Siraj-ud-daula. The Nawab's 30,000 troops had easily overpowered the tiny British forces. Men, women and children had been forced to leap into boats and flee to safety down the Hughli River.

Siraj-ud-daula, an impetuous twenty-seven-year-old with a taste for opium and loose women, had inherited his throne from his grandfather less than two months earlier. What was to happen next was to hurl him into the history books as one of the classic baddies of all time.

Clive and his colleagues were outraged to hear that the cruel Nawab had rounded up the British who had been unable to escape. Ignoring their pleas of mercy, the wicked Siraj-ud-daula threw them into a tiny cell barely big enough to swing a small cat. Panic turned to terror. It was a stinking hot June night and by next morning well over 100 people were dead from suffocation.

The council of Fort St George was outraged at this monstrous war crime. Siraj-ud-daula had to be punished. And it was Clive who was given the job of avenging the tragedy that was to become known as the Black Hole of Calcutta.

Clive would have had Margaret to bid farewell to him before he left for Calcutta. It must have been an emotional moment when the Colonel, as Margaret now called him, set out for the dangers of Bengal.

I was not so fortunate. All I had was Mr Rasnan, the barber. Mr Rasnan was distraught that I was leaving Madras. He was beside himself with grief. He was losing a good customer, particularly as I had been paying him far more than I should have done. He came to my room as I packed my bag. His beaming face changed to one of tragedy. He bowed several times and gave me one of his bear-hugs. Then he grabbed my hand and kissed it repeatedly. I found it all immensely embarrassing.

Five

Clive easily recaptured Calcutta and re-established the 'gentlemen of Bengal'. Siraj-ud-daula had temporarily suspended his ham-fisted politics in favour of tiger hunting in up-country Bengal and was not worried by the arrival of English reinforcements. The Nawab had made no preparations for defending his new acquisition and once again the Union Jack was run up with little opposition.

The 1,000 miles by sea from Madras to Calcutta proved a troublesome journey for Colonel Clive's small army of 1,500 Europeans and 900 sepoys. Storms blew part of the fleet as far off course as Ceylon. Out of ten ships, two failed to turn up with the rest and were lost for months. Eighteenth-century ocean voyages were not easy.

Train travel in twentieth-century India is, thankfully, more predictable. I left for Calcutta by rail in an air-conditioned sleeper. I shared a compartment with a family, who were returning home 200 miles up the track to Rajahmundry. The father had the world on his shoulders and didn't smile once in ten hours. Mother wore ridiculously large Miss Moneypenny-type spectacles and made goo-goo noises over her infant daughter. Their toddler son was reluctant to keep his trousers on and whined through most of the journey. With them was granny, who sat upright in her seat staring at me until I scowled back. Five minutes later, she was staring again. She was very tiresome. One of the family farted a lot. I could have wished for better travelling companions.

The company improved one stop out of Madras. I was joined by Communist Party officials from the South Indian state of Kerala on their way to the Fourteenth CPI (Communist Party

104

India) Conference in Calcutta. One was in his thirties and the other a seasoned political campaigner of seventy-two. They shared their lunch of fish pickle and oranges and I reciprocated with a bunch of bananas and a slab of toffee-encrusted peanuts bought at Madras station.

We talked about communism in India. The first democratically elected communist state government in the world was in Kerala, which is also the only Indian state that can boast one hundred per cent literacy. The men were convinced that all India would be communist by the end of the century. Theirs was the only growing political movement in the country. The next state to fall would be Bihar, followed by Andhra Pradesh, they said. They showed me a copy of the latest CPI manifesto. It contained a long resolution insisting on the removal of South African troops in Angola. The IRA freedom fighters also got a name check. Where, I asked was anything about the development of the welfare state in India? Education, for example. Outside Kerala, illiteracy runs at about sixty per cent with 500 million people who cannot read nor write. (And still the authorities put Mahatma Ghandi's famous slogan outside their schools: 'The destiny of India is determined in the classroom.' To it should be added, 'For those who can afford it'.) The men nodded their heads. Perhaps there should have been more in the manifesto about education. But plans were being drawn up, they said. Education of the masses was on the communist schedule, along with industrial reform. The industry in India, whether it be soft drinks production or agricultural machinery, was controlled by no more than 100 companies, each for the most part with a monopoly.

The older man told me proudly that he had been a communist party member since his youth. Even at seventy-two his eyes blazed with the fervour of a political crusader. He was one of India's so called 'freedom fighters' – Indians who took up arms against their colonial masters. Before Independence, the British had taken exception to his political activities and he had spent three years in jail. 'We were always being beaten up, arrested,' he said. 'The British were not good to us.' There are many freedom fighters still alive in India. They receive a government pension and special privileges such as free first class travel on the railways.

The freedom fighter became quite argumentative. We argued

105

about Czechoslovakia and Hungary. He said the Russians had been quite right to move in with their tanks. 'Otherwise, the reactionaries would have taken over.' He was unreasonably intolerant. I showed him an Indian guide book, written by two Americans. 'Foreigners should not write about India,' he said. 'They will only get it all wrong. Only Indians should write about India.' I pointed out that if one of his countrymen had actually managed to provide a comprehensive guide for the foreign traveller, then I was sure it would sell very well. Unfortunately, so far none of them had and it had been left to foreigners to do the job.

In the early evening the train drew in to Rajahmundry. The family gathered their bags and got off leaving me alone with the communists. I told them about my relationship to Clive. The freedom fighter looked fairly disgusted, although his friend grudgingly admitted that Clive was probably more fondly remembered than other British Indian leaders. 'Your man Lord Mountbatten, for example, was very stupid,' he added.

By the next morning the train hit the outskirts of Calcutta. I stood in the corridor and talked to one of Calcutta's citizens, an engineer called Barun who was returning from working on an irrigation project in Tamil Nadu.

Barun knew a thing or two about water, particularly the water in Calcutta. 'Calcutta is an unhealthy place,' he advised. 'Do not even dream of drinking from a tap. Brush your teeth with cola if you have too. I got jaundice from the water so I should know. Anyone who can afford it drinks bottled mineral water.'

Clive had actually visited Calcutta once before to recover from a bout of fever he had picked up in Madras. After the stifling humidity of the south, Calcutta was popular as a health cure in the cool months of October and November. Listening to Barun drone on, and gazing out of the train window at the fume-laden sky, modern Calcutta did not seem much like a health resort.

I remembered a sad tale I had just read in my newspaper. A youth called Mohamed Nausad bought something called a puchka from a street vendor in the centre of Calcutta. After devouring the last morsel, he complained of stomach pains and was admitted to hospital. Death followed soon afterwards.

'What is a puchka?' I asked Barun.

106

'It is a snack with a lot of very hot spices,' he said. I vowed not to go within a dozen paces of a puchka.

We pulled into Howrah station and I exchanged farewells with the Kerala communists. They had eager looks on their faces and couldn't wait to exchange views with their Marxist colleagues. Barun wished me well. He had warmed to the puchka theme and had got onto the subject of which antibiotics to take in case of amoebic dysentry.

Howrah station has been described as hell on earth, full of diesel fumes, filth and noise. It is a place where you cannot move without tripping over a beggar, a seething mass of homeless all there for the specific purpose of hassling arriving and departing passengers for money.

But the station was surprisingly relaxed. I had known worse chaos at rural bus stands in Tamil Nadu. A surly porter grabbed my bag and we pushed through the throng of people with none of the sleeve-tugging and cries of 'money, master' that I had been led to expect. There was no problem finding a taxi and I asked the driver to take me into the city centre. All in all, a comparatively painless experience.

In the streets outside the station it was another matter: a fantastic confusion and anarchy that is Calcutta's masses. The number of people in the city is one of the East's great mysteries. The official government figure is 11 million. Locals talk of over 20 million. The number climbs alarmingly when food stocks run low in rural West Bengal and peasants advance on the city looking for work. On one day alone you might find 80,000 new residents moving in from the villages. Even in Clive's day there were 400,000 people in Calcutta with only 2,000 Europeans.

Since the time of Clive, various wits have tried to outdo each other in their descriptions of this city built on swamp and surrounded by thick jungle. Clive himself growled that it was 'the most wicked place in the Universe'. British writer Geoffrey Moorhouse, who is responsible for one of the best books about Calcutta, says the place is 'a definition of obscenity', and Mark Twain was quite pithy when he described the weather as 'enough to make a brass door knob mushy'.

It was left to a young Winston Churchill to provide the humour: 'I shall always be glad to have seen it for the same

107

reason Papa gave for being glad to have seen Lisbon. Namely, that it will be unnecessary for me ever to see it again.'

After more than a month in Calcutta I decided, on the basis that things couldn't get much worse, that it was a city in urgent need of a disaster. Perhaps a calamity like a plague, famine, flood or earthquake might stir the inhabitants to positive action for once in their lives.

Calcutta was founded on 24 August 1690, sixty-six years before Clive's first visit. She was the creation of Job Charnock, an English merchant affiliated to the East India Company. Charnock recognised the value of three small villages – Sutanati, Govindour and Kalikata – as an ideal location for 'quiet trade'. Calcutta takes its name from the last of these villages, which in turn was named after the black Hindu goddess Kali. The dreadful Kali is the wife of Shiva, and is portrayed as a bloodthirsty, axe-wielding psychopath, dripping in blood, with the heads of her victims hanging on string around her neck. In normal circumstances the likes of Kali would be taken in for police questioning. But in Calcutta she is revered as the city's patron goddess. The similarly evil appearance of Calcutta must be more than mere coincidence. The forces of Hindu destiny at work again?

Job Charnock was a godly man. He distinguished himself by rescuing an Indian widow, who was about to commit suttee and burn herself on her husband's funeral pyre. Charnock whisked her away and married her the same night in a Christian ceremony. She was a great beauty and Charnock loved her dearly. He was distraught when she died twenty years later. Thereafter, on each anniversary of her death, he sacrificed a live cockerel at her tomb.

By the time Clive reached Calcutta the city was beginning its social climb that would make it the London or Paris of the East. Merchants were on a relentless crusade to make money. Grand Italianate mansions were going up on the banks of the Hughli River. Crates of claret and hock were brought in to water the thirsty inhabitants. Food stores on a level with Mr Fortnum's and Mr Mason's Piccadilly Emporium were importing delicacies like Durham mustard, pickled oysters and reindeer tongue. It was *de rigeur* for Europeans to have a large retinue of servants and everyone competed for the lavishness of their carriages.

Behind the palatial front lines in the native quarter of 'Black

Town', it was a different story. Clive might have seen sights that were splendidly described half-a-century later by Reginald Heber, Bishop of Calcutta: '. . . deep, black and dingy, with narrow, crooked streets, huts of earth baked in the sun, or of twisted bamboos, interspersed with ruinous brick bazaars, pools of dirty water . . . a crowd of people in the streets, beyond anything to be seen in London, some dressed in tawdry silks and brocades . . . religious mendicants with no clothing but their long hair and beards in elf locks, their faces painted white or yellow, their beads in one ghastly lean hand, and the other stretched out like a bird's claw, to receive donations . . . a constant clamour of voices, a constant creaking of cart wheels, which are never greased in India . . . add to all this a villainous smell of garlic, rancid coconut oil, sour butter and stagnant ditches.'

The ungreased cart wheels are still there, but they have been joined by the internal combustion engine. And it is the traffic in twentieth century Calcutta that gets to your senses first.

The taxi, a battered yellow crate, lurched out of the station at breakneck speed. The driver seemed unconcerned that he was in charge of a machine with the aerodynamics of a house brick. Then came the mammoth traffic jam that is daytime Calcutta. The driver sharply decelerated and we crawled over potholes. A multitude of people scurried about their business like deranged locusts. We dodged marauding cows, who seemed to have developed a traffic sense, and goats, who had not. The driver leaned out of his window to shoo the creatures away.

We crossed Howrah Bridge to the east bank of the Hughli. Bicyclists wobbled dangerously in the middle of the road until trucks forced them on to the verge. Policemen in grey-white uniforms blew whistles and tried vainly to look official. You hardly noticed the traffic lights. A grimy layer of dirt covered the bulbs so that they emitted only a dull glow.

The rear bumpers of the buses were decorated with demonic figures and slogans like 'Danger. Use Horn'. This was unnecessary advice in a city where honking your horn is as natural as a West Ham fan shouting encouragement from the terraces. A fire engine, bells a-ringing and firemen clinging grimly to the sides, added to the cacophony. And at the core of this madness were the trams. Long, stately trams, proceeding confidently down the tracks. They set the pace of the traffic and were treated with great respect by motorists and pedestrians alike. A Calcutta tram does not stop for anyone.

The Paragon Hotel was typical of the cheap lodgings in Calcutta's tourist ghetto of Sudder Street. 'Drug addiction prohibited', cautioned a sign in the lobby. The aroma of cannabis wafted from the dormitories. The Paragon was packed with young European backpackers, who insisted on wearing hippy garb like harem pants and embroidered waistcoats over bare chests. All very Jimi Hendrix *circa* '68. The mode of attire must have seemed quaintly old-fashioned to the youth of Calcutta for whom the height of trendiness was a permed, crinkly, slicked-back Michael Jackson haircut, stone-washed denims, fake Lacoste sports shirts, and trainers allegedly made by Reebok, but probably copies knocked up in a Bombay sweatshop.

My first night in Calcutta I shared a room with a Frenchman called Pascal. He lived in Hong Kong where he worked as a film extra playing Westerners in Chinese kung fu movies. His other occupation was smuggling. 'Maybe pocket TVs from Singapore or gold from Hong Kong. It pays for my travelling... and my head.' Pascal tapped his large Gallic nose. He was using heroin and was now considering running narcotics into Europe. I thought he was excessively stupid. He couldn't have looked more like a smuggler, a customs officer's dream. He wore a silk hippy waistcoat over a bare chest. A thin pigtail ran down the back of his neck. Above his ears, the sides of his head were shaved to a fine stubble, leaving a bushy, black thatch on top. He might as well have gone through the green channel at an airport yelling: 'Hey boys! Look at me. I'm a drug runner.'

Pascal was ill. He had become addicted to heroin while bumming around Thailand and now his habit was taking up an increasing amount of his time. I first met him by the entrance to the Paragon. He was going through cold turkey, sniffing and shivering, waiting for one of the many Sudder Street dealers to return with a gram of the low-grade Pakistani heroin that is known as 'brown sugar'. The bulk of India's heroin comes from Pakistan, a country where twenty per cent of the male population is alleged to be addicted to the drug.

My room-mate was not a happy person. The dealer was already three hours late. More than anywhere else in the world, perhaps, it must be a nightmare being addicted to heroin in India. Unpunctuality is the norm; business appointments are

110

seldom met on time and dope dealers are no exception. If the man says he'll be on a street corner at, say, midday, you can reckon on 2 pm. Judging by Pascal's ashen pallor, Bengali black marketeers were worse time-keepers than most. He was shaking and coughing and spitting phlegm into a grubby handkerchief. By mid-afternoon, the dealer had returned and the Frenchman was a lot more cheerful. I found him in our room lying on his bed having smoked some of the brown powder. He looked tediously vacant and would not be good company. I left him and set out to explore the city.

In the alleyway outside the Paragon the filth by the side of the road was worse than at the end of an overcrowded party in a small London flat. Rubbish was piled high. A man threw the murky contents of a bucket into my path, splashing my trousers. A mother sat by a vegetable stall picking lice out of her child's hair. The child cried in pain. The gutters brimmed black with water that seemed to scream, 'Cholera!' The World Health Organisation has reported that 'the Calcutta area . . . forms the starting point for a long distance spread of cholera.' The city's health officials claim the disease is presently in check. This can only be by the grace of God.

In Sudder Street a group of Indians were crowded around an elderly monkey, which had somehow found its way into the centre of Calcutta. I reckoned it must be a pretty senile monkey to want to leave rural Bengal for life in the city. Considering the Indians' often cruel treatment of animals, I didn't give much for the monkey's chances. At Calcutta Zoo, for example, it is considered great fun to poke the animals through the bars with long sticks. But this monkey was attracting a surprising amount of compassion. Its fur was tatty and it was obviously very hungry. A beggar threw an orange. The monkey pounced on the fruit and quickly devoured it. A small boy, keen to show off his macho side in front of his elders, threw a stone at the animal. The crowd rounded on the boy and loudly ticked him off. Perhaps they thought their visitor was an incarnation of the Hindu monkey god, Hanuman. Monkeys are revered in India. The superstitious believe that they were once men, but were given tails and hair for their laziness.

Monkeys have also played a traditional part in sorting out village feuds. Rather than demand satisfaction, an aggrieved party waited until he knew the rains were coming. Then he

111

climbed on the roof of the house of the man who had insulted him and poured rice all over the tiles. From their perches in the surrounding trees the monkeys could see the tempting morsels. They descended on the roof and devoured the rice, much of which had fallen in the cracks between the tiles. The monkeys solved this problem by pulling up the tiles, thus unroofing the house. Then the rain came and the water poured through. The trick was to leave the rice scattering until the last moment before the monsoon broke. If the moment was judged properly, you could ruin your neighbour's property in a matter of minutes.

I left the crowd and walked along Sudder Street dodging hawkers selling Punjabi oranges. 'Yaagh-yaagh,' they shouted. I could not work out whether 'yaagh' meant orange in Bengali or whether the salesmen suffered from a speech defect. I passed kerbside barbers shaving their customer's hair in the light of street lamps; pools of soapy water lay around their stools. Sugar cane juice salesmen were squeezing the cane through huge mangle-like contraptions to which were attached bells. Each time the wheel turned it jangled as if to let customers know that juice was being served. Regiments of cab drivers muttered, 'Want taxi?' to any reasonably affluent-looking passer-by.

I turned into one of the small cafés dotted along Sudder Street where I ordered a banana milkshake. The café's owner lent me his copy of the Calcutta newspaper *The Telegraph*. The paper included a 'Barter Bank', a column where Calcutta's young readers could advertise items they wanted to swap. 'Aquarium, novels and mini soft drink bottles', announced Ajay Gupta from the suburb of New Alipore. 'I offer an aquarium in good condition, two P.G. Wodehouse novels and five Campa Cola mini bottles in exchange for fifty posters of Samantha Fox on roller skates or anything of corresponding value.' Perhaps fifty posters was slightly excessive, and how could the value of Miss Fox begin to correspond with that of Mr Wodehouse? But I liked the roller skates idea.

Was Ajay Gupta typical of Calcutta youth? A party of male students sat on the next table chatting noisily. One of them turned to me and asked the usual questions. Where was I from? How old was I? Was I married? Why not? His name was Vinod, and he had just started studying medicine.

He then asked me a question that I had heard many times already in India. How could he go about getting a job in Britain?

112

He was a young, bright man of twenty-two and he was desperate to leave Calcutta.

He talked about his life in the city. 'India is the black hole of Asia, Calcutta is the black hole of India. There is no future here. I have been trying to get a good job for a year, but no luck. There is too much unemployment.

'When I talk like this to foreigners they ask why I want to leave India. They say I will not like it in the West. There is too much rudeness, it is a bad way of life, they say.' Vinod laughed bitterly. 'It is easy for them to say that. They can leave India whenever they want and go home to good jobs and roads without holes in them and cities where no one sleeps on the pavement. I hate these foreigners for their arrogance. They see India as nicely old-fashioned and polite. I would rather have the rudeness of the West and a good job and maybe a car. Here, if I am lucky, I will have a car by the time I am forty.

'It is easy for foreigners to say there is no need for material possessions because they have them back home. It is easy for them to talk. When they are forty they will have cars, homes of their own and gardens where their children can play. I will not.'

Depressing stuff. I left the café and began my quest for Clive's Calcutta, the city where at least *he* made his fortune. I walked up Sudder Street, negotiated the ferocious traffic on Chowringhee and crossed over to the sprawling expanse of open ground that is the Maidan. This is the two square miles of parkland that has been the site of countless political rallies and where, on weekends, up to ten thousand young Calcuttans turn out to play cricket. Here also is Calcutta's military bastion, Fort William, partly built by Clive and still in use as an army base. The original fort was in a severely dilapidated state when Clive first arrived. It was as Governor of Bengal, on his last visit to India, that he supervised the construction of the present ramparts and barracks.

I moved on to the Victoria Memorial, a lump of solidly early twentieth-century British building standing at the southern end of the Maidan. A statue of Queen Victoria at her grimmest looks down on tourists entering the surrounding gardens. Beautiful is not a word that springs to mind when describing the Victoria Memorial, although it looked quite attractive under night-time floodlights. The Vic is what British rule was all about. It was built with a firm, stately hand and a curious, heavy mix of classical European design with local influences. The man behind its conception, the viceroy Lord Curzon, saw it as the British answer to the Taj Mahal. Needless to say, it goes wide of the mark.

Inside the VM was one of the few statues of Clive still left in India. Until an upsurge of Indian nationalism in the late 1950s there were busts of Clive all over the sub-continent. Bearing in mind that he had been chiefly responsible for laying the foundations of the British Empire in India, the government of Jawaharlal was understandably sensitive about prolonging his memory. The statues had to go. Clive's sculpture in the Vic is a marble replica of the original bronze by Tweed that stands in London. Very imposing it is too, depicting the man as his usual doom-laden self, weighed down by responsibility and nagged by ill health.

I walked until early evening and returned to the hotel via Park Street where the rich have their apartments, a fact that was difficult to believe. It was just like everywhere else in the city: broken sewers spewed filthy water down what remained of the gutters at the side of the wide boulevard; a regiment of beggars stuck out their bowls for alms. You were just as likely to see a beggar, both legs missing, sores covering his body, lying on the pavement outside the entrance to an expensive block on Park Street as in one of the worst slums.

Back at the Paragon, the Frenchman Pascal was still in a semi-comatose state. He planned to take the train next morning to Varanasi, India's holiest city. 'It will be better for my head than Calcutta,' he explained. Bearing in mind his condition, I agreed that he was probably right.

I slept fitfully my first night in Calcutta. Even after a shower, the humidity and grime clung on obstinately. Outside my window in the early hours came the sounds of a series of dog fights; incredible canine battles that sounded as if the One Hundred and One Dalmations had drawn against the Hound of the Baskervilles – and some of the Hound's mates. There was a savage barking and roaring with yelps of pain from the vanquished. At 3 am I left my room to peer into the alleyway behind the hotel. Three dogs, whose ancestry owed much to the Airedale, had set about an animal, whose ginger coat might have been quite elegant were it not covered in mange. Ginger had a torn ear. The smell of blood enraged his attackers. A fight to the death was prevented only by a local resident who threw a flower pot at these canine hooligans. The dogs gave up and fled into the night.

Back to the reason why Clive was in Calcutta in 1757, the year that was to establish British rule in India. It was his task to avenge the deaths of the Europeans who had died in the infamous Black Hole.

English school children will tell you that the Black Hole of Calcutta was the single most important event in Anglo-Indian history. You will hear that on 20 June 1756, the wicked, debauched and French-backed Nawab of Bengal, Siraj-ud-daula imprisoned 146 Europeans overnight in Calcutta's Fort William in a cell no larger than 250 square feet. You will also hear that by the next morning 123 of the prisoners were dead from suffocation.

Worse. A lady was among the prisoners. An English lady at that. Mary Carey survived the night only to be dragged off to Siraj-ud-daula's harem, thereby adding charges of abduction with an intent to rape to the Nawab's already unimpressive record of murder on 123 counts. Shocking stuff. Englishmen were up in arms. They wanted the Black Hole avenged and Clive was the man for the job.

Contemporary historians say the Black Hole story was an example of eighteenth-century British propaganda at its best. According to Mark Bence-Jones the figures are poppycock.

The myth was based on the writings of a survivor, John Zephaniah Holwell, described by Bence-Jones as a 'talented but not always truthful propagandist'. When one considers the size of the cell, Holwell's figures have to be mathematically impossible, and it is now thought that anything between thirty-nine and sixty-nine people were incarcerated, with eighteen to forty-three deaths. But, as Bence-Jones puts it,' 'Even for this lesser number it would have been horror enough to spend one of the hottest and most sultry nights of the Bengal June crowded together in a room fourteen feet by eighteen, unventilated but for two small barred windows.'

Whatever the death toll, the whole sorry affair seems to have been one huge cock-up that started after Siraj-ud-daula was taken not unexpectedly drunk after a twenty-four-hour alcohol and opium binge. Well, wouldn't you celebrate if you'd just captured a fort? The Nawab's exasperated captain of the guard shoved the prisoners into the first cell he could find. In the euphoria of victory everyone was screaming and shouting, and how was the captain to know the room was a bit on the small side? Only acting on orders, guv'nor.

The tag 'Black Hole' is also misleading. Far from being exclusively concerned with events in Calcutta, prison cells in military barracks all over Britain's colonies were, until only one hundred years ago, known as black holes. The London newspapers were also outraged by the detention of Mary Carey, who was described as an English woman. In fact, brave Mary was a foreigner, who only ended up in the cell because she refused to be separated from her English husband. Would the British public have been so concerned about her fate had they known she was a Portuguese half-caste?

Despite the fuss back in Britain, Siraj-ud-daula, chief baddie of the piece, was not in the slightest concerned about his actions. A few days later he was back in his capital of Murshidibad organising an elephant fight and tiger hunt. Anyone who can go big-game hunting after annoying the enemy to the point that they are about to totally disrupt your life has to be quite cool. A case of sod politics, let's bag a tiger.

These days Indians certainly aren't taught in school about the Black Hole. A London-based Calcuttan friend of mine says he never even knew the incident had taken place until he arrived at Eton. Nor is the Indian Government keen on the story. The site of the cell, on which now stands the GPO building in Dalhousie Square, was first marked by a stone memorial erected by our outraged propagandist Mr Holwell. After years of neglect during the nineteenth century the structure collapsed and was replaced in 1902 by a forty-five-foot-high stone obelisk engraved with the victims' names and commissioned by the viceroy Lord Curzon. In 1940, to show willing and appease Indian sensitivities, it was moved to St John's Church, a few hundred yards from Dalhousie, where it remains today.

St John's, modelled on St Martin's in the Fields in London, was built after Clive's time in 1786. But it stands on the site of St Anne's, Calcutta's first church, where he would have worshipped. Having walked the streets all morning, I sought the sanctuary of a taxi to take me there. The driver, a young Sikh, had a fine sense of understatement. 'Calcutta . . . no discipline,' he

116

remarked as a rickshaw, its coolie oblivious to all danger, slewed in front of the car.

The churchyard was certainly suffering from a lack of discipline. A group of small boys were kicking a football around the overgrown graves. Much of the grounds – a sizeable area considering this was in the heart of Calcutta – were taken up by a vegetable patch and an encampment of shacks where the gardeners lived with their families. But at least attempts had been made to grow a lawn and new bushes had been planted.

The Black Hole memorial was streaked with bird's mess. A dead dog lay nearby, its body covered in flies. Grass grew up around the base of the obelisk. It stood in a corner of the churchyard near an ugly clutter of corrugated iron fencing and in the shadow of the tall church spire. I got the feeling that someone had decided to place this embarrassing and none too beautiful testimonial to British sacrifice as far out of sight as possible.

A little way from the memorial were the tombs of Calcutta's founder, Job Charnock, and Admiral Charles Watson, the man who helped Clive recapture Calcutta. The admiral died soon afterwards in a terrible epidemic that claimed the lives of nearly two hundred Europeans and many more Indians.

The church was surrounded by towering pillars that supported the roof above the verandah. It was on the wide steps outside the main entrance that two hundred years ago the bachelor clerks of the East India Company would have viewed the latest talent arrived from England. Starved of female company, the lads would check out the new girls as they walked into Sunday service with their chaperones. Young ladies, who were prepared to undertake the hardship of the seven month voyage from England, were for the most part seeking a husband with good prospects. There were plenty of eligible young men in Calcutta, who were on their way to making decent fortunes.

I walked inside St John's. It was not a lively, airy church like St Mary's. The windows were smeared with city grime so that the daylight struggled to shine through; three electric lamps above the altar emitted a depressing, blood-red glow; the floor was a gloomy, grey marble.

A lonely communion service was in progress. The congregation numbered one man, the verger, who was being administered to by the vicar, the Reverend John Stevens. Tiny congregations were, sadly, nothing new to St John's and it was surprising that the place had survived at all. The only time the church was full was in November when Calcutta's Diplomatic Corps crowded in to celebrate Remembrance Day. Otherwise, it was lucky to see ten parishioners at matins.

I waited until the final blessing was said and then introduced myself to John Stevens. He was a smiling, chubby man with white hair, who had been ordained only three years ago. Originally from Gloucestershire, he had dedicated his life to Calcutta's poor and had worked in the city as a children's social worker for more than twenty years. His transition to the church had come naturally and many people in Calcutta agreed that Stevens was one of the most saintly men they knew. Nothing was too much bother for him when it came to caring for the destitute.

John was about the only person I met who was optimistic about Calcutta's future. 'I think it will become a thriving city again,' he said. 'It has never been dying, although I will admit it has been pretty sick. But it's now overcoming that sickness. There is an aura of hope in the air.

'I know it sounds extraordinary, but I think Calcutta is only just beginning to get over the blow to its morale suffered when the capital of India was changed from here to Delhi in 1911. After that everything began to go downhill. But things are definitely improving. People's attitudes are changing. They are making a bit more effort.'

Perhaps the vicar was being unreasonably optimistic. But it was heart-warming to hear a voice of hope in this quagmire of poverty and deprivation.

The British laid plans to punish Siraj-ud-daula for his cruelty and generally loutish behaviour. On 13 June 1757, Clive and his army marched to meet the enemy.

Or at least the Indian sepoys marched. Rather than a hard foot-slog, Clive and his European officers travelled up the Hughli River in comfort, in boats pulled by the Indians on the banks. With less than three thousand men under his command, Clive was headed for the Nawab's capital of Murshidibad. After a ten-day journey the British were eventually to engage Siraj-ud-daula's forces twenty-five miles south of Murshidibad, at the small village of Plassey.

Six

Travel writers are supposed to be gung-ho. They are supposed to do gung-ho things like cross uncharted African desert single-handed, or narrowly escape death at the hands of the only tribe of cannibals in Papua New Guinea that has not yet taken to wearing rock 'n' roll T-shirts.

The bullock cart episode had been a flop and I felt it was time for a proper adventure. It was with this in mind that I decided on the boat trip.

I would take a boat and retrace Clive's journey up the Hughli River to the battlefield of Plassey. From there I would continue upstream to Siraj-ud-daula's capital, Murshidibad. This would provide a pioneering feel to my travels. And it would be a fitting salute to the colonel.

My researches revealed that Plassey was no more than ten hours away by boat. At least, that's what the Calcutta locals told me. Memo: Don't believe everything you are told in India. For if I had been Clive I would have never even got to the Battle of Plassey – let alone won it. But I discovered all that far too late.

The Great Boat Trip idea started the moment I arrived in Calcutta. But where would I find a boat? The point is that you don't just go boating on the Hughli in the same way that you might spend a few days on the Thames. Boating on the Hughli is not included in the list of great Indian tourist attractions. It is a working river, not a holidaymaker's paradise. The Bengalis simply don't go boating – jolly weather, or not.

There *had* been pleasure cruises on the Hughli, but that was long ago in the last century when rich Europeans would board 'snake boats' 100 feet long for picnics. The Calcutta newspaper-

119

man William Hickey, who later gave his name to a gossip column, regularly set forth in his sleek 48-footer crewed by flunkies in white jackets and red and green turbans.

That was not what I had in mind. I needed a craft of more modest proportions. And that is how I ended up with China.

China was picking his ear with a matchstick when I first met him. He was one of the taxi drivers that hung around Sudder Street and I hired him a couple of times to show me the city sights. Whenever he was worried about something, he had the habit of taking a match and digging into his ear with a frightening ferocity. In the next few days, he was to use a large number of matches.

I got on well with China, despite his Bengali sense of humour. 'China poor man,' he said when we first met. 'But China have big heart. My father say I must never cheat no one. If you not happy with me, baba, you tell me.'

He pronounced his name Cheena. He was a Moslem and had been born plain Mohammed. He had been given the nickname China as a child because of his narrow, Chinese eyes. It had stuck ever since.

China was a short, wiry man of twenty-six. He had a lean face with sunken cheeks and a whispy moustache that twitched violently when he was angry. He was very proud of the fact that his father had earned enough money to send him to school. He had kept up the family tradition and was paying for his own three children to be educated. His five-year-old daughter lived with him in Calcutta. His wife and sons were back at his home village in the neighbouring state of Bihar. He seldom saw them, but sent them 400 rupees (£16) a month. Otherwise they lived off what crops they could grow.

In common with many men in Calcutta, China had left home for the big city at an early age. There was far more to be earned in Calcutta than he would ever hope to make in poverty-stricken rural Bihar.

At first he had worked as a cleaning boy for an Anglo-Indian couple, who taught him English. 'They teach me that I earn more money if I speak English,' he explained. 'They teach me to always say "good morning, sir" when anyone came to call. They say that good manners very important.' After leaving domestic service he worked in a shop where he earned enough to pay for driving lessons. He found a job as a driver for the owner

120

of a fleet of taxis. Now he had saved enough money to buy his own car. It was a 1974 Ambassador, the Indian answer to the Morris Oxford of the 1950s; its body work had seen better days, but it was mechanically sound. China loved it dearly. He had a room in a tenement block, but the car was his base. I would often find him asleep in it, or sitting in the back playing ludo with one of his colleagues.

Since I hadn't a clue where to start looking for a boat, I mentioned it to China. He leapt on the idea like a greyhound on a rabbit. Here was a chance for him to make some money. Of course he could find a boat.

He arrived at the Paragon one morning and we got down to tense preliminary negotiations. We puffed our way through cigarettes. China said that for a small fee he would join me on the trip as official interpreter. He could also cook. It went without saying that the white sahib would need someone to prepare his meals. I agreed that cooking was not my strong point. Anyway, it was likely that Clive was surrounded by an army of chefs and probably couldn't even boil an egg.

'So what you want, baba?' China said. From the moment I met him China called me baba, or master. He also had a habit of saying 'Don't worry, baba' whenever I questioned his judgement.

He continued, 'You want big boat or small boat?'

'A small one,' I said.

'Okay, baba. I go and find one now.' It sounded so easy. I had asked for a boat, so China would find me one.

I arranged to meet him the next day. He was going to meet a so-called broker, to whom I would pay six per cent of the hire fee. The broker would find a boat to my specification. This seemed a lot easier than trailing around endless yards trying to find a craft for hire. Before China left, I told him how much I was prepared to pay for the whole trip. Certainly no more than 4,000 rupees (£160), which would include his fee. So, the less the boat cost, the more he would get. This proposal greatly appealed to him and he set off to meet his broker friend.

China returned the following morning. 'Good news, baba!' he exclaimed. 'I have a boat for you.' It was at this point that I realised he might not have fully understood the gist of our conversation.

'I have found boat, baba. Big motor boat.'

121

'How big?'

'Maybe take thirty people. Very nice.'

It turned out he had found a ferry boat, which would cost 2,500 rupees a day. This was not what I had in mind. I explained that I was not planning to go into the charter business. China looked downcast. I think he had been looking forward to cruising up the Hughli at the helm of what amounted to virtually a small motor yacht.

'No good, baba?'

'No good, China.'

He left to find another broker. Two hours later he was back in high spirits.

'Very good boat, baba. Fast boat. Speedboat!'

Now this was more like it. Perhaps zooming up-river to Plassey in a speedboat was not quite in the spirit of Clive, but I'm sure that if such a craft had been available in 1757, the enterprising colonel would have been the first to take advantage of it.

'Great,' I said. 'Perhaps we can do a spot of water skiing.'

China looked serious. 'No water skiiing in Hughli, baba. Many dead dogs in water. You crash.'

'I know, China. That was a joke.'

'Ah, I see. Joke.' He didn't appreciate the humour.

China fetched his car and we drove down to a boatyard near Kidderpore docks to have a look at the craft. On the way, we passed the Taj Bengal, a new five-star hotel that was being built on the banks of the Hughli. It was a sumptuous looking building in a sort of neo-raj style. It seemed folly for the Taj hotel group to be spending so much money in what most people considered to be a dying city. But at least someone obviously had faith in Calcutta. Rich locals I spoke to were certainly keen on the prospect of an alternative to the Oberoi Grand, which for several years had held the five-star monopoly. I visited the Oberoi only once during my stay. The place looked a picture of elegance on the surface. Marble floors, a jungle of potted plants. A visit to the gentlemen's lavatory revealed a slovenly management. An encrusted layer of vomit in one of the basins. The only towel was grey and grubby and laying on the floor. And not a lavatory attendant in sight – inexcusable in a country where labour is so plentiful and cheap that even the smallest bar will employ a menial to swill out the urinals.

We reached the boatyard, a scruffy compound littered with

old oil drums and wooden launches in various stages of repair. The yard lay on the banks of a backwater known as Tolly's Nullah. This tidal creek winds its way from the Hughli up to the temple at Kalia ghat, home of black Kali. It was named after a Major Tolly, who in 1775 dredged the tributary so that temple pilgrims could bathe before sacrificing goats.

I knocked on the door of the yard's office. I was answered by a grunt and I went in. An elderly air conditioning unit was making a feeble attempt at shutting out the city's humidity. On one wall was a sexy poster advertising Yamaha marine engines. Two Indian girls in wet saris were posing alongside a dinghy with a Yamaha outboard. Forget the Kama Sutra. In twentieth century India a wet sari is the height of sensuality. A pair of nipples trying to poke through damp silk is the biggest turn-on an Indian man can get.

I didn't like the look of the boatyard owner. He had a thick gold chain around his neck, more gold on his fingers, and a gargantuan Rolex watch around his wrist. He sat behind a vast desk in one of those so-called executive swivel chairs. He had an unhealthy browny-yellow complexion and a fat face, which attempted to ooze a sort of slimy charm. He was the very picture of the business smoothy: a sharp operator. I had an overwhelming urge to grip tightly onto my wallet.

There was another man in the office. He was wielding a tape measure and turned out to be Fatty's tailor. Was the boss having a new suit made, I enquired?

'This is correct,' he said. 'It will be a sleeping suit. Silk.'

Fatty was a man who slept in silk pyjamas. As far as I was concerned, he was now known as Mr Silky Jim-Jams.

Negotiations got under way. It became quickly apparent that we were not off to a good start.

'So you want to buy a boat?' Mr Jim-Jams rocked in his chair. It was a question spoken with greedy anticipation in the manner of a pig at the trough.

I looked at China. China looked at me. He shrugged as if to say he didn't know what the man was talking about. Obviously the broker had got the wrong end of the stick.

'No, I do not want to buy a boat,' I said. 'I have no intention of moving permanently to Calcutta and becoming involved in the boating scene on a regular basis. I only want to hire something for a few days.'

123

'That is no problem,' said Mr Jim-Jams. 'I will show you the craft that we have for hire.' He pushed himself out of his chair and we left the office to view the boat. Having picked our way through the flotsam in the yard, we reached the muddy slip at the edge of Tolly's Nullah. Here indeed was the speedboat. And I can say only this: it was not the sort of speedboat that conjured up images of the South of France. It was an ugly vessel with a huge, ungainly canvas awning strung over a tubular metal frame. The fibre glass hull was wide and flat and looked like an over-grown pedalo without the pedals. The colour was garish orangey red. In the boat's favour, it did seem to have a speedboat-ish type of engine, a 25 hp Yamaha outboard that looked in excellent condition. I say 'looked' because I learned later not to judge outboards by their appearance.

'It is a nice boat, is it not?' Mr Jim-Jams flicked a piece of mud off the bows and wiped the fibreglass with his handkerchief. I agreed that it was a lovely piece of design.

We returned to the office to discuss the deal. How long would it take to reach Murshidibad? I asked. No more than two days, said Mr Jim-Jams. Then one day, maybe one and a half days back, as the current would be with us. We discussed the price per day. I had already told China to tell the broker that I would pay no more than 4,000 rupees. Mr Jim-Jams began trying it on. He could not do it for less than 6,000 rupees.

'It is a very cheap price to someone like you from England,' he said. 'I do not make much money from hiring out boats. Indian people are very afraid of the water, you see. British people like boats very much.'

Six thousand rupees was too much. I stood up and made as if to leave the office. Okay, said Mr Jim-Jams, 4,000 rupees it would be. But he would charge extra if we were gone longer than four days. By Indian standards, 4,000 rupees might seem far too much money. But as I said, pleasure boats on the Hughli were hard to come by. There was no way I would find one cheaper.

We shook hands on the deal, which also included the services of a boatman to drive the craft. I did not fancy the idea of China at the helm: he obviously knew nothing about boats.

'There is one problem,' Mr Jim-Jams added. I waited to hear the worst. 'I do not have a licence to hire out boats. If the police stop you, just say you are taking it for trials with a view to purchase.'

'But if the police at Murshidibad decide to haul me in I can hardly say that I've been taking the thing on trials for 200 kilometres,' I pointed out. 'If I was them, I'd smell a big rat.' I did not fancy the thought of being thrown into jail in rural Bengal just because this man was too mean to pay a licence fee. I discovered later that the police were tough on the registration of boats because craft were often used to smuggle contraband downriver from Bangladesh.

'I guarantee there will be no problem. If you are stopped, maybe you can pay some small baksheesh and the police will let you go.'

Mr Jim-Jams asked for a proportion of the fee upfront and announced it was time for his lunch. China and I returned to the car. Now began the problem over the broker's fee. China had rashly promised his contact 1,000 rupees thinking that the boat would have cost me a lot more. I decided to be very firm.

'Six per cent of 4,000 rupees is 240 rupees,' I said. 'Not a penny more.'

China looked worried. 'No more.' I said. China looked more worried. 'Well, no more than 300 rupees anyway.' China smiled. This English baba was a soft touch.

Mr Jim-Jams had lent us two 100-litre fuel drums, which we filled up at a garage on the way back into the city centre. The cans were made of plastic and the screw tops did not fit properly. I told China that with that amount of fuel around, there would be no smoking on the boat. He shrugged, as if to say he did not know what I was worrying about.

By now the crew consisted of three: China, the Sukamar, the boatman, and me. But there was to be one more addition to the party.

Janice was one of the army of English backpackers working their way around India. An effervescent twenty-three-year-old with an infectious giggle, she was the daughter of a retired welder from the East End of London. Travelling was Janice's great love. She had worked as a City secretary as well as three nights a week as a barmaid in order to save up for her trip. She was on her way overland, via the well-trodden backpack route of Thailand and Indonesia, to Australia, where she planned to find work.

Janice was lugging a huge rucksack and storming through India in a happy-go-lucky way. Nothing worried her. There had been one nasty moment on a beach in Kerala when two men had approached her with a view to rape. But her yells and a strong right hook had put paid to that game.

We had met in Madras when I had talked about my plans to follow Clive up the Hughli. Janice thought it sounded like a tremendous jape and asked if she could come along. I said yes. She seemed to have a sense of humour and I had the feeling a sense of humour was one thing that was going to be needed on the trip.

Back in downtown Calcutta, China and I met up with Janice and we all went shopping in the New Market to buy provisions for the journey.

New Market was a large covered bazaar where you could buy everything. We avoided the butcher's hall that was straight out of a Breugel painting: great sides of bloody meat, all but obliterated by carpets of flies, hung from the roof. The stench was horrible; it was a vegetarian's nightmare.

China couldn't understand why Janice and I were so squeamish. 'I am a vegetarian,' Janice said.

'I have just become a vegetarian,' I added.

China looked sad. 'But I wanted to cook my special chicken,' he said. We persuaded him to stick to rice and vegetables.

We moved through the market negotiating the open drains that criss-crossed the floor. Janice distinguished herself by putting her foot in one. A nasty brown sludge of unspeakable origin clung to her ankle.

In the hardware section we bought a kerosene cooker, a kettle, saucepans and mosquito nets. We moved to the food stalls where I paid for two kilos of rice, thirty eggs and freshly ground spices. We stopped at a small shop and bought bundles of candles and enough incense to perfume a large temple. China explained that the incense would keep the mosquitos away.

I adopted the role of chief safety officer. 'When we start lighting that lot, the petrol's going on the bank,' I said.

'Don't worry, baba. China very safe.'

China insisted that we buy some paper plates. I argued that we should take palm leaves and eat off them. After all, that's what the locals did. Indeed, Clive's sepoys would have probably eaten off palm leaves. No, China wanted paper plates. This was

India, 1989, and paper plates were what you used for camping. We bought a packet that had been left over from Christmas and featured a festive holly motif.

Throughout our shopping expedition, we had been followed around by a man carrying a basket in which we put our purchases. When we returned to the car I asked China what sort of tip I should give our bearer.

'Two rupees,' China said. 'Or five rupees if you think he is poor man.'

'Well, he looks quite well fed,' I said. 'Anyway, how the hell do I know how poor he is? I can't exactly ask him, "Excuse me, are you poor today or are there great riches on the way?" '

'He is poor.' China was bored with my procrastination. I handed the man five rupees.

China, Janice and I arrived at the boatyard the next morning. Janice was clutching a plastic Buddha, a gift from a Japanese student. It seemed a little premature to be bringing out the good luck charms. We met Mr Jim-Jams, who was his usual slimy self. He emphasised again that it would take only ten hours to Plassey. 'A very easy run,' he said. 'Very straight. You may be there tonight or at least tomorrow morning.'

He introduced us to our boatman. Sukumar was a Bengali of nineteen with a grin permanently affixed to his face. We shook hands and Sukumar smiled a lot. It soon became apparent that he spoke no words of English.

'But he is a very good boatman,' Mr Jim-Jams said. 'He knows the river very well indeed. Most well. As well as any fisherman.'

I was glad of this. As far as I could work out, as soon as China was away from the congestion of the Calcutta streets, he would be hopelessly lost.

We walked down to the slip and Mr Jim-Jams stood on the bank while we loaded the luggage. Sukumar pulled the cord on the top of the outboard and the engine revved into life. We cast off the mooring lines and Mr Jim-Jams waved us goodbye as we puttered away up Tolly's Nullah.

It was not an auspicious start. The backwater was filthy with an odour similar to that of socks which have been worn for three months combined with the smell of burning oily rags. It was a dreadful clutter of deprivation and poverty. The banks were lined with wooden shacks perched on rotten stilts. Behind the shacks stood crumbling tenement blocks with broken windows. Naked children played alongside mounds of rubbish in the grey muddy sludge at the waterside.

We motored past hooch bootleggers, who had set up shop on the banks. Their trestle tables groaned with rows of bottles containing illegally distilled alcohol, a brown liquid that would blot out the misery of this squalid place. Drinking illegal liquor in India is a dangerous occupation that frequently leads to blindness, brain damage and death. It is very cheap and often made with industrial chemicals. The contents of ancient car batteries make a popular cocktail. But for many people it is the only alcohol they can afford. While I was in India, a batch of bad hooch claimed the lives of more than 100 people during a huge drinking binge in the town of Baroda in Mahatma Ghandi's home state, Gujarat. Another 300 drinkers ended up in hospital, many with permanent brain injuries.

We skirted a stream of sewage that gushed from a leaking pipe under a footbridge. With a yell I ordered Sukumar to slow down. The bridge was so low that it threatened to rip the boat's awning. Sukumar grinned at my panic. At the last minute he reduced speed and we passed under the bridge with only inches to spare. A few minutes later we were accelerating out of the tributary and into the wide open waters of the Hughli.

The Hughli can be a death trap. It is one of the world's least predictable rivers, with shifting sandbanks that present a constant hazard to shipping, particularly the large merchantmen and tankers of today. Skippers hate the Hughli and this explains why Calcutta's importance as a port has decreased rapidly over the years. The river's greatest terror is the tidal bore that charges up the river 144 days each year. The rushing, white surf can reach up to the height of a small house. Boats must be firmly lashed to their moorings less they are swept away and smashed to pieces on the banks.

The outboard churned through the water and we headed north. To the right rose the Writers' Building, the red-brick Victorian pile that had been the business hub of British Calcutta. I began to understand China's remark about dead dogs. The city's doggie population seemed to favour the Hughli as their final resting place. Rotting canine corpses mingled with decomposing vegetation.

We came up with Howrah station on the left. Ahead lay the

eerie, skeletal monster of Howrah Bridge. We passed underneath the huge girders. High above us, ant-sized figures streamed across as the sun glinted off the bare steel. I lifted my camera and took a shot of this monument to the Indian construction industry.

'No,' China said. 'No pictures.' It was forbidden to photograph the bridge on the grounds of state security.

I was amazed. 'What's secure about one of the biggest bridges in Asia that can probably be seen from a spy aircraft at 40,000 feet?' I said. 'Anyway you can buy postcards of the thing in Calcutta.'

China didn't know the reason either. 'Indian people mad,' was the only explanation he could offer.

A fast launch on the Hughli is a star attraction, particularly if it contains two foreigners. After spotting us, people on the banks would wave and shout. I wondered if Clive's army had received a similar reception when they set out for Plassey.

North of Howrah, we had our first sight of the dead bodies that were to become as normal as the discarded banana palm leaves. At Nimtala ghat the Hindus were burning their dead. Sukumar steered around the cadaver of a child swathed in garlands of flowers. Children are not burned. Their bodies are wrapped in cloth and left to float down the river until they either decompose or reach the Bay of Bengal. Or perhaps they will be snagged on the banks where they are devoured by dogs.

The shore either side displayed a chaotic array of architecture: tenement slums, factories and brick-works; long rows of warehouses, now pathetically dilapidated, but which gave a clue to Calcutta's prosperous past. Behind the lean-tos that sprawled along the banks were the remains of once beautiful villas and mansions, formerly the homes of rich European merchants, the Italian-style palaces of Clive's day. We headed towards the city outskirts. We passed the Hare Krishna temple on the west bank, a massive marble complex built at vast expense and paid for by the sect's foreign devotees.

Calcutta sprawled on. The river seemed to become a little cleaner, the dead dog count lower. But perhaps this was our imagination. We had to make frequent stops to free the propeller from bits of debris. Sukumar slowed down to avoid fishing nets strung out dangerously across the river with no regard for shipping. The design of the flimsy, wooden fishing boats would have changed little since Clive's day.

The pollution to the air was dreadful. The new Bali road bridge appeared in the distance in a smoggy haze. To the right, Chitpur power station belched thick, yellow smoke. Above the dozens of brick-works, black clouds spewed from the chimneys. I could almost see the grime landing on our clothes.

We changed petrol tanks. The Yamaha was guzzling fuel at an alarming rate. Sukumar filled up from one of the plastic drums. He sucked on a pipe to create a vacuum and then spat mouthfuls of petrol into the river. Two miles up from Howrah Bridge, we pulled in to one of the ghats on the west bank to rest the motor. Sukumar was obviously not fussy about where he moored up. Was it absolutely necessary to stop by a sewage outlet? The smell was overpowering. People stared at us from the bank. I scowled back. Janice quite liked the attention and practised her royal wave. It never ceased to amaze me how so many people, presumably some of reasonable intelligence, could spend twenty minutes just staring at a boat.

When we set out again an hour later the tide was against us. I reflected on the gruelling task that Clive's sepoys must have been faced with while pulling the officers' boats. We approached the old French colony of Chandernagore, Calcutta's sister settlement of Pondicherry, that like Pondi remained independent from India until the early 1950s. Even by the 1960s it had still retained a French flavour and had been a favourite watering hole for Calcutta's ex-pats, who used to go drinking in the cafés on Saturday nights. But as one old buffer had said, 'It's very grotty now.'

Grotty it certainly was. We moored up again and I walked around Chandernagore's streets. The place was falling down, the mansions a mess of chipped masonry. There were no signs of the French occupation except for a couple of broken stone pillars at the south gate bearing the inscription, '*Liberté, Egalité, Fraternité*'. Buildings that had once been the chateaux of French merchants stood rotting.

In the run-up to Plassey, the British, led by Clive, had begun shaking up the French by attacking and occupying Chandernagore. The French put up a brave defence, but were forced to surrender and Clive moved into the house of the French Director. It was a small but splendid palace set in parkland on the banks of the river.

The park had gone, having been swallowed up by building. But the house still stood. It was a one-storey masterpiece of colonial architecture with a sweeping colonnaded verandah that commanded panoramic views of the Hughli. Since Independence the house had been used as a French institute. However, while I was in Calcutta there were angry letters in the newspapers saying that little was being done to encourage new students.

I managed to stir a caretaker from his siesta. He unlocked the building and showed me round the small museum that occupied part of the house. It featured copies of nineteenth-century Franco-Indian newspapers like *République Française*. Dusty chandeliers hung above nineteenth-century French furniture that was being eaten away by moths. The biggest four poster bed that I had ever seen stood alongside a collection of appallingly kitsch 1930s flower vases.

In one corner the French temporarily forgotten with a tiny exhibition dedicated to the memory of Dr J. N. Sen. Dr Sen, a citizen of Chandernagore, was the first Bengali to be killed in the Great War. He had been a private in the West Yorkshire Regiment and he died in action on 22 May 1916. His personal effects included penknife, a wallet, a pair of shattered wire-rimmed spectacles and a faded, much-fingered photograph of a girl in a sari.

I rejoined the others. Across from Chandernagore was a small island, little more than a sandbank, a fertile strip of soil where farmers were growing rice. The emerald green paddies sparkled in the dying sun. But how long would the sandbank stay there? The continual movements of the river bed meant that farmers could lose their land overnight.

Chandernagore gave way to the old Dutch settlement of Hughli, once the pride of Holland and so rich that the British were prepared to swap it with the Dutch for the island of Sumatra. Now it was just another Calcutta slum littered with bamboo shacks around stagnant ponds. Here were more mansions more than two hundred years old and so neglected that they would have given a National Trust director a coronary. Plasterwork had collapsed like pieces of a jigsaw puzzle to reveal bare brickwork underneath. Walls that had once supported elegant riverside terraces were sliding into the water. Occasionally a curtain in a window indicated that a house was inhabited, probably by squatters. But most were too dangerously unsafe even for the desperately poor, who preferred the primitive comforts of mud and bamboo.

As we continued north, there were hints of rural Bengal on the east bank. The banks were more grassy and the number of palm and mango trees was increasing. Were we at last leaving urban life? We were not. It was only my imagination. Another gargantuan power station appeared up ahead. The trees had lulled me into a false sense of pastoral security.

The light was fading fast. It was nearly 5.30 and the sun was almost down, its hazy glow reflecting in the water. The sound of factory sirens wailed across the river signalled the end of the day's work.

The amount of debris in the river made it dangerous to travel in darkness without a searchlight. We had to find a place to stop. Quickly. The city sprawl was still around us and I had given up all thought of spending the night on a quiet rural riverbank, particularly after repeated warnings from China. According to China, there were people who would creep up at night and rob us. We certainly couldn't just stop tie up and set up camp where we felt like it. China did not have much time for his fellow Bengalis. He referred to 'bad men', who would slit your throat for a farthing.

China echoed the views of Mr Charles Grant, an Englishman living in Calcutta at the beginning of the nineteenth century: 'The Bengalese have not sufficient resolution to vent their resentments against each other in open combat, yet robberies, thefts, burglaries, river piracies, and all sorts of depredations where darkness, secrecy, or surprise, can give advantage, are exceedingly common.' Nor did Mr Grant hold much affection for Bengali women: 'Held in slavish subjection by the men, they rise in furious passions against each other, which vent themselves in such loud, virulent, and indecent railings, as are hardly to be heard in any part of the world.'

I tackled China. 'Well, if we can't stop on a nice grassy bank without being turned over, where can we stop?'

'Don't worry, baba, we stay somewhere.'

The sweeping roofs of Bandel Church came up on the left hand side. It had been founded by Dutch Roman Catholic priests in 1599 and was in a bad state of repair. A restoration pro-

132

gramme was underway, but it seemed to be more of a patch-up job. China spoke a few words to Sukumar and we veered across the river to the opposite bank.

Sukumar headed for a steel pontoon. Alongside was moored a dilapidated ferry boat. There were signs of life on board. A thin spiral of smoke rose from an open cooking fire at the stern. The forty foot vessel dated from the 1930s and, from the look of its chipped blue and white paint, had never been touched since. It was one of the many commuter ferries that criss-crossed the river all day taking workers from one bank to another at a cost of one rupee each way. You would see their skippers at the stern weaving this way and that, dodging the skiffs of the Hughli's marauding fishing fleet. They would stand with one hand on the tiller, the other holding an umbrella to shield off the sun.

The pontoon was a jerry-built steel affair with treacherous, slippery wooden steps. High above it on the bank was a large factory. A sign told us it was the Indian Government Pulp Paper Mill. I could see a stream of men quitting work for their homes in the town of Hazani Nager that lay outside the factory gates.

The speedboat bumped alongside the ferry. Two sweaty deckhands in their vests peered out of a side window. China began a conversation in Bengali. Could we moor up alongside the ferry for the night? The men looked disinterested as if they couldn't care less where we stayed the night. But from the gist of the conversation it didn't sound hopeful. By this time the mosquitos were beginning to bite and the sun was below the horizon. It was nearly dark and there was no way we could go anywhere until first light the next morning.

A figure in a khaki army jumper with shoulder patches walked down the gantry from the bank. He was one of the mill's security guards. China explained our predicament and what we were doing on the river.

At the mention of Clive the guard looked quite interested. But the pontoon was the property of the Pulp Paper Mill and he had no authority to let us stay overnight.

'I cannot let you stop. My boss is not here and I am only Boss Number Three,' he said. Another guard came down the steps. Could *he* give us permission to stop?

'No,' said Boss Number Three. 'He is only Boss Number Four.'

I tapped China on the shoulder. 'Find out where Boss Number

One is,' I told him. China spoke some more Bengali. It transpired that Boss Number One was not available.

'He will be back at 8 pm,' said Boss Number Three.

Oh no he wouldn't, chipped in Boss Number Four. Boss Number One was in central Calcutta and the traffic out of the city was so bad he would not be back until at least 10 pm. It could take four hours to drive the twenty miles from the city centre.

Where was Boss Number Two? The other bosses shrugged. They didn't know. They hadn't seen him since teatime. Perhaps he'd gone home without telling them. I got the impression that the mill's security arrangements were not the height of efficiency.

Boss Number Three explained we could not stay on the boat. But would we mind awfully if we spent the night in the Pulp Paper Mill workers' rest house? That would be lovely, I said. Just show us the way.

At that point Boss Number Two turned up. His hair was dishevelled and he seemed to have just returned from a late-afternoon nap. Boss Number Two scratched his head. He had no authority to let us stay in the rest house, but we could stay on the boat. Did he really mean that? Yes, he did really mean that.

I wondered why we could not have been told this in the first place. China turned to me. 'Okay, baba, so all is fixed. What do you want for dinner? Rice and dal, or omelette?'

I looked at the muddy riverbank and did a quick check for dead dogs. It was not a pleasant place for a picnic. 'And where, China, are we going to cook an omelette?' I asked.

'We cook on boat.' He held up the kerosene cooker. 'Where else?'

'No, we bloody don't cook on boat. Not with more than 100 litres of fuel in leaky plastic drums, we don't.'

China put up his hands in surrender. 'Okay, baba. No cooking. We have bread and an orange instead.'

The men on the ferry boat came to our rescue. They said we could cook on the ferry's roof. It was usually used to accommodate an overspill of passengers with their bicycles. But it would be a safe place to set up the cooker.

China and I hauled the provisions up onto the wide space behind the wheelhouse. The bosses remained standing on the pontoon. They said nothing, but stared at us as China began preparing dinner. It was now dark. I lit some candles while China mixed an onion omelette. Sukumar lit the kerosene cooker.

Boss Number Three looked at the bags of rice and lentils. 'Do you eat Indian food?' he asked me. He sounded a little horrified.

'That is what I have been eating in India,' I said. It was an unnecessary snubbing reply, but the absurdness of the situation was getting to me. Janice and I started giggling. China joined in. We all rocked with laughter.

Boss Number Three took this lunacy in his stride. He wanted a sensible conversation. It was not often that he met Westerners camping on his pontoon.

'Do you know Lucy T?' he asked.

'Lucy T?' I had no idea what the man was talking about.

'Lucy T. Like you. Writer.'

'Never heard of her.'

China tried to help. 'Rucy Tee,' he said.

'Rucy Tee?' I looked to Janice for help.

'Got it!' she said. 'Rushdie. Salman Rushdie.'

'Lucy T! Lucy T!' Boss Number Three nodded excitedly.

Everyone in India was talking about Salman Rushdie, and the rumpus over his novel, *The Satanic Verses*. It was obvious to Boss Number Three that I must know the man because I was also a writer and came from England.

'Well, I've never met him, but I know who you mean,' I said.

I watched the river from the roof. The sound of a melancholy Hindi pop ballad carried softly from a radio in the cabin below. One of the boatmen was singing. From the sound of the deep emotion in his voice, it was a love song. I wondered if the man was married and how often he managed to return home to see his wife. She probably lived many miles away. With the sun deep below the horizon and the smoking chimneys lost in darkness, the Hughli now looked quite beautiful. The lights from the opposite bank twinkled on the gently rippling water. Little fishing skiffs chugged quietly up and down through the mist that was rising in midstream.

The serenity of the river was in contrast to the bankside. The Pulp Paper Mill worked twenty-four hours a day and I could hear the shouts of the men on nightshift. An army of generators hummed in the background. The mill made Silex, a by-product of paper that was used in everything from soap to bricks. The plant had been owned by a British company until the mid-Sixties when it was taken over by the Indian Government. At the side of the mill was a little neo-Tudor summer house, rose garden and bowls lawn where the English managers would have spent their lunch hours. The lawn was overgrown and pitted with holes. The roses had gone wild many years ago.

China tipped the onion omelettes onto the paper plates and handed them to Sukumar, Janice and me with a flourish. Boss Number Three looked on curiously. I beckoned to him to join us on the roof. No, he was quite happy standing on the pontoon. Boss Number Four reappeared. He was wearing an army surplus khaki battle dress top and woollen balaclava helmet to keep out the evening chill. He and his colleague stared as we ate.

Boss Number Four suddenly announced, 'I am in drama.'

'Are you really?' Janice decided to be chatty. 'Well, I must say it's been quite a dramatic day so far.'

He missed the point. 'Yes, amateur dramatic drama. I am doing plays. And TV.' The security guard moonlighted as an extra. His speciality was playing villians and he had been in many films. Janice and I looked suitably impressed.

It was time for the bosses to do their rounds of the factory. They wished us goodnight. I leaned over the side of the roof and shook hands with them and they disappeared up the gantry. China and Sukumar threw their paper plates overboard where they joined the rest of the debris in the river. Janice and I reluctantly did the same. Janice looked unhappy. She did not approve of littering. 'That is so against my principles,' she said.

China organised the sleeping arrangements. Janice would sleep in the bottom of the boat, with China and me on the seats either side. Sukumar found a place down in the stern by the outboard. China would not let Janice and me do a thing for ourselves. He and Sukumar rigged up the mosquito nets and we crawled under them. Much to the amusement – and, I think, disdain of China and Sukumar – I produced a camping lilo. This was not meant to be an SAS exercise and I had no intention of sleeping on hard fibreglass. I blew up my airbed. Janice pulled her sleeping bag around her. 'Isn't it nice to be waited on?' she said. 'Just like in the days of the raj.' And with a yawn and, 'Well, isn't this all very *African Queen*?' she was asleep.

Sleep did not come easily to me. An unpleasant smell came

from the piles of putrefying rubbish under the pontoon. And with the night there also came great clouds of mosquitoes attracted by a bright neon security light on the bank. They were savage brutes, impervious even to tubes of foul-smelling repellent. A hit-squad of insects descended over my net and proceeded to fight their way in. They buzzed loudly in my ears. I dozed until 2 am when I could stand it no longer. My face was covered in bites. China was also scratching violently. I was gratified to see that Bengali mosquitoes had no preference when it came to skin type.

Mosquitoes are bad news in West Bengal. Apart from the obvious problems of malaria – the disease was rife in rural areas north of Calcutta – the insects were also an indirect cause of house fires. Due to a sudden plague of mosquitoes in the district of Midnapore, villagers had taken to lighting fires on the floor in the middle of their wood and straw huts. The smoke worked splendidly at keeping the mosquitoes away, but more often than not the fires got out of hand reducing the huts to ashes. It was not unknown for whole villages to be burned to the ground.

Unable to sleep, I got up and climbed onto the pontoon to smoke a cigarette. The river was now enveloped in a thick mist. The current had slowed and a slick of industrial pollution, in the form of brown-flecked foam, now clung to the speedboat's hull. I was joined by one of the security guards. It was Boss Number Two. He was wide awake and very chatty. He demanded a history lesson. We talked about Siraj-ud-daula's uncle, Mir Jafar, who had commanded two thirds of the enemy troops at Plassey.

It was Mir Jafar who eventually betrayed Siraj-ud-daula and led to his overthrow. In the months preceding the battle, Clive had secretly conspired with Mir Jafar. He had let it be known that if Mir Jafar turned against his nephew, the British would set him up as the new Nawab. Clive's persuasion was successful. On the day of the battle, Mir Jafar and his soldiers refused to fight.

'Very famous man,' the guard said with a big smile. Throughout India, the name of Mir Jafar is used to this day to describe a person who breaks a confidence. But the traitor of Plassey still seemed to command a certain respect from many Indians. It was as if they would have also done the dirty on Siraj-ud-daula had they been in the same position. After all, what's a little cunning and trickery if it makes for an easier life?

We talked for twenty minutes until sleep began to claim me again. I returned to my mosquito net. I had just drifted off when Boss Number Two leaned into the boat and tapped me on the shoulder. He held a bunch of carnations in his hand.

'What the hell's going on?' I nudged China awake. He said something to the guard. 'It is a present,' China said. He rubbed his eyes sleepily. 'The guard has never talked to a foreigner before. It is a great honour for him.'

'Why can't he wait until a civilised hour?' I asked. China could not answer this one. I took the carnations and thanked the guard. He beamed with pleasure. There was something faintly bizarre about being given flowers by a strange man at three in the morning.

The dawn broke at 5 am. Janice awoke with a foul headache caused by petrol fumes escaping from the fuel drum. We were all covered in bites. I reflected that I had never spent a more uncomfortable night. I would be glad to see the last of this mosquito-infested mudbank.

The boatmen on the ferry were preparing to start work. They told China that we were lucky to have stopped here. There were bad men upriver; pirates, who would paddle silently down the river at night and rob boats. The Hughli, particularly on the outskirts of Calcutta, was famous for all sorts of waterborne footpads. Before we left, I asked the boatmen how long it would take to Plassey. Five hours, they said. This was good news. Even with stops to take on fuel, we would be at the battlefield by nightfall.

The morning got off to a good start. Sukumar started the outboard and we continued our cruise up the river. By mid-morning we were clear of the city and moving into the Bengal countryside. China broke out the bananas to celebrate our departure from Calcutta. The bird life increased. Flights of duck took off from the river, kingfishers swooped over the boat, gulls screeched high above us. Herdsmen sat on the banks watching their buffaloes. I envied the beasts, who could wallow for hours, their heads hardly above the water. The sun climbed towards its zenith and we attempted to keep cool under the awning. It was turning into a very hot day.

At around 11 am we ran aground on a sandbank. We were

doing twenty mph at the time and there was a horrible juddering through the boat. The outboard spluttered in protest. We used oars to push ourselves off . . . and ran aground again. Sukumar had failed to notice the shallow water and I was beginning to have doubts about his navigational skills.

The river divided and we stopped by a collection of little fishing punts to ask the way. The fishermen argued amongst themselves. One of the older men told us that Murshidibad was straight on, but we would have to watch out for another fork in the river. He was giving directions on the lines of, 'Left at the big palm trees; right at the mud hut'. There were many palm trees and a lot of mud huts. As an afterthought, I asked how far it was to Plassey. There was more arguing. 'Five hours,' came the answer.

'But the boatmen back at the Pulp Paper Mill also told us it was five hours,' I pointed out. 'And that was three hours ago.'

China was unconcerned and muttered another, 'Don't worry, baba.'

It was at this point that I realised we were rather an amateur expedition; hardly in the tradition of great explorers, who spent months planning their trips. No one on the Hughli had a clue how long it was going to take to reach Plassey, least of all even Sukumar, who was supposed to know the river well. He understood how to operate the outboard, but that was about it. We had a map, but it was very small scale. It didn't even attempt to show all the curves of the Hughli, which was famous for altering its course each monsoon.

The heat and humidity were stifling. Janice and I had both forgotten to bring hats, which, most explorers would agree, was pretty stupid in temperatures of more than 100 degrees. I wrapped a T-shirt around my head in the manner of a Skegness holidaymaker during a surprisingly hot English summer. Janice covered her nose, now an alarming pillarbox red, with sun block. On the plus side we had a large supply of mineral water and there was always my lilo in case the boat sank.

The sun burned down on us and Janice glugged away at the water. Now she badly needed to go to the loo. Sukumar turned the boat close into the right bank. China shook his head. 'No good for toilet, baba. Burning bodies here.' He pointed to a pile of what looked like charred human remains.

'Never mind, I'm sure Janice isn't fussy,' I said.

Janice was disgusted. 'Bloody am fussy. I am not going to the loo near dead bodies.'

Sukumar motored a hundred yards upriver and we turned our backs while Janice found a suitable spot. When we turned back round we saw she had been joined by three labourers, who had left their tomato field to see what was going on. The trio stared while Janice pulled up her trousers. 'At least, *they* are alive,' she sniffed.

After a quick stop for more omelettes (where were all these fancy dishes that China had promised, I asked myself?) we continued on through the heat of the day. We were barely twenty-four hours out of Calcutta and I was beginning to think how bored Clive's army must have become. I felt a momentary burst of excitement every time we rounded a bend to spy a rusted barge moored outside yet another paper mill, but otherwise the landscape was flat and unchanging. There was little to look at except for more palm trees and more mud huts. The sandy riverbanks changed to muddy riverbanks and then back to sand again. The simple charms of water buffaloes bathing themselves and village women doing their washing no longer appealed. Even the bodies in the river had become two a penny. And above us, there was not even the occasional plane to look at. In the west we take the presence of light aircraft for granted. In India you very rarely see anything smaller than a passenger jet.

Boredom turned to deep depression when we reached Katwa at two in the afternoon. Sukumar manoeuvred the speedboat alongside a large covered punt containing a government research team. They were using weights on the ends of pieces of string to study the depth of the river. One member of the team spoke English.

'Excuse me,' I began, 'any idea how long it will take us to reach Plassey?' With a T-shirt wrapped around my head I must have presented a ridiculous sight.

He gave me the bad news. Plassey was at least eight hours away. But – like everyone else on the river – he wouldn't like to swear to it. Twelve hours was probably a safer bet. If we were lucky, we would reach the battlefield half-way through the following day.

It was time to make a decision. Sukumar switched off the engine and we settled down for a pow-wow. I worked out that it would cost me another £250 in fuel. There was at least one, possibly two, extra days' boat hire to add to that. I'd heard of budget travellers who had survived on £250 for six months in India. I was about to get through that amount in two days. It didn't seem right to continue burning up petrol just for the sake of a story. Janice agreed with me. China looked unhappy. He had not got me to Plassey and he was beginning to feel it was his fault. He had failed as tour leader.

Sukumar wanted to keep going. He was optimistic. He was certain that it would take no more than eight hours. 'Yeah,' Janice said. 'Eight hours in one of those power boats they have in *Miami Vice*.'

China picked his ear with a matchstick. He looked at me dolefully. 'We go back, baba?'

'We go back, China.' There was no more we could do. I thought of Bala. He would have said that going back was my destiny. It was meant to happen. Still, it was a bit of a cop-out. Certainly Clive would have been disgusted by my lack of moral fibre, but I wasn't going to spend another penny on petrol and, anyway, *I* didn't have a battle to fight. For all I knew, Plassey was twenty-five hours away. Trouble was, most of the river people we had spoken to had probably never travelled further than a couple of miles from their villages. I also suspected that their judgement was clouded by the smoke of more marijuana than was good for them. Plassey and Murshidabad seemed to be mythical places, visited only in dreams. Plassey was always five hours away, regardless of where you were on the river.

Sukumar reluctantly turned the boat around. He opened the throttle and we shot forward. The current was now with us and we almost doubled our speed.

No one spoke for several minutes. Then Janice tried to brighten us up. 'Never mind, we've seen an awful lot of river already,' she said. The sun was burning her fair skin and she glowed like a stop light. Now that we were going home, caution went to the wind. China and I lit cigarettes in schoolboyish defiance at the fuel. I brought out a bottle of brandy that I had planned to open at Plassey. I handed it to Sukumar. The spirit went straight to his head and he giggled inanely as we weaved down the river. China fell asleep in the sun. Janice applied more block to her face. I recited part of *Albert in the Lion's Den*. Young Albert and his mum and dad '. . . didn't think much of the ocean 'cos the waves were piddlin' and small. There were no ships and

141

nobody drowning. In fact, nothing to laugh at at all.' The Hughli was like Blackpool: nothing to laugh at at all.

The big drama happened half-way through the afternoon. Sukumar had sobered up and was staring ahead as if hypnotised, his fingers clamped tightly around the throttle of the outboard. The engine was becoming louder and louder. I didn't like the sound of it.

I woke China. 'Tell Sukumar to slow down a bit,' I shouted above the noise.

'Don't worry, baba.' China went back to sleep.

Five minutes later the outboard began to do a fair impression of a chainsaw.

I panicked. 'Cut the engine!'

Too late. A puff of blue smoke emerged from underneath the cowling. With a small popping sound, the outboard stopped. The silence of the river was overwhelming. We drifted with the current.

Sukumar unscrewed the outboard from its mounting block and began to dismantle it. Indians love to tinker with engines and Sukumar was no exception. Nuts and bolts and bits of metal soon littered the bottom of the boat. Sukumar's hands got oilier and oilier. His face took on a puzzled look. I did not have great faith in him as a mechanic. Suddenly he held up a bit of blackened metal and said something to China.

'What's the problem?' I asked. Outboard motors were not my strong point.

'Defect in engine, baba.'

'I know there's a bloody defect in engine otherwise engine wouldn't have blown up. What *is* the defect?'

'Don't worry, baba. We mend defect.'

Sukumar was not so sure about this. He looked worried. He looked closely at the engine and tapped it with a spanner. He cleared his throat and pronounced his verdict.

'Engine no good,' he declared. This had been an immense effort for him. They were the only words of English that Sukumar spoke the entire trip.

It emerged that the Yamaha's cylinder head was cracked; well and truly buggered, as a British mechanic would say. In less than two days the outboard had received more of a pounding than ever before in its life. It had decided to pack up for good, or, at least, until Mr Jim-Jams paid a hefty repair bill. Sukumar

142

screwed on the reserve motor. It was a tiny thing meant for emergencies only. Sukumar pulled the cord and it put-putted into life. We set of downstream at an altogether more leisurely pace.

The reduction in speed created a problem. We had less than two hours in which to find a place to stop overnight. Then the light would go. In the distance we could see the ominous black haze hanging over Calcutta thirty miles away, the smoggy pall that indicated we were returning to urban life.

The afternoon turned to evening and the light faded quickly. The soft orange glow of the sun was reflected in the still water. Every so often we caught the fragrance of evening lilies. Up ahead, a vast power station, all eight chimneys pouring smoke, was silhouetted in the sunset. The smoke pulsated upwards until the breeze caught it and carried it like an arch across the river towards the east and Bangladesh. It was a strangely beautiful sight. In the shadow of the power station squadrons of tiny fishing craft were leaving the banks to pursue the evening catch. The fishermen would use one hand to play their nets while they operated the paddle using the combination of their other hand and a foot.

I suggested that we should stop where we were – in the countryside. China would not hear of it. 'Bad men here,' he said. 'We get robbed.' I thought that the rural Bengalis looked quite friendly. After all, they had spent all day waving at us. But China seemed to see 'bad men' around every bend.

'So what do you suggest, China?'

'Shall we go back to Calcutta, baba?' he asked.

'Certainly not tonight,' I said. There was no way we were going to negotiate the sandbanks and dead dogs in darkness. I was the only one with a torch, and the batteries were nearly flat. I added, 'So where are we going to stop?'

China gritted his teeth. 'Where we were last night, baba?'

'Not the . . .'

'Yes, baba. Pulp Paper Mill. Nice men there, nice guards.'

Oh God, another night on the mosquito-infested mudbank. The thought was too much. Janice and I looked at each other in despair. We began scratching at imaginary mosquito bites. We were all sweaty and dirty.

China smiled. 'Never mind, baba. We have good evening. China cook special dinner tonight. Better dinner than best meal in London.' China leaned back. He closed his eyes to dream of culinary preparations.

We approached the mill. Across the river the ruins of French Chandernagore seemed to gloat at me. Ha! The family of Clive finally scuppered! We bumped alongside the pontoon just as the sun disappeared. The mist began to close in on the Hughli. I had an awful sense of *déjà vu*.

The bosses had seen us arrive. They lined up in the gantry. China explained the problem. They were quite pleased, if a little surprised, to see us.

'What about Plassey?' Boss Number Four called down to me. 'What about Robert Clive?'

'Sod Clive,' I growled. 'Where's Big Boss?'

'He has gone, but you can stay here. You will always be welcome here, sir.'

That was very kind of him, but I had no intention of ever returning to sample his hospitality. We climbed onto the ferry-boat's roof and China prepared dinner. He was in his element and had decided to give us kedgeree. He mixed rice and lentils together in a sort of porridge. This was added to boiled potatoes ground up in Sukumar's fist – a distinctly grubby fist that only an hour earlier had been covered in a thick layer of Yamaha grease. 'Think I'll give the potatoes a miss,' Janice remarked. The kedgeree was accompanied by chips, strongly spiced with chillies, and onion salad. What China's food lacked in subtlety was made up for with the remains of the brandy, which we demolished before bedding down in the boat.

It was a miserable night during which I was kept awake by the squeaking of rats that scuttled about on the riverbank. The mosquitoes descended with a vengeance and China's kedgeree was doing ghastly things to my digestion. Several times I had to leave my sleeping bag to squat over the side of the pontoon. No one else slept and at 4.30, as the first hint of light appeared, we said goodbye to the bosses for the last time and moved out. Sukumar started the engine and began the homeward stretch to Calcutta.

Four hours later we were back under Howrah Bridge. As the steel girders loomed up above us, China, Janice and I broke out into a chorus of 'No photo!' This had become a running joke. I switched my camera to motor drive and banged off a dozen shots in defiance of the Indian Government's absurd security regulations.

The Hughli's dreaded tidal bore was expected at any moment. Sukumar steered the boat towards the conglomeration of shipping moored a few hundred yards downstream of the bridge. We tied up alongside a small freighter. The crew invited us on board and we waited for the tide.

It came in at a terrifying speed. In the distance we could see the crest of a huge wave, which sped up the river violently rocking any boats in its way. Suddenly waves were crashing around the freighter. We sat on the freighter's deck and attempted to fend off the speedboat with our feet as it crashed against the ship's side. After twenty minutes the flow subsided and the waters began to calm.

We clambered back into the launch. Sukumar declared it was now safe enough to leave the Hughli for Tolly's Nullah, the route back to Mr Jim-Jams' yard. This was a mistake. The stream looked suspiciously fast as we turned into the backwater. We shot down the creek narrowly missing two fishing boats. We passed under a road bridge. It was crowded with people, who had noticed the fact that the boat contained two Westerners. They cheered and shouted, and as we emerged under the other side of the bridge we were greeted with a hail of coconut shells. 'I suppose they think that's funny,' Janice said as she protected her head with her hands.

A dredger loomed up ahead. It was moored mid-stream by a series of steel hawsers that stretched across to both banks. Mr Jim-Jams' yard lay a few hundred yards behind. But there was no way we could safely get past. Sukumar slammed the outboard into reverse. The feeble engine was no match against the torrent. We crashed into the dredger. There was a splintering of fibreglass and the boat lurched over to a forty-five degree angle. Janice looked terrified, the engine roared. I could have sworn that China yelled, 'Don't worry, baba.' Just as I thought we were about to capsize the boat righted itself.

Sukumar muttered a Bengali oath. The current was now pinning us to the front of the dredger. We were stuck there for twenty minutes until the waters quieted enough to allow us to push and pull our way underneath the hawsers. The dredger's crew stared down at us with blank, unsmiling faces. They were totally unconcerned about our predicament. They were tough and mean in the way that you would expect Calcutta dredger-men to be. And they had no intention of helping us.

A crowd had gathered on the bank. They looked hostile and seemed disappointed that they had been deprived of the sight of us capsizing. We extricated ourselves from the dredger's hawsers. A couple of youths threw stones in our direction. They landed by the boat, splashing us with water. 'Bad people,' China said. 'They think you and me rich because we are in speedboat. They not like rich people.' Looking at this unbelievably foul, stinking place, I did not blame them.

Mr Jim-Jams was not pleased to see us. We unloaded the gear and went to his office. He was sitting, bloated as ever, in his executive chair. The wet sari Yamaha girl pouted down from the poster.

'You are back,' he said.

'Yes, we are,' I replied flatly.

'You are one day early. Why?'

'Your engine is broken. And anyway,' I added crossly, 'what you said about Plassey and Murshidibad being ten hours' away is rubbish. It's more like twenty-five.'

This went right over the head of Mr Jim-Jams. He couldn't care less that he'd misled us about the time the journey would take.

But the engine was another matter. He was very worried about the engine.

'The outboard is broken?' It came out as a stutter.

'Yes.' I was quite gleeful. 'Sukumar says it's a cracked engine block.'

Mr Jim-Jams put his head in his hands. This was bad news. 'I will have to import the part from Japan.' he wailed. I inquired if he was insured. No, he wasn't. Mr Jim-Jams did not look like the sort of businessman who wasted good money on insurance premiums. I made sympathetic noises. He got out a hanky and wiped his nose.

I suggested that in view of the fact that I had paid for three days boat hire and we'd only been gone two, it would not be unfair of me to ask for a portion of my money back. China looked at me as if to say I didn't have a dog in hell's chance. Bengalis did not have a policy of refunding customers' money.

Surprise! I suddenly saw Mr Jim-Jams in a new light. No, he agreed, it would not be unfair of me to ask for a refund. China

146

looked astounded. But I wasn't quite there yet. Mr Jim-Jams looked very sad. Melancholy oozed from every pore. He was the picture of a man under great emotional strain. Did I realise that he would be making a loss out of the deal? Did I not feel just a little responsible?

No, I did not. 'It's not my problem if your engine blows up,' I said. 'That's one of the perils of being in the boat business.'

Mr Jim-Jams stared sadly at his feet. I noticed that he had one of those jokey, novelty signs on his desk: 'Without a smiling face, do not become a merchant.' He looked miserable, but I would not be moved. Eventually, he dug into his pocket and handed over a wad of notes.

Before we left the office, I suggested that he go home, get into his new silk sleeping suit and have a lie down. Mr Jim-Jams allowed a small smile. 'Perhaps this would be a good idea,' he agreed.

Seven

The boat trip had been a fiasco. And in the end I followed the trail of Clive to Plassey and Murshidibad by car on the Calcutta-Assam highway that runs parallel to the Hughli. This was hardly in the same adventurous spirit of Clive, but it was a damned sight easier. China polished his old Ambassador especially for the trip and we set out through the Calcutta suburbs at five in the morning.

The Ambassador is modelled on the 1950s British Morris Oxford. It is low on refinements but built with a suspension that could support a small truck. Until recently, it was about the only car you could buy in India. But now Fiat are building a hatch-back called a Maruti. The Maruti is hopelessly unsuited to Indian roads. China and his mates laughed at them. Most would be on the scrap heap in ten years' time whereas Ambassadors made fifteen years ago would still be trundling along, gears crashing, springs creaking, after endless patch-up jobs. Try getting a family of six and a couple of goats in a Maruti. Reclining seats with go-fast stripes are no match for leather upholstery. And who needs fold-down interior vinyl sun visors when you can have a huge steel sunshade bolted on the outside? Why have flimsy plastic ashtrays when you can flick your stubs out of the window? What is the use of a car that can do ninety mph when the roads allow you to travel at no more than forty? Unlike the massed forces of Ambassador drivers, I noticed that Maruti drivers tended not to use their horns much. A feature of this new status symbol is a headlight flasher. Much smarter to warn other drivers with your lights.

But ancient Ambassadors do have their drawbacks. After twenty minutes' driving, the brakes failed. China put his foot on the brake pedal to pull up behind a lorry. The pedal went down to the floor and we cruised sedately into the back of the truck. Thankfully, we were doing no more than 5 mph, but there was a tinkling of glass as the Ambassador's headlights smashed.

China drove the car onto the verge. The lorry continued on into the distance, its driver oblivious to the incident. A crowd of pedestrians stopped and gawked at the car.

'Lucky we weren't going faster,' I remarked.

China shrugged and inspected the damage. The broken lights were a minor irritation, but that was all. A little thing like a brake failure was nothing to be unduly worried about. Especially if you weren't travelling at speed.

'Don't worry, baba. You wait here.' China walked away up the road. Twenty minutes later he was back. 'Okay, have found mechanic. We go.' And with that he got into the driver's seat, started the engine and put the car into gear.

I was horrified. 'But China, we haven't got any brakes, for God's sake. This thing's a death-trap. Can't the garage come to us? Don't they have breakdown trucks in Calcutta?'

'No breakdown truck. We go to garage.' China was not in the mood to argue. We crawled slowly up the road.

The great advantage of driving an Ambassador is that they comprise ninety per cent of the cars in India. This is good news when it comes to spare parts. You can find spares everywhere, and virtually every motor mechanic in the country understands the workings of these cumbersome beasts.

We reached the garage and an oily Bengali looked at the car. He quickly identified the cause of the brake failure. Two simple rubber seals — costing no more than two rupees each — had perished. This was a common problem with the Ambassador, he explained. The seals were replaced whereupon I got a demonstration in panel beating, Indian-style. The force of the blow had put the driver's door out of line so it would not shut properly. The mechanic disappeared into his workshop and came back with a heavy hammer and steel chisel. He started bashing the door. He bashed and he bashed. For five minutes. Sweat dripped off his brow. Still the door would not shut. More bashing. The paintwork flaked off the Ambassador revealing bare steel underneath.

I looked at China. 'Is this really a good idea?'

'No problem, baba. You wait. When you come back to Calcutta next year my car will look like limousine. New paint, new seats . . .' Finally, the hammer and chisel method seemed to work and the door clicked shut. China handed the mechanic a few rupees and we continued north towards Calcutta's outskirts.

The roadsides were crowded with street vendors hawking everything from scrap pieces of cardboard to glass chandeliers. On one stretch of road, hundreds of chandeliers, strung up on cane frames, glittered in the morning sun. As we turned on to the main road, China stopped the Ambassador at a small temple. He got out and pushed two rupees through a hole in the wall. It was a puja, an offering to God, the guarantee of a safe journey.

'Too many crazy bus drivers, baba,' he said. 'Road very dangerous, but God now with me. I drive slow and we not crash.'

We badly needed China's god on that road. Smashed up cars and coaches littered the verges. We were overtaken at frightening speeds by trucks overloaded with Malaysian timber bound for building projects in Assam. The metalled road was just wide enough for a car to pass a lorry. A lorry passing another lorry was forced to leave the road and thunder along the dusty verges, which were crowded with bullock carts, bicycles and rickshaws wobbling under the weight of bundles of sugar cane. And as if the road was not crowded enough, women were drying rice on the hot tarmac. Most vehicles gave the grain a wide berth. Sometimes a truck ploughed through the rice, scattering what would keep a family in food for a week. The villagers did not seem to complain. They simply brushed it up again.

Calcutta's wooden shacks gave way to mud huts. Here the communists were more in evidence. The walls were painted messily with red hammers and sickles. By each collection of huts children swam in stagnant pools of water, their brown bodies caked with mud. The sweet, sickly smell of shredded sugar cane was everywhere.

China slipped a tape on the car stereo. The Ambassador was filled with the voice of a singer called Tarzan. He was warbling what sounded like a Bengali version of *Chirpy Chirpy Cheep Cheep*. Tarzan was big in Calcutta. I had seen his name promoted on T-shirts and posters. It was the only tape China possessed and after five hours of this music I felt that I would never become a big fan. When we returned to Calcutta I bought China a Dire Straits cassette. I don't think he liked it very much. Who needs the guitar skills of Mark Knopfler when you have a local hero called Tarzan?

Six hours after leaving Calcutta we arrived at the battlefield of Plassey. It was noon – the same time of day that the battle had turned in Clive's favour. At midday on 23 June 1757, the heavens opened and a thirty-minute deluge of rain soaked the ammunition of Siraj-ud-daula's artillery.

I attempted to give China a history lesson. The night before the battle, the British were camped in a mango grove south of the enemy lines. Here they would have heard the sound of war drums coming from the Nawab's camp. As dawn broke, a heavy mist lay on the ground and black clouds filled the sky. Siraj-ud-daula's forces included a squadron of war elephants and a detachment of French artillery. They outnumbered the British by more than fifteen to one. It must have been an anxious moment for Clive, a mere thirty-two years old and inexperienced at dealing with such formidable opposition.

The outcome of the battle rested with the Nawab's uncle-by-marriage, Mir Jafar, who was commanding three quarters of the enemy army. Like the British, Uncle Mir felt no great love for his nephew and Clive had been secretly negotiating with him for over a month. But as the battle got underway, with fierce cannonades coming from both sides, Clive was still uncertain about Mir Jafar's loyalty.

Clive need not have worried. Mir Jafar had absolutely no intention of getting involved. The commander and his soldiers folded their arms and watched the British rout what was left of Siraj-ud-daula's army. The Nawab's elephants were not a great help either. Their hides stung by musket fire, the beasts turned tail and trampled their own men. The deaths of several officers further demoralised the enemy. At the last moment, Siraj-ud-daula tried to bring forward cannons pulled by oxen. Clive's men began firing on the animals. What with enraged oxen and stampeding elephants, anarchy broke out in the Nawab's camp. The battle was lost. Siraj-ud-daula mounted a camel and hot-footed it back to Murshidibad. Mir Jafar cannot have been his most popular uncle that day.

The historian Philip Mason describes the action at Plassey as 'the most miserable skirmish ever to be called a decisive battle.'

Casualties were light. The English lost only four Europeans and fourteen sepoys. About 500 enemy soldiers died. But whatever the figures, it was a great victory as far as the British were concerned. And Clive was hero of the day.

The battlefield lies to the west of the village of Plassey, now known by the Bengali name of Palashi. China drove off the main road and we continued for a mile along a bumpy dirt track flanked by sugar plantations and rice paddies towards the Bhagirathi River. Anglo-Indian history was not China's strong point. While I explored, he went to sleep in the car.

Clive's triumph was commemorated by a sixty-foot high memorial. Like the monument to the Black Hole, it was in a sorry state. Graffiti covered the stonework. Was it absolutely necessary for 'cycle tourists' D. Basak and S. Dutt to leave behind a permanent, scrawled reminder of their visit? It looked as if the structure had once been surrounded by iron railings, but these had obviously been stolen for scrap years ago.

For five minutes I was alone on the battlefield with just a few vultures for company. The birds were noisily tearing leaves off the top of palm trees. But like anywhere in India, I was not alone for long. I was soon surrounded by five young brothers, who emerged from their parents' riverside hut. I took photographs of them waving sticks and looking warlike. They shrieked with delight.

The famous mango grove where Clive had struck camp was all but gone. Once known by the Bengali name of Laksha Bagh, or Orchard of a Hundred Thousand Trees, most of the trees had been cut down to make way for an ugly sugar cane factory. Sugar production, along with rice and jute, is one of the big industries in West Bengal, a solidly agricultural state where more than sixty per cent of the population are employed on the land.

The hunting lodge, which Clive made his headquarters, was demolished years ago. It was here that he is alleged to have slept during the battle – malicious gossip put about by his enemies. In the place of the lodge was a small bungalow, a scruffy tourist rest house, sitting under what remained of the mango plantation. Inside the bungalow the visitor could study a dusty scale model of the battle. On the wall above it someone with a sense of irony had stuck a World Council of Churches poster. The caption read: 'With so much blood being shed in the name of religion, will there be tears to shed tomorrow?'

152

Fourteen years after the battle, the area around Plassey continued to see plenty of bloodshed. But this time the victims were animals.

In 1781 Plassey was visited by a Bombay-based Englishman called James Forbes. The portly Mr Forbes was a part-time diarist, who produced a grandly-titled book called *Forbes's Oriental Memoirs*.

'The country surrounding Plassey abounds with beasts of prey, and game of every description,' wrote Mr Forbes. 'A gentleman lately engaged on a shooting party gave us an account of their success in one month . . . in which space they killed one royal tiger, six wild buffaloes, 186 hog deer, 25 wild hogs, 11 antelopes, 3 foxes, 35 hares, 15 brace of partridges and floricans, with quails, ducks, snipes and smaller birds in abundance.'

Which might explain why the only wildlife I saw at Plassey was the vultures. Perhaps their forefathers had seen rich pickings in the aftermath of the battle.

From Plassey we continued north to Murshidibad. Here, the Indian Army of today was much in evidence. The town was perilously close to the Bangladesh border and was under the protection of the 32nd Battalion of the Border Security Force.

Murshidibad had known grander days. Until the last century it had been one of the most noble cities in India, a thriving centre for the taffeta and silk industry. Now it was crumbling away. The place was littered with decaying palaces, mosques and tombs: relics of a princely past with broken roofs and entangled with creeper. The two largest palaces in the centre of the town overlooked a huge expanse of park, now Murshidibad's chief cricket pitch, on the banks of the Bhagirathi. The 200-yard long Imambra Palace, completed in the nineteenth century to accommodate a descendant of Mir Jafar, reminded me of Cair Paravel, the ruined castle in C. S. Lewis' story *Prince Caspian*. The windows were boarded up, roofs had fallen in, and squatters occupied the stable block. Years of neglect had all but obliterated a glorious history.

I bought a copy of the official Murshidibad guide book. It was a quaint little pamphlet in which the author had written about someone called Lord Clave: 'Lord Clave compared Murshidibad with London for its population, area and prosperity. The city was more pompous for its beauty and riches than that of London. But, alas! Murshidibad today is an irony.'

An irony. No question about that. Nothing but a small pile of bricks marked the spot of Siraj-ud-daula's palace of Mansurganj. Further downstream of the Bhagirathi his tomb still stood at the Nawabs' ancestral burial ground of Khosbagh. Hammers and sickles were splattered carelessly on the outside walls of the mausoleum. There was no inscription on the simple grave stone, but a guide assured me this was the final resting place of Clive's opponent.

Mir Jafar's powerbase lay to the north of the town. Once a splendid palace, only one wing remained. The building is now known by the Bengali name of Nimak Haram Deori — Home of the Traitor. More than two centuries after Plassey, the memory of Mir Jafar's appalling treachery still lingers on in Murshidibad, and, indeed, in India as a whole. Indians still use his name to describe someone who breaks a confidence. Some politicians have been described as Mir Jafars. And I suspect that a thousand years hence, the man's behaviour on the battlefield will still not be forgotten. God cannot have looked on him too kindly either. He was a cripple and opium addict when he finally died in his seventies, a victim of leprosy.

A couple of weeks after Plassey, Siraj-ud-daula was spotted in the town of Rajmahal, 100 miles north of Murshidibad. Mir Jafar's henchmen were alerted and the defeated Nawab was brought back to Murshidibad in chains and quietly done away with. It is unclear who exactly was responsible for his death. Tricky Mir Jafar insisted later that he had never given the order, but that the assassination had been carried out by some over-enthusiastic soldiers. Whatever the answer, Clive must have been relieved not to have been faced with the responsibility of putting his foe on trial.

The guide at the remains of the traitor's home grabbed me by the arm and led me excitedly across the overgrown courtyard. He showed me a small room.

'This was where Siraj-ud-daula was stabbed to death,' the guide said. He pointed at a sword hanging on the wall.

'And that, I suppose, is what killed him.'

'That is right, sir. How did you guess?'

The story sounded pretty fanciful, but, as far as the guide was concerned, it was good for business.

After the battle Clive and his chiefs of staff followed Mir Jafar into Murshidibad. For two weeks Clive stayed at Moradbagh, a large mansion on the west bank of the Bhagirathi. The house was demolished years ago, but it was there that he set out on accruing his fortune. Mir Jafar, now installed as the new Nawab, handed over a gift of £180,000 worth of gold and gems. To an Englishman of thirty-two this was an immense bonanza. To the traitor it was peanuts: Mir Jafar is said to have looted more than £1 million from his nephew's treasury.

Clive visited Murshidabad once again, five years later in his position as Governor of Bengal. On that visit he stayed in the Palace of Motijhil, or Pearl Lake in Bengali. Motijhil must have been the most beautiful estate in Murshidabad. Here the river curves to give the impression that you are on an island in the middle of a lake. It is a wonderfully serene setting. The rhapsodic Mr Forbes described a Hindu water festival that was held a few years later:

'The boats are of a singular construction, particularly those called moor punkees, or peacock boats, which are made as far as possible to resemble the peacock. In the most commodious parts of these boats are laid carpets, cushions and pillows, covered with silk, satin, fringed and embroidered with gold and silver. These boats, all in swift motion . . . and enwreathed with flowers, the songs and dances of the choristers . . . gave a lively interest to the scene.'

However, the God-fearing Mr Forbes, who concludes that Christians should unite to convert the 'Hindoo heathens', was unimpressed by the dancing girls. 'The attitudes of the dancers before the images were frequently not only indelicate, but disgusting,' he raged.

China declined my invitation to trail round the sights and spent most of the afternoon asleep in Murshidabad's only hotel. It was a grubby flea-pit called the Hotel Historical, an apt name if only for the plumbing. Judging from the red stains on the walls, the previous occupants of my room had spent much of their time spitting betel nut juice.

That evening we dined on chapatis and chilli omelettes. China sent out a boy to buy some beer. It could only be found on the black market at an absurdly inflated price since no one in the town was licensed to sell alcohol. The hotel's dining area was packed with locals. They crowded around our table. As I explained my relationship to Clive, I realised how much the man's name still means to Bengalis. It was touching to discover that even the most simple peasant farmer knew who I was talking about. Mention of subsequent British leaders like Hastings, Curzon and Mountbatten aroused little interest. But Clive, now, he was different, a big hero. Robert might have not always acted in the best interests of the Indian people and his skulduggery with Mir Jafar was unforgivable, but he was remembered as an almost fairytale figure, a fine leader of men, who earned the undying loyalty of his sepoy troops.

I chatted to a small man called Uday, who taught chemistry at one of the schools in Murshidibad. Uday remembered a colossal statue of Clive that used to stand in the town. 'I am afraid that it was pulled down after Independence.' He was quite apologetic about this.

Uday went on: 'The story of Clive is one of the most important chapters in Indian history. Everyone in Murshidibad knows all about him. He was a very great man. No doubting.'

Why were the palaces being allowed to crumble away? Why was the West Bengal state government not doing more to promote tourism in Murshidibad?

Uday looked at me sadly. 'We are only forty kilometres away from Bangladesh. Today we are friends with Bangladesh, but tomorrow, who knows? If they wanted to, they could fire their missiles right into this room. And that would not be good for tourism.'

Looking around at the Hotel Historical's peeling paint and yards of exposed electrical wiring, I mused that perhaps the arrival of a Bangladeshi missile would not be such a bad thing.

Next morning a party of tourists from Calcutta arrived at the hotel. I came downstairs to find two girls in saris perched on a table attending to their make-up. They were students from Calcutta's Kaliani University and were weekending with their boyfriends. In separate rooms, of course. In a country where you are likely to be spat upon if you make a show of affection in public, unmarried girls and boys do not share hotel rooms.

China appeared from his slumbers and pinched yet another of my cigarettes. I had taken on the role of chief keeper of the fags. We left the hotel and had breakfast up the street in a ramshackle lean-to that called itself a restaurant. A dog lay in the doorway crunching its way through a dead bat. Later we sat on the steps of a small Hindu shrine outside the hotel. The day warmed up. People jogged in front of the Imambra Palace. Schoolboys set up stumps on the cricket pitch.

Sitting by the shrine I had a remarkable encounter. I was talking to a group of male students, explaining that Clive was my five-times great-grandfather. Hearing this, the students became very excited. They gesticulated wildly and someone dragged forward a youth, who had been standing shyly at the back of the group.

'This man is a relation of Clive!' The students grabbed the young man and pointed at me. 'Tell him who you are!'

The young man was very reluctant to say anything. But after some coaxing he admitted to being Syed Mol Iman, a nineteen-year-old student of Urdu at Calcutta University. He was also the eight-times great-grandson of Mir Jafar.

It was a momentous meeting in which photographs were taken and addresses exchanged.

Syed was a big chap with a heavy beard. He looked like a warrior. I could see him in battle, dressed in leather jerkin and turban astride a fast camel, his fist clenched around the handle of a swishing scimitar.

He did not smile much. He explained that he was staying the weekend in Murshidibad with his uncle, also a direct descendant of Mir Jafar, and son of the last Nawab. All his uncle's property had been seized by the government after Independence and he was now very poor. The family of the traitor was still paying for his sins.

Syed patiently listened to my questions, but he was reluctant to volunteer an opinion of his ancestor. Could I have a chat to his uncle, perhaps? No, his uncle did not like visitors, and anyway he would not talk about the past.

What had started out as an epic encounter was turning into a disappointment. Despite the enthusiasm of his fellow students, who were gathered round listening eagerly, Syed was a rather sticky conversationalist. Did he have any hobbies? Well, he quite liked Western pop music.

'Do you like the Beatles?'

'Oh yes, very much,' he said. 'John Lennon very good.' The eight-times great-grandson of the traitor of Plassey was a Beatles fan.

I took Syed's telephone number and promised to look him up in Calcutta. Unfortunately, he must have written it down incorrectly and we never did get to meet again. After much hand-shaking with him and his friends, we left. China coaxed the Ambassador into life and we headed back to Calcutta.

Forty miles south of Murshidibad we nearly became the victims of a nasty accident. We had reached a small village near the town of Krishnanager when the traffic suddenly came to a standstill. China got out of the car and asked the villagers what was going on.

A truck had run over and killed a cyclist, a man of twenty-five. The lorry driver and his mate had run for it. A wise move. In rural India it is quite common for drivers involved in fatal accidents to be beaten to death by the victim's relatives. Shortly after the accident, a policeman had arrived at the scene only to have been threatened with a broken bottle. The village was out for blood. Years of poverty and grievances against the system had come to the surface with the death of a friend.

A long jam of cars and trucks was building up behind us. A crowd gathered around the car. They had seen me, a European and a rare bird in these parts. Someone banged their fist on the boot. People stuck their heads through the window and stared. I felt threatened. The villagers had developed manic grins. Warning: when a Bengali starts grinning manically, get the hell out of it.

China was arguing loudly with two men. He quickly got back into the car and slammed it into gear. He swung the Ambassador in a U-turn and we gunned it back down the road. The engine screamed frighteningly.

'India people fucking mad,' China yelled. We ran over a chicken. 'India people mother-fucking crazy.'

China's happy-go-lucky side had given way to anger. In between bouts of colourful language, he explained that we had only just escaped serious trouble. Having been robbed of the chance of reprisal on the truck driver, the villagers were prepared to take out their vengeance on any strangers. A white man, presumably carrying large amounts of money, was a good target.

'They say there is big trouble for me,' China said. 'You foreigner and I from Calcutta. They not like me. People ask me for baksheesh. They say I have much money.' It was an indication of the poverty in rural Bengal, where most of the population do little more than survive on what crops they grow

158

themselves, that they thought anyone from Calcutta was a rich man.

China was very worked up. He was not going to let the matter rest. 'Bloody bastards,' he muttered as we turned onto a dust track that took us on a thirty-mile detour around the accident. His driving became more erratic. A cyclist swerved to avoid us and drove into a ditch. I hung on to my seat and offered a prayer to China's god when we reached Calcutta in one piece.

Eight

The bawdiness began back in Calcutta. Up until now my progress through Clive's India had ranged from the historical to the spiritual. Now came the sleaze.

After the Murshidibad expedition China felt we both needed to relax with some good old Calcutta entertainment. There were plenty of cinemas showing both Hindi and English films, but they were impossibly crowded and stiflingly hot. I had been to the zoo, but that had been a big disappointment. Like everything else in Calcutta, the famous white tigers are actually grey. No, I needed to sample the night life.

One afternoon I was drinking tea with the combined corps of Sudder Street taxi drivers. China was throwing biscuits at the drivers' adopted mongrel dog, Mutti, when he had an idea.

'You must see mujra, baba,' he said.

'What, China, is mujra?'

'Mujra, baba. Magic show.'

'Oh, you mean a conjuror. Well, it wasn't something I'd thought of, but yes, it might be quite nice to see a conjuror.'

'Maybe 350 rupees.' That was about £30. It seemed a bit steep for a magic show.

'No, not expensive, baba. Magic show with negative girls.'

'Negative girls?'

'Yes, baba.'

'Look, China, I haven't a clue what you're talking about.'

China was becoming impatient. 'Yes, negative girls. *No clothes!*'

The penny dropped with a loud clang.

'Ah, you mean naked girls.' China nodded violently. But where did the conjuror fit in? The mind boggled.

China looked at me intently. He studied my reaction.

'Maybe 700 rupees for two girls, baba; 1,500 with boys as well.'

'With a magic show?'

'Yes, magic. Private room. Only you and me, baba, and the girls.' China's eyes glittered at the thought.

'Look China, I'm not sure about this. I'm here to do serious research into Clive and I haven't come all this way to end up in some Calcutta clip-joint.'

China looked downcast. 'Well, all right,' I said. 'We'll give it a try.'

Actually, I was not straying too far from Clive's path. As a young man, Robert spent much of his time – and money – amusing himself with Indian girls of a professional nature. He was expert at 'gallanting the ladies' and, in the words of his friend and fellow clerk John Dalton, he was 'clapped' more than once.

Dalton was a bit of a lad, and together they would go whoring in the brothels of Madras's black town. Even by the time Clive was courting Margaret, he was still enjoying the company of other women. Dalton wrote from Trichinopoly that although he had heard dark rumours that Robert was on the verge of matrimony, he was relieved to hear that 'you fuck as usual'. But Clive must have restrained himself after his marriage and not even the enemies that he attracted in later life ever suggested that he was unfaithful to his wife.

That evening I met China by his car outside the Lytton Hotel. He was wearing his best safari suit, whistling merrily and playing the role of lad about town. With him was a friend called Moktar, our chauffeur for the evening, and another man called Ivran. China was paying Ivran to stay with the car all evening. Such was the vandalism and theft in Calcutta that China did not leave his car unattended – day or night.

We set off for an area called Sonagraachi, meaning Tree of Gold in Hindi. Sonagraachi is one of the best-known red-light areas in the city, a long street of tenement blocks where more than seven thousand girls are said to ply their trade.

Seven thousand might sound a lot in such a small area, but it is nothing compared to the total number of prostitutes in Calcutta. There are no official figures for 'working girls', but China and his chums reckoned 30,000 was not far off: 'Maybe more, maybe less, baba. When girls are hungry they work. When they have money to eat they stop . . . until they are hungry again.'

In his hugely entertaining book *India – The Perpetual Paradox*, Calcutta journalist Sasthi Brata reasons why there were so many prostitutes in India: 'What has always intrigued me is the phenomenon of domestic servants in every middle-class Indian home. There are males who come from the villages into the cities, work for pitiful wages, and return home once a year on unpaid leave for a month. For the rest of the time, they sleep three or four to a room or on staircase landings in modern apartment buildings, and have absolutely no means of indulging in sexual activity within normal circumstances. Naturally, they resort to the brothels . . .'

Sonagraachi has a long history of prostitution. Brata adds that it is a place 'where the ripe old tradition of men never spending the night with their wives is still decrepitly maintained.

'The landed gentry in the city would always keep a dozen or so concubines in this area some hundred years ago, in whose company they would retire after having consumed dinner in their palatial establishments. It was thought to be the mark of a sissy if you stayed home and slept with your wife at night, other than for the purposes of procreation, which was strictly an annual affair.'

The first thing that struck me about Sonagraachi is that it did not look like a red-light quarter. I could have been in any urban area in any Indian city. China parked the car and I stepped out into a thriving self-contained community of Bengali brashness where girls were inclined to approach you with, 'We go fuck now. Quick!'

Children played under hand pumps and girls shouted across the street. Old ladies gossiped on the pavement next to the inevitable living flotsam curled up asleep under rags. Fat ladies sat in their front-rooms, windows wide open so that they could show off their massive, white Kelvinator fridges, a mark of great affluence.

Our pimp, or llal in Bengali, was Rajiv. He was twenty-four and wore a well-groomed moustache of the type that is much admired in Bombay film studios. He had coiffured hair, designer stubble and looked quite suave. He wore a brilliant white traditional Moslem cotton suit, with a kurta, or long shirt, and

162

pyjama trousers cut tight at the ankles. Rajiv never stopped working. He was always on the look out for customers wanting to be introduced to girls. He smiled the smile of a worried man, letting the corners of his mouth drop when he thought I wasn't looking. He took his job very seriously.

China had telephoned earlier. We met Rajiv on a street corner on the edge of Sonagraachi. He introduced himself as a broker. He was not a pimp in the Western sense of the word in that rather than running the girls himself, he was the contact for clients looking for action. The client would pay the broker 100 rupees and then another 400 to the girl, who would then return a portion of her fee.

China had known Rajiv for several years. He was a good man, who would not rip us off. China launched into his 'poor man, big heart routine'.

'If you not happy, baba,' he announced, 'China not happy.'

We walked to one of the tenements. Outside in the street a group of old men were crowded around a radio listening to the cricket. They were the brothel runners, who earned small tips for going for bottles of beer, cleaning rooms and changing sheets. The girls were complaining that they couldn't get the men to do any work tonight. India was playing the West Indies and it was always the same when a test match was on.

Rajiv took us into a large building with cracked walls and stained floors. Inside it was bedlam. We climbed the staircase, squeezing past small children and beggars, who stuck their hands under my face. In Calcutta you find beggars everywhere – even in cat-houses. An old woman with a wooden bowl grabbed my sleeve and demanded money. Rajiv growled at her. She cowered and hurried away down the stairs.

We stopped at the first floor. A long corridor ran in either direction. Leading off the corridor were rooms each lit by bulbs in varying shades of mauve, green and red. After the squalor on the stairs, the rooms were surprisingly clean and tidy. Pink was a popular colour for the walls and on the beds were clean, starched candystriped sheets.

The rooms were full of girls aged from around fourteen upwards. They were dressed in a mixture of traditional Indian and Western clothes; some in saris, others in jeans with flowers in their hair. Such is Calcutta's housing shortage that up to five girls occupied each room. They sat chatting on spacious double beds and talking. When a customer turned up, the girls he did not require would temporarily move into the corridor while he completed his business.

Some of the rooms contained whole families, including grandparents and babies. Rajiv explained that if a family wanted to rent a room in Sonagraachi, at least one of the daughters must be on the game. Whenever she found a customer, her family joined everyone else in the corridor.

Punters were cruising the building. Two sikhs passed me in the corridor. One held a radio to his ear. He too was listening to the cricket at the same time as popping in and out of rooms to inspect the girls.

'What's the score?' I asked.

'130 for three.' The sikh looked into a room and shook his head.

'Not found what you're looking for?' I added.

'No, she was here last week. I will find her soon.' He headed off down the corridor, the voice of the commentator crackling out of the transistor. In India, cricket comes well before sex.

Rajiv took us along the corridor and showed us into a small room. It was furnished like a cheap London bedsit with an emphasis on Formica; more pink walls, neon strip lighting, a gargantuan 1960s Kelvinator, a stereo cassette player and a wide, low bed with a quantity of pillows. A ceiling fan rattled above. On the walls were Hindu religious prints, pictures of Vishnu, around which hung withered garlands of flowers.

Rajiv asked us what sort of girl we would like. 'We have everything here,' he said. 'All sorts of girls – big and little.' I looked at China. He said we had no preference. I thought he was being a little rash.

Rajiv fetched our hostess. A girl entered the room. She was called Sunaina and she had a sulky face with a ski jump nose. Her pinched lips were painted with a swipe of bright red lipstick. Her figure was hidden by a baggy silk shirt, although we discovered later that she had large biceps and a slightly bulging tummy. To me she seemed a Weightwatchers' disaster. But from the look on China's face she was very attractive to the average Bengali male, who likes his women on the large size. China was fascinated by her.

We ordered beer and sat on the bed. I paid Rajiv his 100 rupees broker's fee. Sunaina grudgingly added her percentage.

It seemed to be the girls, rather than the brokers, who were in charge. Rajiv wished us a pleasant evening and left.

Sunaina poured the beers and put a tape on the cassette player. It was a compilation of Hindi pop songs that included the big hit of the moment, *Ek, Do, Teen, Chaar (One, Two, Three, Four)*. The music was distorting horribly. The tape had got stretched in the sun and was speeding up and slowing down at an alarming rate.

'You like Indian magic, baba?' China slapped me on the back.

'What magic?'

'Magic!' China began singing along to the tape. The penny dropped for the second time. He was having trouble with his English. Thus, substitute magic for music. I was disappointed. I'd been looking forward to the odd Indian rope trick or two.

China improvised the lyrics. 'If you have money, you have honey,' he sang. 'No money – no honey.' I think he had been secretly rehearsing this rhyme for my benefit.

The honey in question now proceeded to take her clothes off. This was a complicated process, which involved a rudimentary light show such was Sunaina's coyness when it came to undressing in front of strange men.

Besides the neon strip, the room was lit by a dim green bulb, and a red bulb that was a little brighter than the green one. First Sunaina turned off the neon. Then she switched on the green bulb, plunging the room into virtual darkness. There was a certain amount of scuffling before she switched the red light back on. She was now down to bra and pants. She gyrated self-consciously to the music for a few minutes.

Another click of the switch. The red light was replaced by the green and off came the rest of her clothes. The green light stayed on. Sunaina was not going to let us see too much of her. And despite the fact that virtually the whole street outside was on the game, she didn't want any old person looking in. The window was firmly shut and with the absence of fresh air the room soon became an inferno. Sunaina was perspiring heavily and she wiped away the sweat with her T-shirt. Occasionally she suddenly stopped dancing, cleared her throat and spat into a corner. From the look of the marks on the wall, this was a popular place to spit. The television was still switched on. But she did not approve when her customers talked too much. And she fixed China and me with bolshie stares whenever our attention wandered.

It was a relief when it was all over. The neon came back on and the excrutiating Hindi pop switched off. Then the mood suddenly changed.

Sunaina wept. Her tears began like little diamonds in the corners of her eyes. Then they flowed down her cheeks. She was still standing by the light switch. She screwed up her face in a look of utter desperation. Her arms flopped hopelessly at her sides. China looked at her and then at me.

'What is going on, baba?'

'I don't know, China,' I replied. 'You'd better ask her.'

'What is the matter, mama?' China got up from the bed and put an arm round Sunaina's shoulder. China spoke softly in Bengali. Sunaina pushed China away and sat heavily on the other side of the bed from me. China stood in the middle of the room looking awkward. He spoke some more words of Bengali. Sunaina replied with little sobs.

'Is she all right?' I asked.

'I ask why do you cry, mama,' China said. 'She says she hates this job. She thinks we were laughing at her. She only dances and goes with men because she has to eat. She says she is very worried because no man will want to marry her. It is very bad in India if a girl cannot get married.'

It transpired that Sunaina had been a prostitute for less than two months. She was barely sixteen. This explained her shyness. She came from a very poor family. Her father was sick and could not work. She had younger brothers and sisters. It was her job to feed them. Her body was her only means of earning money.

Rajiv walked into the room. He looked at Sunaina. Her face was puffy from crying. Rajiv shrugged and muttered something. They did not sound like kind words. Sunaina got up from the bed and attempted to compose herself. Then she nodded briefly to China and me before leaving the room. Rajiv raised his eyebrows and tut-tutted as if to say, 'Women! They're all the same.' At least China had been touched by Sunaina's tears. I dug my hand in my pocket and brought out some notes. I handed them briskly to Rajiv and thanked him for his time. China and I showed ourselves out.

On the way back to the car China returned to his 'big heart'

166

mood. He had momentarily sobered up during Sunaina's sudden outburst. But now the alcohol was back, circulating around his brain again.

'Are you happy, baba?'

'Very happy, thank you, China. But it was a pity about Sunaina.'

'I know, pity. But if you not happy, I kill myself. Anyone make you unhappy, I kill him.' He pronounced kill, *keeeel*. I assured him that I was very happy indeed and that there was absolutely no need for him to kill anyone.

China decided our excursion into Sonagraachi was not enough. Why have 7,000 prostitutes when there was an area with 30,000? For this was Kiddapore, Calcutta's docklands and the city's biggest flea-pit of vice.

The following evening we set off for another boys' night out that was going to lead to my meeting with Colonel Sexy.

There were seven of us in China's car, including five of his taxi driver mates and a Japanese man of twenty-three. The Jap was a strapping lad of six feet three inches, who was wearing shorts and a T-shirt bearing the slogan 'Sport'. He had a completely unpronounceable name and for the sake of simplicity the Sudder Street drivers had christened him Tojo. One of the Indians in the car spoke Japanese and was acting as his interpreter.

Tojo had been in Calcutta for only a week, but he was already famous in Kiddapore for his extraordinary libido. 'One night, three, maybe four girls,' giggled China. Having been travelling around India for six months, he was running short of funds and had just sold his camera to pay for another sexual rampage.

We drove across Calcutta via the Maidan. Across the park, the Victoria Memorial was lit up with floodlights. China slipped a tape of Hindi pop in the cassette player, and turned it up loud. This got us in the party mood and soon we were all singing along to Tarzan.

In Kiddapore there were more people sleeping on the pavements than I had seen anywhere else in Calcutta. Sonagraachi had been smart by comparison. Hundreds of people lay by gutters brimming with rotting vegetation or on wasteland covered with shacks. We walked through a maze of dog-infested, urine-smelling alleys to a three-storey tenement block. We walked up past men asleep on the stairs to the second floor.

Here the rooms were grouped around an open balcony above a central well.

A boy hardly out of his teens appeared from a doorway followed by a much older woman. He adjusted his clothes and handed her some money before hurrying self-consciously past us down the stairs. Most of the men I saw in Calcutta brothels were in their twenties or younger. The majority of Indian girl-friends forbid sex before marriage so the men resort to paying for it.

We were met by a frail, elderly Nepalese woman. She turned out to be a sort of informal madam, who washed her girls' clothes and brushed their hair. She led us along the balcony and into a tiny room furnished with only a bed, table and chair. On the wall was a poster of Sylvester Stallone in the guise of Cobra: The Strong Arm of the Law. Underneath was the caption: 'Crime is a disease . . . meet the cure'. If Calcutta men went wild over Samantha Fox, then Rambo was the biggest turn-on for women.

There were two girls in the room, both of Nepalese extraction. Bobby was the tart in charge. She was about nineteen with a bawdy sense of humour. She had a habit of lightly thumping any men who got in her way as she busied herself distributing glasses and pouring the beer. She shouted like a fishwife and ruffled my hair. She sat on China's lap and tugged at his moustache. She was a very sweet girl and very bright. She had a better chance than most of leaving this hovel. Bobby's friend Sumita was older. She was very noisy and gave us all loud, smacking kisses. Both girls owned padlocked metal attaché cases in which they stored their money and a few, precious pieces of junk jewellery. Burglary was common here.

The girls gave Tojo a rousing welcome. This was his fourth visit in a week. China's Japanese-speaking Indian arranged for him to see what was on offer. Various other girls were brought into the room. They paraded in front of him. Tojo looked at them closely. He chose an imp of seventeen with a pencil figure. She seemed quite flattered. After all, the money was good — foreigners could always afford to pay more than locals. The pair disappeared onto the balcony and into another room.

With Tojo out of the room, Bobby and Sumita began making crude jokes behind his back. They were quite impressed by him. Other Japanese men they had encountered in the course of their work were no bigger than 'little mosquitoes'. Tojo was a different proposition altogether. He was a Samurai warrior, as insatiable as a sex-crazed tiger. Or, as Sumita put it, 'He very strong fucky.'

China explained that the Englishman had only come to talk (don't they always say that?) and that he was researching a book. Bobby said she didn't mind as long as I was generous with the baksheesh. She added that we could stay as long as we liked. She would cook us a meal of mutton curry. We talked about Bobby's life as a prostitute. She had been on the game since the age of fifteen. It was a good living, she said. Otherwise she would starve. What else could a single girl with no money do? I raised the question of AIDS. She was not keen to talk about it. AIDS was bad for business. But she admitted that she was worried. And no, her clientele did not wear condoms. They were too expensive. She had heard stories of people catching AIDS, but did not know any personally.

We knocked back beers and sat on the bed eating the mutton with our fingers. I was armed with my camera and I took snaps of everyone. There was much whooping and laughter and more Hindi pop blared from a cassette player. Sumita stood on a stool and did a spot of impromptu go-go dancing.

Then a girl I had not seen before stuck her head around the door.

'Police! Police! Her voice was a rasp. The local constabulary were raiding the building. Bobby gave orders. There was to be no talking. No one was to move. She turned off the light. We sat in darkness for fifteen minutes. The only sound was the soft whirring of the ceiling fan. China and I got the giggles. The thought of being caught by police in a Calcutta cat-house was quite funny. Bobby tried to hush us. In the darkness I could feel her hand cuffing the back of my head. We waited. Somewhere else in the building I thought I could hear the sound of raised men's voices.

Our silence obviously paid off. The law never came and fifteen minutes later the same girl popped back into the room to give the all-clear. The police had given up their search and moved on to another tenement down the road. Bobby stood up and switched the light back on.

She explained that there were police scares like this at least three times a week. However, there was no question of a crowd of girls being thrown into the back of a Black Maria along with their trouserless customers. Usually the police just demanded money, which was a bore and would have made it an expensive evening. The girls were keen that the police should not find me, a foreigner, on the premises. Foreigners paid more than locals. Therefore the girls would have more money on them. The police would demand a much larger pay-off than usual.

The party resumed and China got drunk. He pinched the girls' behinds and spilled beer down his front. He lapsed into his 'I keel' mood: 'I keel anyone who cheats China or cheats China's good friend, Peter. Peter like brother.' I suggested that he go easy on the beer – particularly as he was driving home. I moved onto the balcony and chatted to Sumita.

It was now that I got the sniff of a good story.

Sumita told me about her colonel. She swigged at a bottle of beer and between burps, she told me that she had an English boyfriend.

'Oh really?' I said.

'Yes, he is a colonel in the British Army,' she said. 'He very sexy. I call him my Colonel Sexy.' She bared her white teeth and howled with laughter.

'How fascinating,' I said. This sounded like fun. A Kiddapore hooker with a British Army colonel. As old India hands would have said, Colonel Sexy had 'gone jungly' and taken a native mistress. Clive had been a colonel in Calcutta. I wondered if he'd had a mistress like Sumita.

'Do go on,' I said, all smiles. She took a card from her pocket and proudly showed it to me. It was a visiting card and it gave the name of L/Col___MOD with an address at a British Embassy in the Middle East.

'How absolutely fascinating,' I said. I reflected that the fact that Colonel Sexy spent his spare time with a Bengali tart would not be much appreciated by either the MOD or his wife.

'Oh yes,' Sumita added. 'He have wife in England. And children. He show me photo of them.'

'How nice to have a boyfriend like that.'

Sumita grinned broadly. Yes, it was nice. He was a very nice boyfriend because he gave her lots of money and bought her lots of nice presents.

'And how often do you see this colonel?' I asked.

'Whenever he comes to Calcutta.' Then, much to my surprise,

she added. 'He is coming tomorrow. I go to airport to meet him.'

Frankly, I did not believe her. I suspected that she was trying to impress me, that her colonel was nothing more than a punter who had visited her once or twice. After all, it was not every Calcutta call-girl who went to the airport to pick up a high-flying British Army boyfriend.

Still, I gave her the benefit of the doubt and planned to return next evening in the hope of meeting the chap. This was too good an opportunity to miss.

Sumita was on the balcony when China and I arrived. She rushed up to us beaming with pleasure. Colonel Sexy had come off the plane that morning. I must meet him. We were both English so we would have lots to talk about. (I bet we will, I thought.)

Then she added quickly, 'Don't you dare say you know he in Army. He not like people to know he in Army.'

Too right, I thought. British Army colonels do not like to be discovered by journalists in Calcutta brothels. I could only imagine that Colonel Sexy would view me with extreme suspicion. Here I was in a Kiddapore cat-house, camera slung around my shoulder, and no intention of jig-a-jig.

Sumita grabbed my arm and pushed me into her room.

He was lying on Sumita's bed. He was fully clothed, but had kicked his shoes untidily onto the floor. A beer bottle was in his hand and he had made himself at home. He had greying hair, was in his late forties and his voice was pure public school. He also looked very fit, a keen squash player possibly. He was certainly not the stuffy colonel-type you see in cartoons.

We introduced ourselves. I was careful not to let on that Sumita had told me he was in the army. I explained that I was doing research into prostitution in Calcutta.

To give Colonel Sexy his due, he was very relaxed. But he mentioned not a word of his true profession. Instead, he explained he had just flown in from Saudi on his way to do business in Hong Kong. That was it. He was in business. And, of course, there was nothing unusual for a jet-setting business-man to break his journey in Calcutta for a couple of days of fun and games.

Once the colonel got going, there was no stopping him. He

was very chatty and told me about his relationship with Sumita. His nickname for her was Kala, after Calcutta's patron goddess, black Kali. Sumita had very dark skin.

Sumita sat on the bed and put her arms around him. The colonel said: 'Don't you think she is the most beautiful girl in the world?' I agreed that she was absolutely ravishing. Sumita lapped up the attention.

The pair had met seven years ago when he paid his first visit to Sumita's boudoir. He had never forgotten her and they wrote regularly to each other from across the world. The customer-tart relationship had blossomed into one of friendship and even love. It was all quite touching.

Sumita snuggled up closer to her gallant officer. He announced that it was time for her to leave Kiddapore and give up her business while she was still young.

And maybe leave India, I thought. I certainly wasn't going to let the colonel know I had blown his cover by suggesting it, but it crossed my mind that someone based in a British embassy should not have much problem finding a British visa and work permit for a single girl. British residency would be a fine thank-you present for a seven-year relationship.

The colonel took a swig of beer. While he was not looking in her direction, Sumita mouthed, 'No photo,' at me. I shook my head. Of course I wasn't going to snatch a picture and give the man perfectly reasonable grounds for breaking my camera and probably my nose. Gentlemen found in whorehouses do not appreciate having their photographs taken.

We chatted for a few more minutes, but the atmosphere was becoming rather sticky. I got the impression that the colonel had only just arrived from the airport and was keen to get down to matters of business. We shook hands and I wished him a successful 'business trip' in Hong Kong.

It was after midnight when China dropped me back at the Paragon. He too had been fascinated that a senior British Army officer had a bit on the side down in Kiddapore. 'Good story for you, baba,' he said before he drove off.

Inside the hotel some of the staff were busy drawing posters. They were preparing for a strike. The owner of the hotel lived in a big house in one of the suburbs and only drove in once a day to pick up the takings. Strikes are a way of life in the city. There are plenty of opportunities for industrial action if only

172

for the fact that there are 16,000 unions in India, 7,500 of which are in Calcutta alone.

The staff's wages were pathetically low – little more than 200 rupees a month. They were demanding a minimum of at least 1,000 a month. They did not plan to strike just yet, but were encouraging all the hotel employees to unite against their capitalist master. The message on the posters was one of solidarity: 'Pet dog of the owner, be careful!' This was a reference to the manager, a sour-faced individual to whom I had taken an instant dislike. 'Dog living on the money of the owner be careful!' Not a popular chap, this manager. 'Dog live no more!' Time for the manager to find another job.

I bade them the best of luck and retired to my room to dream of mad dogs and sex-crazed colonels.

Victory at Plassey led to a new job for our hero. He was appointed Governor of Bengal, and, as befitted his new position, he now searched for a grand country mansion. He found a suitable house a few miles outside Calcutta at Nager Bazaar in the village of Dum Dum. The one-storey brick building dated from the 1730s when it had been a Dutch or Portuguese factory. It occupied high ground and offered superb views of Calcutta. The East India Company were suitably impressed and agreed to buy the property for Clive, who added a second floor and laid out a formal garden.

Dum Dum is now part of Calcutta's urban sprawl. The suburb is home to the city's airport and is probably best known for the exploding bullet of the same name. The munitions factory where this hideous weapon was invented was still in operation, standing, incongruously enough, next to the India Toy and Metal Works.

The morning after my meeting with Colonel Sexy, China and I drove out to the house. We were both nursing hangovers and after several U-turns we managed to find Nager Bazaar. It was a largely Bengali area and relatively prosperous by Calcutta standards. We turned off the main Jessore Road by a shop called 'The Buy Spirit From Us Saloon' and continued up a rough track. Clive House, as it is known, lay ahead in a large expanse of waste ground.

By God, it was a dismal sight. 'Turning in one's grave' is a well-used cliché, but if Clive could have seen the place now, he would have turned like a pig on a spit. His beloved mansion looked like it had suffered an arsonists' attack. Either that, or it had been used for hand grenade practice. Scorch marks covered the walls; windows hung lopsidedly from their mountings. The house was typical of so many eighteenth- and nineteenth-century mansions in Calcutta; a rapidly deteriorating wreck that would be lucky to see the next century.

China stopped the car by the house. A man came out to meet us. He introduced himself as Mr Bose, spokesman for the 100 Bangladeshi refugees who now occupied the building. They had been there for forty years since the partition of India and East Pakistan. Fifteen families lived in the house and outbuildings.

'Fifteen families?' I was astounded. 'But the place is about to fall down.'

'Yes, it is a little dangerous,' Mr Bose agreed. 'But we must have somewhere to live. Things were better when we first came here, but we do not have money for repairs.'

Mr Bose was an earnest little man in spectacles. He announced that he was a tailor and, like everyone else in Calcutta, he was very poor. This was the cue for baksheesh. I handed over a few notes. Mr Bose beamed. He would show me around the house.

We walked up a flight of stone steps to a grand entrance hall that now functioned as a cowshed. Mr Bose pushed a couple of heifers out of the way and pointed out the two massive pillars that held up the ceiling – or rather, what remained of the ceiling. One corner of the hall was cordoned off with coconut matting to make a bedroom for one of the families. High on the wall was a plaque stating that Clive used the house as a country retreat 1757–1760 and 1766–67.

The place was on its last legs. Floors threatened to collapse at any moment. Slabs of plaster had fallen from the walls and ceilings; vegetation sprouted from the cracked brickwork. Even China looked horrified. 'Be careful, baba,' he said, adding with considerable understatement, 'house no good.'

Mr Bose started up the staircase. We followed him gingerly. There were large gaps in the rotten planks and I could see the cows below. Mr Bose was very concerned about my safety. I took a step forward. He shook his head violently, grabbed my arm and steered me in another direction. 'No, you must not go where you please, sir. It is most dangerous.'

At the tope of the staircase was a wide colonnaded verandah.

Between the pillars were washing lines festooned with quantities of clothes. Mr Bose led us into the long salon where Clive would have entertained his guests. It was now a storeroom for bundles of incense made by the occupants of the house to sell in local temples. The original panelled doors were still in place, although the wood was bent with damp and scrawled with graffiti. What would have once been an elegant waxed teak floor was stained and splintered and littered with dead pigeons. At either end were fireplaces that Clive's servants would have lit on cool winter evenings. Mr Bose looked a little sad. 'It must have been a beautiful room once,' he said.

Standing in that drawing room, I became quite sentimental. I imagined what the house would have been like in Clive's day. It was always full of guests: the Colonel smoking one of his diamond and ruby-studded hookahs and playing cards with his chums; the bottles of Hock and Madeira consumed during long discussions about Bengal politics; the sound of Margaret Clive playing her harpsichord and the chattering of her tame mynah bird. And of course, rowdiness. Such was the brashness of Calcutta society, that the house would have reverberated to the sound of noisy dinner parties at which, according to Bence-Jones, 'the throwing of bread pellets was a recognised diversion'.

Come sunset and the Governor of Bengal might stand on the roof surveying his domain. From here he could see the whole of Calcutta, from the Hughli to the West and the tiger-infested jungle to the East. Today there is no such view. The once magnificent panorama has long since been blocked by later buildings.

Mr Bose guided us back down the staircase and round to the rear of the house. More refugees were living in outhouses little bigger than coal sheds. Dirty water ran along open gutters. The pot-holed brick paths were caked with cow dung.

I met the oldest resident, Mr S.N.Brattachayee, a retired academic book publisher in his late seventies. He lived in a small room that was once part of the servants' quarters. He lay on his bed wrapped in a woollen shawl.

'So you are a descendant of Clive's, eh?' Mr Brattachayee's nose twitched like a ferret's. He gestured at the simple furnishings in his room. 'This is not what your ancestor would have known, is it? I do not see the chandeliers or fine French furniture. Do you?' He pulled the shawl around him. 'There are only poor people living here now, you see.'

Mr Brattachayee bade me sit on a chair next to his bed. With a self-satisfied smile and a gleam in his eye, he told me about the latest saga of Clive House. It sounded like a typical Calcutta cock-up.

The house had been owned for many years by a property tycoon who wanted to demolish the mansion and sell the site for building. Or at least the tycoon *thought* that he owned the house. For as far as another Calcutta businessman was concerned, *he* owned the property. There had been a row over the deeds, which, several years later, were still the subject of prolonged legal argument.

Mr Brattachayee had the expression of a child toying with a lollipop. 'Of course, this is very good news for us,' he said. 'We have squatters' rights, so no one can get us out. We have tried to pay rent, but no one wants it. But while these men squabble between themselves we are left alone. There is a court case against us, but like everything else in Calcutta the decision is a long time coming. We have said that if we are given half the land free of charge, then the owner can have the other half. We would be very happy with this.'

Was this not blackmail? 'Blackmail? Oh no.' A hint of sarcasm appeared in Mr Brattachayee's voice. 'I think this would be a very fair arrangement. Otherwise, you see, our families will be in this house for ever and ever. And what use is that to the owner?'

I asked Mr B. if he would mind if I took his picture. Yes, he did mind. 'You go and take pictures of little boys. I do not like photographs. I am an old boy.' And a charming old boy at that.

Mr Bose led me around the grounds and pointed out a huge tree that was standing in Clive's day. There were no signs of Clive's formal garden, or of the menagerie where Margaret kept a young tiger, a bear and two porcupines.

A group of schoolboys were playing football. They saw me and crowded around, clamouring to have their photographs taken. One of them was keen to demonstrate his knowledge of English. 'Happy birthday to you,' he sang in a squeaky treble. It was many months to my next birthday, but the boy's cheerfulness helped dispel the gloom of Clive House.

Here was a prime example of Calcutta's rot and the state's

blindness to preserving its history. The housing authorities were throwing up concrete blocks that looked battered within a year. Yet the city was saturated with old mansions and villas that could be renovated and occupied again. The problem was simply that no one cared.

Before we left, Mr Bose had an idea. 'Our government is not interested in old houses. You should ask your government to pay for renovations. Clive was an important British man, yes?' I replied that unfortunately Clive wasn't such a big draw these days. If, say, Churchill had lived there, the government might be more prepared to put a few bob into the place. Mr Bose was not convinced. Which Englishman was more famous in India than Clive?

As China and I drove away I noticed a queue of people on the main road. They were standing underneath a sign saying 'Clive Stoppage'. It was good to know that even after the house fell down, the victor of Plassey would be remembered by a bus stop.

Nine

How are you supposed to react when a woman, whom you have never met before, launches into a conversation with, 'My people come from Wimbledon, you know?' Are you impressed? Or do you feel terribly sorry for her?

That was how I met Violet Smith, the proprietress of the Fairlawn Hotel, not the most luxurious lodgings in Calcutta, but certainly the most eccentric.

Clive would have appreciated the Fairlawn's thoroughly British feel. Even in the plastic 1980s there was a sense of doing things the proper way. Forty years after Independence, the spirit of the raj lived on in this magnificently dotty establishment.

The land on which the Fairlawn stood in Sudder Street was originally purchased by a European in 1781. The mansion was completed in 1803 and became a guest house early this century. Now it was run by Ted and Violet Smith, a British couple in their sixties. Vi was of Armenian extraction: she combined the genteel enunciation of a Tunbridge Wells landlady with the guttural laugh of an Yerevan inn-keeper.

Once a year the Smiths returned to England, where, according to her husband, Vi spent most of her time in Harrods' cosmetic department. The couple always stayed with their daughter in Wimbledon. Their granddaughter attended Whispers, a smart school for young ladies near Guildford. 'A very clever girl, you know,' Vi said. Her grandson was at Charterhouse. She was very proud of him.

I moved into the Fairlawn towards the end of my stay in Calcutta. China approved. Better that the white sahib stay here rather than a backpacker's grot-hole like the Paragon. China did not trust the Paragon. 'Bad tourists, baba. Steal your money.

178

Break your padlock.' In common with most cheap Indian hotels, there were no locks on the Paragon's bedroom doors. You had to provide your own padlock.

I arrived at the Fairlawn at the same time as a party of Russian tourists. They had just defected from the Lytton Hotel next door where they had been unhappy with the accommodation. The Lytton was not a patch on the Fairlawn. Whereas the Fairlawn's bedrooms boasted Edwardian furniture scented with the aroma of moth balls, the Lytton was drearily G-plan and Holiday Inn. 'Oh dear,' Vi said, 'I don't think the Lytton will like me very much this morning. It's awful taking their business, but we are a much better hotel, you know.'

The Smiths made no effort to compete with the 'international' service of Calcutta's five-star establishments. They offered graceful living with more than a touch of Noël Coward. By the reception desk was a poster of the engagement picture of the Prince of Wales and his Lady Diana. I counted no less than twelve other pictures of the Royal Family around the hotel: first snap of mother and father with Prince William; HRH The Queen with corgis. In the upstairs salon the Smiths' own wedding photographs of forty-five years ago sat on side tables topped with lace doileys.

Arriving guests were informed of Vi's strict meal times. She had a habit of putting on a foreign accent in the belief that her non-English speaking clientele would understand her better. 'Deener ees at eight o'clock,' she would say. The dining hall was staffed by a retinue of grizzled old retainers in white suits and turbans. Before meals Vi prowled around the tables as if on a military recce. Was the cutlery laid out correctly? Were the cruets all full? She directed operations with a fly-swat, ordering the servants to change a table cloth if it bore the minutest stain. On each table was a fly-swat for use of guests. Mrs Smith was keen on fly-swats.

There was a curry lunch and English fare at night. Bread and butter pudding and a savoury of Welsh rarebit rounded off a dinner of mulligatawny soup and slightly overdone lamb chops. There was porridge and kippers for breakfast. Afternoon tea, with a slice of fruit cake, was served at a quarter past four – precisely. At Christmas, guests were treated to turkey and plum pudding after which they were entertained by a conjuror.

There were several Americans staying in the hotel. They did

not seem to get the joke. I suspected that they believed we still carried on like this back home in England.

Outside the Fairlawn's palm green pillars, a shady courtyard provided a sanctuary away from the bustle of the street. It was a glorious place for sundowners. Here you could sip an evening burrapeg while surrounded by a jungle of plants in red ochre pots. In the centre was a mass-produced plaster copy of the Venus de Milo. The tables were covered in green marble effect Formica.

Violet Smith would have been Clive's sort of woman. Clive was not a handsome man and sarcastic friends nicknamed him 'Beauty'. But he liked fine clothes and saw himself as a bit of a dandy. 'To a countenance which was saved from vulgarity only by the expression of decision and natural intelligence which pervaded it,' wrote the biographer Gleig, 'he added a figure without symmetry or grace, which he rendered doubly conspicuous by the elaborate care with which it was his custom to adorn it.'

Clive would have much admired Mrs Smith. Elaborate care about her appearance was Vi's hallmark . . . It is a little after four o'clock in the afternoon and we are about to witness one of the last great colonial spectacles in India. Violet Smith, a lady just a trifle past the peak of her maturity, emerges from her boudoir after an afternoon nap. She has a truly splendid fullness of hips and bosom that would raise the blood pressure of the most decrepit ex-Indian Army colonel.

Vi descends the staircase. Her face is liberally applied with preparations by Elizabeth Arden, a beauty spot is delicately affixed to her chin. She is dressed in the purest white chiffon blouse and perfectly creased blue skirt. A charming burgundy silk cravat is tied neatly around her neck. On her feet are black court shoes. Her hair is flawless. She is a goddess. A picture of elegance rarely found outside a Paris *salon de thé*, and marred only by the presence of a plastic fly-swat in her right hand.

Following Vi down the stairs are her troops. Her maid remains a respectful one step behind, occasionally reaching forward to tease her mistress' locks. A male servant takes up the vanguard. In his hands are two red leads to which are attached a pair of brilliantly white poodles. The dogs are a little on the elderly side and they take careful steps.

Vi reaches the foot of the staircase. She spies one of her guests, a pretty Swedish girl. Vi affects one of her many accents, this time a little-girl Marilyn Monroe squeak. 'Hi, honeybunch,' she calls out. The Swedish girl is mystified by this familiarity.

Vi switches sharply to Hindi. A servant is in trouble. He has not swept the reception area. Why not? She brandishes the fly-swat. The skivvy looks terrified and scuttles away to find a broom. A young Indian enters the hotel. He is from a video hire shop and has brought two films to be shown to guests on the television in the residents' sitting room. Vi grabs the cassettes and studies them through *pince-nez*. 'Rubbish,' she snarls. The films are *Rambo III* and something called *Curse of the Killer Ninja*. 'These are rubbish. You take them back and find something decent like *Gone With The Wind*.'

The video man cowers like a trapped rabbit. 'But you had *Gone With The Wind* last week,' he stutters.

'Then we'll have it again.' An imperious command. The man exits quickly. You do not argue with Madam.

Vi is joined by her husband, Ted, who vaguely resembles Arthur Lowe in *Dad's Army*. He walks with an arthritic limp caused, perhaps, by a surfeit of square-bashing in Army days long past. It is also likely that he has bashed a few pink gins in his time. A product of the Grenadier Guards, he is dressed in cavalry twills, striped city shirt and brigade tie. Vi lifts a dainty hand. She checks whether her nail varnish is dry before picking a stray hair from her husband's tweed jacket.

The couple leave the hotel for their car, an uncommonly clean Ambassador. Vi settles in the back while Ted takes the driving seat. He is the chauffeur. It is quite clear who is boss. The servant places the poodles in the front next to Ted, who slowly manoeuvres the car out of the Fairlawn's yard. From here the Smiths travel less than half a mile to the Oxford Book Shop in Park Street. This is a daily excursion that is done for one reason alone: so that Ted Smith can buy his three-day-old copy of the London *Daily Telegraph*. He reads it chiefly for the cricket. Vi never leaves the car. 'I do not like walking in the streets,' she says. 'Far too dirty, you know.'

It was my last night in Calcutta and I was enjoying a beer in the Fairlawn's courtyard to kill time before China arrived. He promised me a special treat. I had dared not inquire what he had in store.

181

Vi was doing the rounds of her guests. She loomed over me and asked if everything was to my satisfaction. No problems, I explained. But there was one thing I wanted to ask. How on earth did she keep her poodles so brilliantly clean and white in such a filthy place as Calcutta?

'Easy,' said Vi. She launched into a verbal delivery like a machine gun. 'I have them washed once a week. Know I shouldn't. Bad for them, you know. My daughter in Wimbledon has a bloody great hound. Can't think what it is. Washes it once a year. Stinks like hell. Walks it in Nonsuch Park near Epsom. Of course you know Nonsuch Park.'

'Er . . .' Of course I didn't.

'Really?' Vi sniffed and walked away. How extraordinary that an Englishman had never heard of Nonsuch Park.

China had turned up and was hovering by the main gate. I invited him to join me for a beer. It was not possible, he said. Mrs Smith would throw him out. The lower orders, like Indian drivers, did not mix with her guests. We adjourned to a chai shop across the road and sat down.

I looked at China across the table. 'So, what's this special treat you're promising?'

'Ah, baba. Very special treat.' China was in his element. He looked quite the young swell in his grey safari suit. His hair was neatly combed and I detected a smell of aftershave. 'Tonight we go see girls in sari,' he announced. 'Very special mujra.'

'Oh God, China. Not again.' I had expected the worst.

'But very nice girls. Not full negative, but very nice.'

'Look, I've told you before, it's naked, not negative. Anyway, can't we go to the cinema or something like that?'

China wasn't going to give up. He pushed on enthusiastically. 'Muslim mujra. Like Siraj-ud-daula would have done. After long day, Siraj-ud-daula relax with girls and hookah. You know hookah?'

'Yes, it's a pipe.'

'Yes, pipe. And there is music with tabla. You know tabla.'

'Yes, China, it's a drum.' I sighed. China's enthusiasm was definitely not catching.

'Yes, drum, baba. And sarangi.' A sarangi was a sort of Indian violin. China began humming and got up from the table. He closed his eyes and began dancing like a gypsy fiddler. The other customers in the chai shop looked at him oddly. 'And music and nice girls,' he murmured. He was lost in thought about the delights of the nawab's court.

'And then what?' I asked. 'What does Saraj-ud-daula do next?'

China's eyes brightened. 'He pom-pom all the girls.'

'Pom-pom?'

'Yes, pom-pom. Like jig-a-jig.' His voice rose a notch.

'Monkey Business!'

'What? *All* the girls?'

'One, two, maybe all. We go tonight, Baba?'

'Well, if it's the sort of mujra Siraj-ud-duala would have known, I suppose we ought to. But it stops at the music. No funny business.'

'What? No pom-pom?' China looked mortified.

'Look,' I said, 'I'll be a celibate Siraj-ud-duala and you can be an oversexed Mir Jafar for all I care.' He grinned. This image appealed to him.

The Nawab Siraj-ud-daula's mujra would have been rather different to the wham, bam and bumps-a-daisy version of today's Calcutta. The Muslim rulers of eighteenth-century India took their mujra very seriously. It was a princely ritual strictly reserved for the ruling class. While gentlemen back home in England were retiring to their libraries for bawdy stories and a decanter of port, the Nawabs were relaxing with a smoke of opium and the company of their favourite courtesans.

It is a warm evening in Murshidibad. Siraj-ud-daula sits on deep cushions on the roof of his palace beneath a linen canopy, or shahmyanah, decorated with gold thread. From the roof he can see the moon's reflection in the waters of the Bhagirathi. His favourite hunting cheetah, fastened to a gold chain held by a servant, lies purring at his feet. The Nawab is surrounded by courtiers and friends. Glistening, ebony black Abyssynian slaves serve sherbert perfumed with rose water. The air is filled with the sweet smell of jasmine from the royal gardens.

The musicians assemble. With the company relaxed with their hookahs, the ladies enter. They are delicate and olive-skinned, their hair scented with sandalwood. They perform the ritual mujra. There are elaborate dances and the Nawab's praises are sung. The girls recite love poems. Perhaps Siraj-ud-daula requests the ancient muslim song of Selima, an anguished ballad of unrequited love:

'Lamp of my life and possessor of my heart; my first, my only love! In vain do I call upon thee, but thou hearest not the voice of Selima, once the most favoured of thy slaves!

'My king! Thou hast decked me with diamonds of Golconda and covered me with pearls of Ormuz. But what are diamonds and pearls to her that is forsaken? Give me thy heart!

'The shawls of Cassimer and the silks of Iran presented by my lord have no longer any charms for thy Selima. Thy palace, thy baths, delight me no more. Give me thy heart!

'The gardens and groves, once the fond retreat of thy Selima, afford me no pleasure. The mango and pomegranate tempt me in vain. The odour of spices I no longer enjoy. Give me thy heart!

'Return, oh my lord, to thine handmaid, restore her thy heart and every pleasure will accompany it. Oh, give thy heart to thy Selima, restore it to its first possessor.'

When the mujra is over the Nawab sprinkles his guests with precious drops of attar of roses before presenting them with lavishly embroidered shawls. A bigger and better present follows as each guest retires to his room in the company of a girl specially chosen by his host . . .

China's interpretation of the mujra was rather different.

We left Sudder Street and drove to a part of town called Bahu Bazaar. On the way China gave me the impression that we were going somewhere smart. 'Muslim area, baba. Many rich people.' This sounded more like it. I was looking forward to an upmarket evening of music and dance in a nice, salubrious club.

It was not a promising start. As we drove into Bahu Bazaar I looked out of the Ambassador at sights that were all too familiar after my evenings in Kiddapore: dog-infested alleyways; streams of black effluent oozing their way down the gutters; mounds of rubbish that had been festering for weeks.

China parked the car and I stepped out onto a pavement littered with the customary legions of homeless. China spotted a man sitting on a bench across the street and went over to talk to him. It turned out to be Alum, our broker for the evening. China introduced me. 'This is Peter. I am his secretary.' Secretary? This was new to me.

Alum was very fat. A massive paunch bulged under his long shirt and he wheezed asthmatically, punctuating his sentences with bronchial coughs. He waddled rather than walked. Considering we were supposed to be in Calcutta's poshest red-light area, Alum was by far the sleaziest pimp we had encountered so far. He reminded me of one of those touts that hang around outside Soho strip joints.

Alum and China put their heads together and negotiated the fee for the evening. Singing and dancing only. Definitely no pom-pom. One hour would come to 400 rupees, which seemed pretty steep to me.

Alum led us into a building and we climbed to the second floor. It was another cat-house like all the others with the same sort of rooms leading off the same long corridors. But the girls were different. They were mostly Indian and smartly dressed in brightly-coloured expensive saris. Unlike with the Kiddapore girls, there was no giggling here, only serene looks, an air of sophistication. And, without exception, they were all very pretty. Oh yes, this was a classy clip-joint.

Alum was puffing loudly after the climb. He coughed, turned away, and spat into a corner. He turned back to us with a grunt and introduced us to a slightly chubby girl with a petulant, but pretty face, who was standing in the corridor outside one of the rooms. She was called Versha, and she was wearing an elegant dark brown silk sari decorated with gold braid. A single red rose was pinned in her hair. She looked at me and burst into a fit of giggles.

China said, 'Versha mean "come running".'

'Come running?' What sort of name was that for a call-girl? The mind boggled.

Thankfully Versha didn't speak any English. I say 'thankfully' because Alum and China then started speaking in broken English, discussing her merits in the art of pom-pom. Alum said that to pom-pom with the Englishman would cost 2,000 rupees. China shook his head vigorously. This was far too much. Okay, said Alum, he could manage it for 1,000. China said that was better. Hang on, I said, this Englishman has no intention of pom-pomming. Why can't we get on with the mujra?

'There is a problem,' said Alum. He looked at his watch, a Taiwan-made copy of a Cartier. 'Versha has another man in her room and he has twenty more minutes with her.'

'Well, whoever's in the room must be pretty pissed off if he's paid for Versha's services and she's outside on the landing chatting with us.'

China intervened. 'Don't worry, baba. Other man has finished pom-pom. He has been here since lunchtime. A lot of pom-pom. He quite tired now. Just want to talk and have quiet smoke and a whisky.' I was not surprised. More than twelve hours of pom-pom was enough for anyone. Even Siraj-ud-daula.

Versha said that her customer wouldn't mind if we joined him. I explained that I was quite happy to stand outside for a few more minutes. She insisted that we join her. In a country of more than a billion people, privacy was no big deal. And it was no different in a brothel.

We entered the room. It was lit by a single strip of neon. A bed took up most of the space. It was an enormous bed and, apart from a television, was the only piece of furniture in the room. At one side of the bed was a velvet curtain that screened off a narrow passageway to the bathroom. There were tatty Hindu posters of Vishnu on the walls. I felt that Siraj-ud-daula might have expected a little more. Although perhaps the Nawab would have been impressed by the bed's easy-wipe melamine headboard.

Versha's client was reclining on a heap of cushions covered in cherry-coloured easy-wash dralon. He was a thirty-year-old motor parts dealer from Assam, who was on business in Calcutta. I got the impression that Versha was an old flame.

China and I sat awkwardly on the edge of the bed while Versha leapt onto the cushions to join the man from Assam. She pouted at him. He pouted back, blew a little kiss and put his arm around her. He offered me his other hand and we introduced ourselves. His handshake was wet and flabby. On his little finger was a diamond ring of intensely vulgar design. Half a dozen thick gold chains hung around his neck. I was quite surprised to see him there. He looked more like the sort of chap who preferred boys.

I chatted for a few minutes to the man from Assam. But in common with most motor parts traders he was not particularly exciting. I turned to Versha. China interpreted for me and I learned that she had been born in Agra, home of the Taj Mahal. Her parents had moved to Calcutta twelve years ago. She was nineteen and had been a mujra girl for barely a year.

A small boy stuck his head round the door. Did we need drinks? The man from Assam ordered whisky for all of us. He punched me playfully on the arm.

186

'You like MacDougall whisky? Yes?'

I had no idea whether I liked MacDougall whisky, but at least it sounded Scottish. The boy returned a few minutes later with a bottle that featured a label with a lot of tartan on it. Versha brought out some glasses from under the bed and poured the muddy brown liquid. She then drowned it with water. A wise move. It tasted more or less like whisky, but I suspected it was made from cane spirit.

The man from Assam delicately grasped his glass so that his bejewelled pinkie stuck out at a right angle. He gulped down the alcohol. He stood up and explained that he had enjoyed our company very much, but he had to meet a business colleague for dinner. He straightened his tangle of gold chains and sighed loudly. The motor parts trade was a demanding occupation, he said. After more sticky handshakes, he left.

I nudged China. He had taken a great shine to Versha and was drooling like a Labrador.

'So where's this mujra, then?'

'Don't worry, baba, We wait. Good mujra soon.'

Versha and China giggled together. After ten minutes, we were joined by a trio of musicians. One of them set up a small, portable harmonium. He pumped the instruments with one hand and let the fingers of his other run over the keyboard. The tabla player put his drum of stretched leather between his legs and beat out an intricate pattern. The violinist, an old man with a creased face, shouldered his sarangi and added a squeaky accompaniment.

China and I sat cross-legged on the bed. Versha knelt opposite us. She smoothed down the folds of her sari and clasped her hands together as if in prayer. She opened her mouth and softly began to serenade us. The mujra had begun.

The ballads came first. Hindi love songs in which the girl prayed for the safe return of her sweetheart from a long voyage. Versha sang with a deep, hypnotic, resonance. She had a lovely voice, full of emotion. Here was a tart of many talents. China was wallowing in the opulence of it all. He reclined contentedly on the cushions, the glow of whisky on his face. 'Ah, baba,' he murmured, 'here is proper mujra. Mujra for rich man.' I had to agree that it was a pleasant change from mutton curry in Kiddapore.

The drum beat increased and sweat poured off the musicians'

187

faces. The elderly violinist struck up a frantic jig and Versha moved on to a jolly drinking song. It was a sort of Indian equivalent of *Roll Out The Barrel*.

China translated: 'She is saying that she is very sad because her husband doesn't think she is sexy anymore. But she thinks she is very sexy. If her husband doesn't want her, she says that is no problem. She go out and find another man.' China howled with laughter and spluttered on his whisky. He found this shriekingly funny.

While Versha crooned her earthy little number, China threw ten rupee notes at her. He told me to do the same. This was one of the traditions of the mujra. You showered the singer with money to show your appreciation. Versha then passed the notes to the musicians. They responded with wide toothy smiles as they pounded away at their instruments.

The entertainment ended an hour later when fat Alum returned to collect his money. With him was a man selling garlands of sweet-smelling lilies. Versha took one of the chains and hung it around my neck. She did the same to China. He was delighted.

'Now we can walk through the streets with flowers, baba,' he said, 'and everyone will know we have been to mujra.'

'Siraj-ud-daula mujra.'

Out in the street, China put his arm around my shoulder. 'Come on baba, why don't we find you nice girl and you take her home?'

'Certainly not, China,' I said. The thought of being caught by Mrs Smith in the Fairlawn in the company of a Calcutta tart was too appalling to even contemplate.

The days of the Raj live on not only in the Fairlawn. Shortly before I left Calcutta, I accepted an invitation to have dinner with an English couple called Bob and Anne Wright.

Bob Wright was one of the best known of the ex-patriot Brits in Calcutta. The British contingent in the city totalled only 100, including diplomatic personnel, and were outnumbered 2–1 by the Russians. ('Pretty poor show', according to Bob.)

Bob was in charge of the Tollygunge Club, the only country club in Calcutta, and a wonderful anachronism that tried hard to epitomise the days of the Raj. If the Tolly, as it was known, had been functioning in Clive's day, the colonel would have undoubtedly been a member.

I travelled down to the Tolly by metro. Calcutta's underground network was three years old, but should have been in operation long before that. Construction progressed slowly during the 1970s not least because of thousands of Bangladeshi refugees, who took up residence in the concrete pipes through which the trains would run while they were still at ground level awaiting installation.

This hiccough over, the metro was about the only orderly thing in the city. Around five times as expensive as the buses, it was used only by the well-off professional classes. There were no beggars or vagrants down here. It was built for the well-off as a means of getting around the city without the inconvenience of repeated traffic jams. When I got on it was rush hour and yet there was no queue for tickets and the train was not even full. After the turmoil of the streets overhead, the journey was a marvellously peaceful experience.

Reality returned with a jolt. The road from Tollygunge station to the club was like any other road in Calcutta: snarled-up traffic, meandering cows and goats, the familiar shattered pavements on which the ragged poor were setting up camp for the night.

But suddenly I was out of the squalor and walking through the gates of the Tolly to an extraordinary display of wealth. Just a minute after leaving urban chaos behind I was in an indecently calm rural oasis. The noise of honking horns was replaced by the twittering of birds in jacaranda trees. Neatly clipped lawns flanked the long drive.

I could have been in one of those gin'n'jag country clubs outside Guildford. A garden boy in threadbare T-shirt solemnly watered a herbaceous border. To the right were the tennis courts, bathed in floodlighting. Players in white tennis kits lethargically lobbed balls at each other. Beyond the courts were the swimming pools, the polo stables and golf course. The club house lay at the end of the drive. It was a gloriously elegant, pillared eighteenth-century mansion built in 1788, fourteen years after the death of Clive, by a tycoon called Richard Johnson. The building had been a club since 1895 when it was known as Sahibangicha, 'the garden of the white man', and served as a surburban retreat for Europeans wishing to escape from the bustle of the city. These days the members were mostly rich Indians.

The entrance hall contained a portrait of the Queen diplomatically positioned next to Prime Minister Rajiv Gandhi. Clumpy leather armchairs were scatterd around the highly polished floor. A sign warned: 'No spiked shoes.'

A club servant at the reception desk announced my arrival to the Wrights. He used an ancient wind-up field telephone that might have seen service at Passchendaele to ring upstairs to the couple's apartment. I was to go up immediately.

A cigarette dangled from Bob Wright's mouth. He welcomed me with a raffish grin. 'Ah, Holt, isn't it? Think we're expecting you.' He led me into a lofty room with copious ceiling fans and acres of parquet floor on which stood antique tables and dressers bearing silver picture frames with the Wright family photographs. At his heels were three unruly Labradors led by a brute called Bertie.

With his well-brushed moustache, Bob resembled an overweight David Niven. He was dressed in well-worn tropical kit – beige safari suit and sandals. His voice was the type you used to hear in Second World War naval cinema epics made by Euston Films. 'First class!' was his stock expression followed by 'very, very, very good', the 'very' pronounced 'vairy'. But despite his kind face and bluff exterior, I got the impression that he was the sort of old Indian hand who took no nonsense from the staff.

Bob handed me a beer in a heavy, cut-glass tumbler. He pointed me in the direction of a chintz-covered sofa where Anne was sitting. She greeted me with an outstretched hand. Bob apologised for the dogs that threatened to knock me over. 'The pack belong to me,' he said. He indicated a pair of sleepy cocker spaniels that lay in a corner of the room. 'Those two are hers. Keep the labradors well away, you know. Inclined to savage them.'

Anne Wright was draped in a long blue tent-like dress. 'Keeps the mosquitoes away from my ankles,' she explained. After forty years in Calcutta, the Wrights still hadn't mastered the art of insect control. They were trying out a new, electric anti-mosquito gizmo. It burned tablets that gave off the sort of sickly rose smell found in lavatory fresheners. Anne wrinkled her nose. 'Godawful pong, isn't it?' she said.

I chatted about my disastrous boat trip. By remarkable coincidence, it turned out that Bob knew the dreaded Paper Pulp Mill very well. He had worked there briefly as a young man when the plant was still under British management. 'It was a damned good little factory in those days,' he said. 'I remember that we doubled its output of paper in one year. Probably bloody awful now.' I agreed that it was not my favourite spot.

India had been Bob's home for forty years, the last eight spent at the Tolly. Both he and Anne were active in various charities helping Calcutta's poor. Both had received MBEs for their efforts. One of Bob's friends told me later, 'Calcutta would not be the same without him. I can't imagine him ever leaving. I think you could say he is deeply in love with the place.'

The couple also ran a wildlife encampment 400 miles away in Maydar Pradesh with tiger spotting for paying guests. It was called Kipling Camp, after Rudyard who was said to have written *The Jungle Book* there. 'It's our bolt hole,' Anne said. She was most insistent that it was not a commercial enterprise. 'We certainly don't encourage tourists, just friends, and friends of friends.'

The wail of bagpipes drifted through the window from across the Tolly's polo ground.

'Good lord! Is that the bagpipes?' I said. 'Sounds like an eightsome reel.' Bob looked at me as if to say what else did I expect to hear in the middle of Calcutta.

He explained that the piper was an old friend called George Mackenzie, who was staying in one of the Tolly's guest bungalows and was also due for dinner. 'Famous bagpipe player. Heard of him?' No, I hadn't.

George and his wife Viv arrived to a ferocious welcome from the pack. The labradors skidded and barked their way down the wooden floor. Mackenzie was a jowly man in his forties with a soft Scottish accent and a ruddy, laughing face that suggested he would be good fun at parties. He wore an open neck shirt with a natty white cravat. Bob poured more drinks.

George was another old Indian hand. He had been born in Assam and was an ex-Gurkha officer, who had first met the Wrights when stationed in Calcutta in the 1970s. After quitting the Army, he had emigrated to Australia, married Viv, and now ran a guest house in the Blue Mountains outside Sydney. I got the impression that the guest house was more of a hobby than a serious business venture. Playing the pipes was George's main occupation and his greatest love.

He was nostalgic for the old Calcutta days. 'Bloody good fun,' he said. 'I was stationed about fifteen miles from the centre at Barrackpore at the Gurkha supply depot. When I got the posting everyone else in the regiment said, poor you, you'll be bloody miserable. I was the only officer at Barrackpore and I used to have dinner on my own in this huge mess waited on by ten servants.

'When I arrived, I found my predecessor was drunk and had been so for quite a considerable time. I thought, well, I'm not going the way of you, old chap, and I spent the time getting bloody fit.' He slurped on his whisky and slapped one of the Labradors hard on the rump. The dog wagged its tail and grinned stupidly.

George went on: 'Weekends were a different matter. I used to come into the city for parties with the other European bachelors who worked in banks and businesses. I could keep going all Friday and Saturday night because I was so fit. I stayed in friends' flats all over the city. Just dossed down where one got drunk and there was the chance of a poke. For all I know I've still got clothes hanging in flats all over Calcutta.' George leaned back in the sofa and smiled nostalgically. 'Time of my life. Loved Calcutta. Still do.'

Staff in white suits served dinner. We dined off a long table covered in the Wright family silver. Bob produced a bottle of Burgundy – a great treat in India.

All went well during the fish in lemon sauce, but as the servant passed round the chocolate pudding, the row started. I had brought up the subject of Calcutta's beggars and what a nuisance they could be. You could not walk anywhere in the city without children tugging your sleeve and demanding money.

'Don't be so hard, Peter,' Anne said, 'you should always give something, even just a tiny amount. I always give a few paise.'

This was too much for Bob, who was sitting at the other end of the table. He roared like an enraged tiger.

'Balls!' The room went horribly quiet. 'Balls, woman! It's stupid women like you who cause all the trouble in the first place. If no one gave money to beggars they'd soon give up asking for any. Much better to write out a big cheque and give it to a charity.'

192

George and Viv looked embarrassed. Viv made the mistake of taking Anne's side. 'Well, I agree,' she said. 'It doesn't do any harm to give a little money to beggars.'

Bob glowered at both of them. He launched into a lecture about the system of begging in Calcutta. It worked as a sort of mafia. In prime spots, like around the tourist hotels in Sudder Street, it was well known that the beggars paid protection money in order to stay on their patch. It was a network of organised crime in which able-bodied racketeers were the winners. There was a good chance that of the two rupees you gave to that appealing little urchin with a runny nose, one rupee would go to a hood up the street. And there was certainly no way that any old beggar could simply move in and start work.

Despite an excellent dinner with quantities to drink, the evening ended rather sourly with the Wrights engaged in a full-scale domestic battle that seemed likely to continue long after the guests had departed.

Nor had I helped the atmosphere. I had innocently suggested that perhaps the Indians had sometimes – and I emphasised the perhaps and sometimes – been given reasonable grounds to complain about their British masters.

'Balls!' Bob rounded on me and delivered another lecture, this time about the increase in government corruption since Independence. 'That's the trouble with you people who come here on holiday. You don't know what it was like in the old days. We ran a fair administration with a proper judiciary that couldn't be bribed. Now everyone's on the bloody take.'

A whisky and soda later and it was time to go. I left the Tolly with the cries of 'bloody tourists who don't know what they are talking about' ringing in my ears. It had been an excellent evening.

Ten

Blustering Bob Wright exaggerated when he said that everyone in India was on the take. Perhaps what he should have said is 'nearly everyone'. But corruption is a way of life, and the Indians are the first to admit it. Bribery reaches from the top (for example, Prime Minister Rajiv Ghandi's alleged involvement in the Bofors arms scandal) to the lowly telephone repairman, who accepts 'speed money' as a legitimate fee for getting things done faster.

But many Indians claim that it was Clive and his associates who started the rot in the first place.

Clive gave up his position as the most important man in India in 1767. He resigned as Governor of Bengal and sailed home to set about spending the vast fortune amassed during his years in the sub-continent. He had two substantial country estates, Claremont in Surrey and Walcot in Shropshire, as well as the grand townhouse in Berkeley Square. He also spent thousands rebuilding the ancestral home, Styche, for his parents. And he equipped his houses with expensive antiques bought on a grand tour of Italy.

He had fits of generosity, lavishing money on his friends and family. Each of his five sisters received £2,000; Major Stringer Lawrence, his military mentor, got £500 a year to ease his financial problems. Gossips estimated that Clive was worth £1,200,000, although the correct figure was probably half that.

Even so, he was one of the richest men in Europe, an eighteenth century answer to Getty. And his enemies did not like that. He was too flashy and he needed to be put in his place.

One of the first snubs arrived when he was given an Irish peerage – Baron Clive of Plassey – rather than a British one, a

194

great disappointment that kept him away from the House of Lords and the corridors of power. Then came the allegations of bribery and malpractice. His enemies accused him of milking India of her riches and accepting bribes from the Indian rulers he had kept in power. The public turned against Clive and newspapers were started for the sole purpose of maligning him. The hero of Arcot and Plassey was now a figure of national scorn.

In 1770 Bengal was hit by a terrible famine, which claimed millions of lives. According to Clive's biographer R.J. Minney, 'People gnawed at the barks of trees for nourishment. Mothers fed on their dead infants. Children ate their dying parents . . . Hundreds of villages were left without a single survivor.' England was shocked, and Parliament was determined to find a scapegoat.

Clive was treated, in his own words, like a sheep stealer. On 13 April 1772, his greatest enemy, Colonel John Burgoyne – a man of bastard birth who later was to lose us the American colonies – stood up in the House of Commons and demanded a Committee of Inquiry. Clive was brought before the house and ordered to explain himself. What about the money that Mir Jafar had given him? Clive replied it was for services rendered. He pointed out that Mir Jafar had actually offered him a lot more, but he didn't want to overdo it. 'By God,' Clive announced to the packed chamber, 'at this moment I stand astonished by my own moderation!'

But he was not off the hook. A year later, Burgoyne put the resolution before the House that Clive had 'illegally acquired the sum of £234,000 to the dishonour and detriment of the State'. By now, this bitterness had left Clive tired and depressed. He stood up and answered back with a moving speech, saying he was broke – 'I can look upon myself as having nothing left but a family estate of about £500 a year, which has belonged to us for many generations . . . I believe that those that do know me know that I have supported prosperity in moderation . . . I may be distressed, I may be ruined, but as long as I have a conscience to defend me, I will always be happy.'

Clive added, 'Leave my honour, take away my fortune,' and walked out on the verge of tears. The House was stunned. Then the cries of 'hear, hear' began to break out and several members burst into tears themselves. Burgoyne was forced to withdraw his resolution. Clive was all but exonerated.

But Indians still blame their problems on Clive. While I was in Calcutta, a blistering attack on Clive appeared in the daily newspaper *The Telegraph*. 'Lord Clive's cavalier theft of Indian wealth and raw material knew few bounds,' raged journalist, Minhaz Merchant. 'The East India Company came to trade and stayed to profiteer. Its masters, the British Crown, looked the other way as long as the refined looting indulged by Clive and his men was done in the long-term interests of Her Britannic Majesty.' But in the end even the Crown was embarrassed by Clive's brazenness. 'So the East India Company invented tidier ways of thriving. It created special shares, which only senior officers of the company could buy and sell, to skim off money and raw material from the princes. It was all done with spit and polish.'

The fiery Mr Merchant added that the ancient Hindu scriptures proclaimed that death was preferable to dishonesty. 'But modern Indian politics is more influenced by eighteenth-century trading ethics. The freedom stuggle led by Ghandhi brought the promise of a new ethic to India's moral character, ravaged by over 150 years of British conquest and expropriation. If the British could cheat so could the Indians. Thus were laid the roots of the petty corruption seen today.'

It is a cosy argument. But does it really explain why Calcutta's traffic cops spend their days stopping trucks for absolutely no reason and refusing to let the drivers continue until they have handed over thirty or so rupees? I saw that happen a couple of times while driving through the city rush hour. Anyone you talk to in Calcutta will tell you that the police are bent.

And what about the tea stall in Sudder Street? It was a sordid little incident. A man had set up a shop on the pavement with a paraffin burner and a kettle. He did not have a licence to trade – nor could he probably afford one – but he was trying to scratch a living by selling a few miserable cups of tea. He had been in business for barely two hours when I saw a police car roar up. Three plain-clothed officers piled out and slung him in the back. They threw his pots into the boot of the car before driving off. I learned later that the owner of a restaurant across the road had complained to the police that the man was taking his business. And because the restaurant was keeping the police happy with kick-backs, they were only too willing to stop the competition.

Corruption of another kind reaches the tourists in India. And I admit that I readily fell into this trap.

With dormitory accommodation costing around fifteen rupees a night, an extra couple of rupees in the pound can make a lot of difference to one's spending power. So the first thing I did on reaching Calcutta was to change money on the black market. There comes a time when you want to change your foreign cash and you think you're being clever if you get more than the official bank rate. But dealing on the black market can be a headache.

One morning I tackled one of the many money changers hanging around in Sudder Street. He was a man of about fifty who seemed tired with life. He had a bald head, a pockmarked face and the shifty look you expect from a black marketeer. He also had a habit of constantly readjusting his dhoti, that length of cloth tied around his middle. The Indian man seems to have a mania about his dhoti. He is always re-tying it, changing the dhoti's shape. On occasions the dhoti is pulled up high around his thighs. At others it is around his legs so that he resembles a baby with a full nappy. At the beginning of our conversation, the dealer favoured the mini look. The discussion progressed. The dhoti was untied and reset to a more modest length.

I explained that I wanted to change £100 in £20 notes. We struck a deal at twenty-nine rupees to one pound – two and a half rupees above the official bank rate. I expected him to go off and get the cash so that I could meet him an hour later and do the deal. It was not going to be that simple. The next minute we were sitting side by side in a taxi and heading across Calcutta. 'We now meet my boss,' the dealer said. Ten minutes later we stopped outside a row of shops.

The money changer's 'boss' turned out to be a thirty-year-old spiv, who owned a tatty souvenir kiosk. I stayed in the taxi while the money changer got out and had a brief conversation with him. The dealer returned. He looked shifty. The dhoti was hauled up almost to his groin.

'It is a Sunday,' he said.

'So what?' I said. I didn't like the sound of this.

'It is a Sunday so the black market rate comes down – twenty-eight rupees for one pound.'

'But how is that possible? How can the black market shift one rupee on a Sunday when the bank rate has hardly moved in a week?' I was being done – good 'n' proper.

I got out of the taxi and argued with the spiv. He would not budge. Twenty-eight rupees or nothing. I lost the argument and after much shouting I settled for twenty-eight rupees. I pointed out to the spiv that for the sake of a few quid it was a lot less hassle to go to a proper bank where I would not have to deal with sharks like him. He simply smiled.

On the way back to the hotel in the auto rickshaw, Baldie put on a pained expression. He wanted a tip, baksheesh. I pointed out that he had fouled up the deal. If, as a middle-man, he had made some money from his boss, that was fine. But I wasn't giving him a thing.

Baldie tried the 'have a heart, guv' approach. He put a hand in his shirt pocket and produced a much-fingered piece of paper. It was a hospital docket stating that he had been tested for tuberculosis and that the test was positive. I looked at the date on the docket. It was four months old.

'I am a very sick man,' he said.

'Bollocks – with a capital B. If you're so sick, how come you can trundle around Calcutta each day changing money?'

'I not lie, I not cheat.'

We parted company outside the hotel. The dhoti had moved again and was now crooked. The knot at the front resembled a large growth. Baldie looked pitiful and put his hand out. This was too much for me and I grudgingly handed over ten rupees. He managed a weak smile and I headed into the hotel. When I last saw Baldie he was preparing for another deal and was about to get his claws into a pair of Swedish backpackers. Perhaps the Swedes would have more luck with their Kroner.

After six weeks, Calcutta was beginning to get me down. The squalor of the streets had become unbearable; the continual hassle from the touts and hawkers was no longer amusing. Like most foreign visitors to the city I eventually succumbed to a vicious stomach attack. I spent my last days in Calcutta confined to my hotel room where I read the complete works of Neville Shute that I had found on a second-hand bookstall.

It was a relief when it came to the day I was due to leave. China picked me up and drove me to the airport. I clutched my stomach as we bumped over the all too familiar potholes of Calcutta's roads.

'You not happy, baba?' China said.

'Blame it on the bloody food in Calcutta, China.'

'You take medicine?'

'Yeah. Antacid tablets.' And I thought of Walt and how he would have laid his hands on my stomach and filled me with his so-called love energy.

At the airport China helped me with my bags to the check-out desk. We hugged each other goodbye.

'China poor man, big heart.' This was the cue for China's tip. I handed him some notes. 'You come back next year, baba, and you see China with smartest car in Calcutta. I spend lots of money on my car. You tell your friends that when they come here China is best driver in Calcutta.'

'Yes, China,' I said wearily. 'And watch out you don't get into too much trouble with the mujra girls down in Kiddapore.'

China grinned. 'Don't worry, baba,' and he turned and walked away.

Epilogue

Ramesh telephoned me a few months after I returned from India. He had been in America and was now on a week's holiday in Britain before returning to Pondicherry.

Ramesh was in a jubilant mood. He had just completed a successful lecture tour of the States where he had visited Princeton University. Princeton had given his work with human energy fields an enthusiastic reception. University statisticians had studied his data and pronounced that it was ninety-eight per cent accurate. The human aura was slowly on its way to being accepted as a perfectly sound way to detect cancer. But Ramesh conceded that he had a long way to go. 'The trouble with most conventional doctors,' he muttered darkly, 'is that they don't believe in anything unless it has been invented by one of the big drug companies.'

While in the States, Ramesh had travelled to Cleveland to see Walt. Alas, Walt no longer had his Methodist ministry. His congregation had found it bad enough when he began faith healing. But when he had returned from the East with news that he was the New Messiah (and a reincarnated Indian New Messiah at that), it had been too much for their unwordly Ohio souls to bear. He had parted company with his flock by mutual agreement.

I invited Ramesh to stay the weekend at my home in Shropshire. It was his first visit to Britain and he was keen to see the English countryside. And the English at play.

I took him to the annual open-air Ludlow Shakespeare Festival, set in the courtyard of ruined Ludlow Castle. This year it was *Julius Caesar*, which fascinated Ramesh since he had once played Mark Anthony in a school production in Madras. We were in the third week of July and, needless to say, it poured with rain through most of the performance. The water streamed off us as we watched Caesar's gory death while huddled under hastily provided bin liners.

'Do the British always watch Shakespeare in monsoon conditions?' Ramesh asked me with an amused glint in his eye. 'Perhaps that is the real reason why you always have the advantage over us Indians.'

'British people mad,' I said, thinking of China.

It rained all weekend, but the ceaseless deluge did not deter Ramesh's spirits. 'I want to see where Clive came from,' he said. 'I would like to see where he is buried. Perhaps we will feel vibrations at that place.' And so we drove to the little village of Moreton Say.

Clive's family quickly hushed up the real reason for his death. After all, suicide was a criminal offence and victims of suicide were often buried at a cross roads with a stake through the chest. Within forty-eight hours Robert's body was taken from London 160 miles north to the church of Moreton Say where he was hurriedly buried in the family vault. The funeral was conducted quietly, with as little fuss as possible, and with nothing to mark his resting-place, not even a humble headstone. It has been suggested that Margaret wanted no publicity for fear that her husband's enemies might defile his grave.

The gossips had a wonderful time that week. As black-humoured Horace Walpole remarked, 'Lord Clive has died every death in the parish register; at present it is fashionable to believe he cut his throat.'

The first newspaper reports suggested he had suffered an epileptic fit. Then came the rumours of an overdose. 'He had taken opium for many years, and finding the disorder in his bowels very painful, he took a double dose against advice, and died in a fit,' wrote Mr Robert Pardoe, a London lawyer. 'He had several of those fits before, some friends of mine have seen him seized with them in the Rooms at Bath.' The penknife theory is now generally accepted as being most likely, although, understandably, Margaret wanted it kept quiet at the time.

Ramesh and I turned off the A41 to Whitchurch and plunged into a labyrinth of country lanes flanked by high hedges. The downpour continued. I could hardly see the road through the slashing windscreen wipers. Ramesh looked out of the window with an expression that bore a mixture of amazement and sympathy. 'Are your English summers always like this?' he asked.

This was rural England at its most sodden and unspoilt. Here you still found the rotted wooden platforms outside farms from where the milk churns were collected before the days of tankers. In the fields, bedraggled Friesian cows stood under oak trees gloomily sheltering from the rain. Overflowing brooks thundered and gushed beneath thriving willow trees. From the edge of the saturated corn fields came the occasional rumbling shot of a bird-scarer.

We turned left at a junction by one of those pre-war metal roadsigns that could be swivelled around in order to confuse German para-troopers (or so the story goes). After a few hundred yards we turned down the rough, farm track that led to Styche Hall. I parked the car in front of the house and we got out. The torrent of rain suddenly increased and Ramesh tightly buttoned up the Barbour jacket I had lent him. A tweed cap was perched on his bushy shock of black hair. I think he found the effect quite amusing. You do not see many tweed caps in India.

Styche was as dismal as the weather. Clive demolished the old gabled Tudor house that had been his birthplace and hired the architect Sir William Chambers to build his parents a mansion that he felt befitted their position in the Shropshire squirearchy. It was an anonymous sort of place that sat on a small rise overlooking the fields: Georgian architecture of the dullest kind, originally painted white, but now streaked with grey. After a short spell in the 1970s as a commune for affluent, middle-class hippies, the house had since been converted into flats. We tried the doorbell but there was no one around.

At the back of the house lay the stable block, now a comfortable old people's home. The owner, Anthony Kinson, seemed pleased to see us. He grabbed an umbrella and gave us a tour of the walled rose garden and lake, also built by Clive. Beyond the lake was a stretch of lawn bordered by oak trees, some of which had been cut down after the Second World War to repair the damage to the House of Commons.

We all squeezed under Mr Kinson's umbrella. 'Over there is a walnut tree that Clive planted,' he said. 'And here is a curry tree that Clive brought back from India.' He pointed at a craggy specimen that was cloaked in thick foliage.

202

Ramesh plucked one of the leaves and ground it in his hand. He sniffed it.

'No, it's not,' he said. Mr Kinson looked alarmed. 'This is not a curry tree. Curry trees smell of curry.'

'But everyone says it's a curry tree,' Mr Kinson said. 'Ever since we came here seven years ago we thought it was a curry tree. It's got to be a curry tree.' He was rather upset. What was this Indian interloper doing by telling him he did not own a curry tree after all?

'Perhaps,' I suggested tactfully, 'after more than two hundred years in this ghastly climate, it's given up trying to smell of curry. Maybe nature told it there wasn't much demand for curry in Shropshire and it just sort of packed up.'

'No,' Ramesh said. 'Definitely not a curry tree of any description. I suppose you could put it in a biryani, but I'm not sure what good it would do.'

Mr Kinson looked utterly dejected. I apologised for spoiling his day and we returned to the car.

Cock pheasants squawked at us through the mist as we motored to Moreton Say. In the centre of the village stood the church surrounded by a slumbering graveyard. The building dated from the thirteenth century, but was encased with brick in 1788 so that Clive would not have recognised the place where he was baptised and where he worshipped as a boy. We sprinted through the rain to the porch. It was dark inside the church. I found a light switch and we walked slowly up the aisle with echoing footsteps. The only memorial to Robert was a simple tablet. It was to the right of the altar next to inscriptions in memory of other generations of Clives. The plaque had been erected in 1911 – 'Robert Clive, K.B. is buried within the walls of this church'. It bore his coat of arms featuring an elephant and ended with the words: *Primus In India – First in India.* There was nothing more. No grand statue, no further eulogy to the founder of British India.

A young, fresh-faced man breezed out of the vestry. He introduced himself as the Reverend James Graham, vicar of Moreton Say. I asked him if he knew exactly where Clive was buried. 'Well, we're fairly certain that he's in the family vault under here.' The vicar pointed below the lectern. 'I would say that he's definitely not in the graveyard. If you were important in those days, you were buried in church in a coffin. Mere commoners were wrapped in sackcloth and dumped outside. And Clive was not a commoner. Even at death there had to be a social divison.'

Clive's remains are said to have been discovered once, in 1900, when a man was hired to refloor the building. The rector at the time was puzzled why one portion of the floor was taking so long to complete. He walked in one day to see a queue of people each paying half a crown to view Clive's coffin.

It was still raining when we left the church. We got into the car and sat in silence for a moment. Then Ramesh spoke: 'A Hindu of that importance would be remembered in a far grander way. It's not much of a memorial to a man who was so great in India, is it?'

'No, it's not,' I replied. And we left Moreton Say and drove back through the misty Shropshire lanes.

Selected bibliography

Bence-Jones, Mark, *Clive of India*, Constable, London, 1974

Corner, Miss, *The History of China and India*, Dean and Co., London, 1847

Dubois and Beauchamp, *Hindu Manners*, Oxford Clarendon Press, 1906

Forbes, James, *Oriental Memoirs Volumes I and II*, Richard Benntley, London, 1834

Gleig, Rev. G. R., *The Life of Robert, First Lord Clive*, John Murray, London, 1848

_____ *India, 1989 Annual Review*, Competition Review Ltd, New Delhi

_____ *India, A Travel Survival Kit*, Lonely Planet Publications, Victoria, Australia, 1981

Malleson, Colonel G. B., *Rulers of India: Lord Clive*, Oxford University Press, 1988

Minney, R. J., *Clive of India*, Jarrolds, London 1931

_____ *Miss Fane in India*, ed. John Pemble, Headline, London 1988

Muthiah, S., *Madras Discovered*, Affiliated East-West Press PVT Ltd, New Delhi, 1987

Nicholson, Louise, *India in Luxury*, Century Hutchinson, London, 1985

Sinclair, David, *History of India*, SPCK Depository, Vepery, Madras, 1906

Thangarai, R. H. and Yawalkar S. J., *Leprosy for Medical Practitioners and Paramedical Workers*, Ciba-Geigy Ltd, Basle, Switzerland

Index